Were You Born
on the Wrong Continent?

Were You Born on the Wrong Continent?

HOW THE EUROPEAN MODEL CAN HELP YOU GET A LIFE

Thomas Geoghegan

THE NEW PRESS

NEW YORK
LONDON

Requests for permission to reproduce selections from this book should be mailed to:
Permissions Department, The New Press,
38 Greene Street, New York, NY 10013.

Published in the United States by The New Press, New York, 2010
Distributed by Perseus Distribution

LIBRARY OF CONGRESS CATALOGING-IN-PUBLICATION DATA
Geoghegan, Thomas, 1949–
Were you born on the wrong continent? : how the European model can help you get
a life / Thomas Geoghegan.
p.   cm.
Includes index.
ISBN 978-1-59558-403-8 (hc)
1. Socialism—Europe.   2. Well-being—Europe.   3. Europe—Social conditions—
21st century.   4. Europe—Economic conditions—21st century.   I. Title.
HX238.5.G463 2010
330.12′6—dc22   2010010889

The New Press was established in 1990 as a not-for-profit alternative to the large,
commercial publishing houses currently dominating the book publishing industry.
The New Press operates in the public interest rather than for private gain, and
is committed to publishing, in innovative ways, works of educational, cultural,
and community value that are often deemed insufficiently profitable.

www.thenewpress.com

Composition by NK Graphics
This book was set in Fairfield

Printed in the United States of America

2 4 6 8 10 9 7 5 3

To Samuel Hutchison Beer

Contents

Preface:
I'm No "European Socialist"

I had better say: I'm no "European socialist."

A few months ago the uproar d'jour was: is Barack Obama a socialist? Yes, he was to the extent that, like George Bush, he wanted a bailout of the banks. The cover of the February 16, 2009, *Newsweek* announced: "WE ARE ALL SOCIALISTS NOW." The argument is that U.S. government spending is nearly as high as Europe's. A decade ago, the U.S. government was spending 34.3 percent of GDP, compared with 48.2 percent in the "euro-zone," which is Europe without the UK. Now, while the Continent is at 47 percent, we have gone up to 40.

And, in fact, I think the U.S. will close the gap. But in a sense, the more we spend, the less socialist we become. For whether it is health care or education, we use the private market to pay for the distribution of public goods. In other words, we pay socialist-type taxes so that the private insurance companies, drug companies, and, yes, doctors can profiteer.

That's the crisis of our time: we're paying for European-type socialism, without getting the equivalent payback.

Still, isn't it worth it to keep capitalism?

Yes, of course, but if we took Europe as a guide, we would do a lot better at capitalism. The Germans make money off the same global economy that leaves us in hock. And the longer the hours we work to be competitive, the deeper in debt we seem to go. How is it that *they* are the ones who aren't in debt when they get six weeks' holiday every year?

I have to say again: I'm no European socialist. But as a patriot I would like to ask: which model, ours or theirs, is more likely to keep us out of the clutches of foreign creditors?

It's bad enough that, with the Wall Street crack-up and the war in Iraq, we are no longer a superpower. What worries me even more is that we have compromised our sovereignty. One day our creditors—China, Saudi Arabia, even Honduras, God help us— could assemble into a creditors' committee that tells us what to do.

What bothers me is that Europe does better than us both at capitalism and socialism. It's unfair that they seem to be beating us at both.

Still, I'm no European socialist. On the other hand, I think back to one of the original arguments against socialism. The case against socialism, Oscar Wilde wrote, is that it takes up too many evenings. We end up going to political meetings instead of going out to dine. But in my own personal life, I have to say the case against our capitalism, our kind and not Europe's, is that it takes up too many evenings, working late at the office, and it takes up weekends, too. What fascinates me about Europe is the possibility of having an interesting job and still leaving the evenings free.

On what continent is it easier to go out and dine?

Still, even if I could start over, I'd hate to make the choice between soaring to the top in a free-fall U.S. or putt-putting in neutral in a cozy little EU democracy. Is it possible to have a world where we get a bit of both?

In most of what follows I will be talking about the Germans. Like all of you, I deeply regret I didn't write about the French. Yet for all the lack of sex appeal, it's still Germany that presents the starkest alternative to the way we live today. It's the only country with a system that, after the collapse of Communism, continued to push for a certain very limited form of worker control.

That's only one reason why I picked the Germans. After all, I'm a union-side labor lawyer. But at the moment I also worry about the future of my country. The Germans seem to have the secret for getting out of debt.

I hope I have cleared up that I'm no European socialist. Now let me explain how I ended up in darkest Germany when I might have had my evenings free in France.

May 2010

Were You Born
on the Wrong Continent?

PART ONE

Which Side of Paradise?

1

I Know No Europeans

March 1997. When I came back from Europe, after two months, I thought, "My God, where's my furniture?" Then it hit me: I'd never had any. In the middle of the room was a NordicTrack, which someone, maybe me, must have dragged out and—forgot. It looked as if I'd fled.

It was a shock to me, still, that I had left at all. Two months, away from work! Before I went, most lawyers I knew said, "Two months? In Europe? But what about your practice?" While other lawyers would say, "That's nice, but what about your practice?"

And still other lawyers would just say, "*What about your practice???*"

And all I could say was: I don't know! I don't know! I don't know! I had court dates, court calls, and I was on trailing trial calendars, which wrapped around my ankle, up my leg, and around and around my shoulders. Go to Europe for two months? Tangled like this, how could I even move? I had decided to drop the idea, it was ridiculous, but then one friend who was a lawyer called and left a voice mail, which I heard late at night, and all he said was: *"Vacation courage!"* Because he and I are in a kind of support group to tell each other, it's okay, we can take vacations: "Yes I can." But later, when he heard my plan was to go for two whole months, he called up and said, *"What about your practice?"* Because in our lives today, two months off is like two years off. It's like the time that an explorer such as Richard Burton would take to travel up the Nile.

Well, for an academic, a social scientist, a two-month trip like this would be a joke. "You can't find out anything in two months," they'd say. But I figured that for a lawyer, to find out what Europe is like, it's almost too long. One all-night binge to pound out a brief would be enough, wouldn't it?

Obviously, I'm kidding. I should probably repeat that for any Europeans: I'm kidding! No, the truth is, I am scared to go to Europe. Why? First, I'd just hate to be in Paris and be—alone. Second, I'd hate to be anywhere and be alone. In a sense, to be in a city like Paris, alone, is to be in a state of sin, mortal sin, the kind of sin a Jesuit describes on a tape I have at home. In the end, he says, sin is the condition of being alone. That is, it's the condition of being isolated, cut off, from everything that is human.

In other words, it's like all the Paris trips I took when I was in my twenties.

It means walking around all day without talking to anyone. It's knowing I don't know any Europeans. "Oh Paris—isn't it wonderful?" Sure, it's great. But after two days in Paris, every demon I hammer down under the floor here is flying up through the air. For years, I have kept a big photo of Paris in my law office: it's huge, what one used to call a panorama. It's a wide-angle, 180-degree black-and-white photo of Paris in 1927, with little Model Ts tooting to the Louvre. Sometimes, a client, like a teamster, might stare up at it, look at the Paris metro map next to it, and say, "Hey, you must like Paris, huh?"

Ha.

It's in my law office, like a skull, to remind me how unhappy I will be if I ever go to Europe. No human contact, not a word of speech. I think of poor Jim, back in college: one summer, as a junior, he went around Europe by himself with his *Let's Go Europe*. And as he went, he got lonelier, and lonelier. Finally, he stopped eating, then talking. He ended up in Glasgow, unable to move. Somehow he got to a phone and made a call: to his mother, in Boston, for money for the plane. When his mother saw him at the airport, she burst into tears. "My God, what's happened?!" All he could do was stare—he'd not talked to a human being in two or three weeks. Still, the photo, over my desk—it's haunting. What if my real life is over there, ticking away, and I'm not being allowed to live it?

Just the other night, I opened *Pilgrim's Progress*. On the first page, the Evangelist comes up to Christian—Fly from here! I shivered. Didn't we come to this country as Pilgrims, to be free? I'm not free at all. When was my last vacation? I can't remember.

Shouldn't we all get on a plane and fly?

Yes, my life is ticking away somewhere, etc., and I'm not being allowed to live it! But what makes me think, in these wild moments, that it's going on in Europe? For years I've thought the most "political" part of the *New York Times* is the Sunday travel section: "It's got the real news about Europe." For years I read the front page about European unemployment, the collapse of social democracy, etc. But then I'd flip to the travel page and get the real news, the news that they don't dare put on page one, that every year in Europe, the whole place keeps getting nicer. It may be that in our time, the real political news, the specter that is haunting our civilization, is only in the travel section of the *New York Times*. It would murmur in a whisper what the "serious" parts of the *New York Times* would deny: maybe, just maybe, Europe was moving past us.

Reading the travel page, I think of all the European cities I might have lived in. Just think, for example, of the ones that start with "B," like Barcelona, Brussels, Bologna, and even Bruges. What do we have, over here? Oh, we've got Baltimore, Baton Rouge, and let's toss in Bayonne, too. In these cities that begin with "B," for the kids at the bottom, the "B" should stand for "bullet." From ages eight to twenty, it seems most live under fire. Am I being unfair? Let's go to the next letters, "C" and "D": they've got Copenhagen and Deauville, and we have Cleveland and Detroit. Or let's take the ones that begin with "E," then "F"—and when we get down to "Z," I have to bring up Zurich.

I admit, Zurich is the main reason I came to write this book. It was 1993, and I was on my way to Moscow. Why? Well, I could say: I had to go because of the collapse of Communism. It seemed to me this was the biggest event in World History, in my entire lifetime. Shouldn't I go to see it, even if I was a little too late? So yes, I could say: the collapse of Communism. But it had more to do with the collapse of a relationship in Chicago, and while grieving I met Ms. O. and decided to go.

Yes, I went to Moscow, to see a girl. Now you know.

But since it was a long flight, I decided to have a day's stopover in the middle. Get used to the time change. I didn't want to get there and then, like Communism, collapse. So, for no specific reason, I came to Zurich.

Zurich: I expected to be bored. True, I'd not been to Western Europe in many years. But the adventure would be Moscow.

That's the only city that was burning in my brain. In Zurich, I would snooze.

Ms. O. would laugh: "Zurich! That's where you keep your money." And if you lived in a city where they spike vodka with diphtheria, you'd be right to scoff at Zurich. What kind of kick could Zurich be?

Still, as I walked the streets, I had to gasp: My God! I had never seen a city not just opulent but opulent in such an elegantly intelligent way. How could a continent like Europe change so much in ten years? I now saw what ten good years of GDP growth can do! Much of Europe, from Milan up to Stockholm, had climbed up to us, in America, and a few countries, like Norway, were even above us in GDP per capita.

But that's not the shock. It's not the per capita on paper. It's the per capita in the street. I mean, these are social democracies. The richest, like Sweden, are the most Red, i.e., on the left. Which means everybody's got dough. That's why in a social democracy, even plain old Cologne has a whiff of cologne, while out in the parks even our most elegant cities have a whiff of urine.

Just count the elderly poor: in the U.S., 24.7 percent of old people are in poverty; in Sweden, it's 7.7 percent; and in Germany, 10.1 percent (mainly in East Germany). Dare I mention children? Ours is 21.9 percent, and in Germany, it's 9.0 (again, mainly in East Germany). So think of "U.S. v. Europe" not in terms of graphs and tables, but sensually. Sight. Touch. Even smell. Over there, in the really social democratic parts, I can inhale whole cities like banks of violets.

That's what made me gasp: where there's equality, there's so much more in an affluent country to see, to taste, to touch—it's so much easier to roam around. There's more order. But it's the order of not having the disorder of mass poverty. And because of this order, in a city like Zurich everything can be perfect. The perfect cup of coffee. The perfect bowl of muesli. Even when something was out of place, it was perfectly out of place, in a certain way. Couldn't the U.S. be like this?

Of course. But in a country with mass poverty, there has to be disorder, and the disorder makes it impossible for everything to be perfect the way it is in Europe. I was stunned at the way Zurich seemed to work when no one seemed to try. But isn't Zurich one of the nicer ones? Yes, of course, but there seem to be a hundred cities of which I could say, in the same way: "But isn't that [Copenhagen, Lübeck, etc.] one of the nicer ones?"

Up and down I walked in Zurich that afternoon. Block after block. Boutique. Café. Perfumery. Global bank. Bank of violets. Each perfect, in its way. I saw how the lack of poverty can open up a whole city as one's own, as if it were an art gallery. When there is a relative lack of poverty in a highly developed country, the private sphere can pour out its well-being into the public sphere, which becomes like a bonbon one consumes.

So I had bonbons all day and never bought a thing.

Late in the day, between a perfumery and a boutique, I came upon a tiny bookstore, all in white and yellow. When I went in, the books were all in white and yellow too, as if the books themselves were trying to make a fashion statement.

Then out came a clerk: a young woman, in white, who seemed to have stepped out of the pages of *Elle*.

Say something to her! (Ah, I couldn't think!)

"I, uh," I said, "I wonder if you, like, have any books in English?"

"Oh!" she said, "I'm so sorry, but the only books we sell here are . . . German philosophy."

Sure: of course.

And as I stumbled out the door, I could hear Schopenhauer, in the back, splashing on cologne.

Oh God! How can I leave this for Moscow, which seemed like such a nightmare? I had to call Ms. O. I had to tell her: I've stumbled into Eden. I . . . I went back up, halfway up a mountaintop, to my hotel, and sat on the terrace, and looked down upon peaceful little left-wing Europe, where nothing's going on.

Call her. "Look, O., maybe . . ."

No, she's expecting you.

But I want to stay here! In Moscow, there's bubonic plague. What about Chernobyl? So far as I knew, O.'s apartment, at this moment, could be glowing with radiation. Oh God. Not now. Just in from west of Eden, why must I go east? I would call her: "Look, I need a few more days here." But I went. And it was worse than I had imagined. There was a coup. Yeltsin sent troops around the parliament. The old guard, inside, opened fire. Why did I leave and go to that? I lost my nerve.

In Moscow, I kept talking to O., to everyone, about what I had seen in Zurich. "You should see how nice it is." Or: "It's the most amazing thing I've ever seen!" Of course, all they wanted to talk about there was the civil war, the shootings. But how could that compare with what was happening every day in Zurich?

Anyway, being an American, how was I to know that Europe had gotten so nice? For years, in the business section of the *New York Times*, the *Wall Street Journal*, I had read, and I believed, that the whole place was in collapse. The joblessness. High labor costs, etc. "It can't go on." That's all I knew. "The economy's awful, terrible." Maybe it was. But now I'd seen the way that Western Europe *looked*! I mean the part that runs from Milan to Paris and then over to the Rhine and up to the very tip-top of Norway.

And other people say East Asia, or part of it, is even nicer. Maybe it is. But I haven't seen Asia: I've only seen this. And that's

my real case for Europe, aside from the economic data that we
Americans can consume like Big Macs without getting any taste.
Go over and see it.

Europe's in collapse? Fine. I'm not going to argue. Go there.
See it. Then come back here and look around. And don't tell me
our GDP is higher. Or our GDP per capita. Or our employment.
My eyes tell me it's not. As for Europe, are you going to believe
the business page or the travel section? Look at the pictures.
Don't read the words. But on that day in Zurich, it was not just
the opulence but the look on people's faces. It's the look on the
faces of people who speak two or three languages. I wish I didn't
notice that—but over here, I'm used to the look on the faces of
kids who have had Lady Gaga or worse blasted into their baby
brains.

Aside from that, Europe's cheap! Let's put fluctuations of currency aside. That night, I stayed halfway up the mountain, in a
place that was like a resort, and ate out on the terrace, under the
vines and trellises, and looked down on Zurich, for $125 a night.
It's not that the dollar was so good in 1993, though it was. At that
time, a place like this, with a garden, waiters, a stunning view of
the city, would have cost $1,000 a night in the U.S. Yes, even a
union lawyer like me could live well.

That's the night I discovered: America may believe it's set up
for the middle class, but, as my friend Lee put it, Europe is set
up for the bourgeois.

Or let's put it this way: America is a great place to buy kitty lit-
ter at Walmart and relatively cheap gas. But it's not set up for me,
a professional without a lot of money. That's who Europe's for: it's
for people like me and Lee.

Okay, maybe it is.

Still, as a union-side lawyer, it's really set up for my clients, or who used to be my clients before the unions in America collapsed. Let's put my own self-interest aside: where would my clients, who are not poor, who make $30,000 to $50,000 a year, and yet keep coming up short, maybe by $100, $200 a month, really be better off? That's easy. Europe. I think I can answer that as their lawyer, the way a doctor could answer about their health. The bottom two-thirds of America would be better off there. I mean the people who have not had a raise, an hourly raise, in maybe forty years, and who do not even have a 401(k), nothing but Social Security, and either have no health insurance or pay deductibles of $2,000 or more. Sure, they'd be better off in Europe. When unemployed, they'd certainly be better off in Europe. Over there, even single men can get on welfare. And in much of Europe, contrary to what we hear, unemployment is much lower than over here.

But one of the ways Europe is set up for the bourgeois—including, perhaps, some of the readers of this book—is the very fact that it's also set up for people who make $50,000 or below. Since it's set up for these people too, the bourgeois—Lee, others, maybe you—get the political cover to have it set up for them. Besides, what the people-in-the-unions get, people-from-the-good-schools also get. Indeed, often Lee et al. are *in* the unions. They get the six weeks off, the pension like a golden parachute. And the higher up we are in terms of income, the more valuable these things are. In America, they don't tell us: social democracy, or socialism, or whatever Europe has, pays off biggest for people in the upper middle class, just below the top.

What are all the ways it pays off? Wait till the next chapter: in my head, at least, I started writing that chapter long ago when I looked around in Zurich. For if Zurich looked this good and Chicago looked as broken down as it did when I had left, and if

America had such a high GDP per capita and Chicago was one of America's crown jewels, maybe there was something wrong with GDP per capita. It's not that the numbers "lie" in any crude way: GDP, productivity, unemployment. But past a certain point, maybe these numbers mislead us as to where we're better off.

For to look at the numbers, who would guess that Zurich looks gloriously like Zurich all over, and that Chicago looks so glorious in Lincoln Park, dumpy west of Pulaski Avenue, and gulag-like by Twenty-sixth and California? But forget the look of the place. It's also the way of life. The numbers say, on paper, I have a better way of life in Chicago. But are these numbers right? It may be that, past a certain level, an increase in GDP per capita pushes my living standard *down*. I don't mean this in a spiritual sense: I mean it in a cold, neutral, out-of-pocket sense. Example: if I make more by working longer, I might subcontract out more of my life and incur other "costs," like losing a trip to Zurich, which may be of far more value than the extra income. Or another example: if I get a raise, I might be worse off. I might widen the gap in income with others around me. Who cares? Well, by doing this, I might be spreading poverty, which, like everything, is relative. I might make my public space more of a hellhole than before.

Now people at the Cato Institute love to scoff: "Oh, our poor in America are so well off in GDP per capita." Go ahead. Argue. I'll let you win. But I dare the Cato types, when the argument is over, to go outside and walk around.

In other words, the farther ahead we get, the more our standard of living drops. Let's say, as a European, I work 1,500 hours a year. Now, let's put me at 1,800 or even 2,300 hours, like many Americans, and while I've moved to higher GDP per capita, I've also got:

No six weeks off.

No perfect cup of coffee to sip at some place other than the office.

No city to inhale like a bank of violets.

I look at this table and marvel that we're ahead.

PER CAPITA INCOME
(PURCHASING POWER RATIOS)

	1989	2000	2007
U.S.	33,477	41,236	45,604
Germany	26,365	31,159	33,880
Denmark	26,830	33,742	37,185
France	25,768	30,430	32,906
Netherlands	26,519	35,221	38,118
Switzerland	33,684	36,097	38,842

Source: Economic Policy Institute, the Conference Board.

Technically, we seem far ahead, but don't drool. The U.S. superrich gobble well over two-thirds of the increase. In 2005, the real hourly wage for production workers in America was approximately 8 percent lower than it was in 1973, while our national output per hour is 55 percent higher. So it's dubious whether most Americans have gained even a penny in purchasing power since 1989. And even skewed by all this U.S-type inequality, we understate what Europeans at the "middling" level are able to get for free, i.e., public goods like education, health care, cities like banks of violets. Even apart from the grotesque U.S. inequality, the net purchasing power disparity after we toss in the public goods is not so great.

Then I look at the table on page 14 and I'm in despair. Aren't the Europeans coming near us with one hand tied behind their backs?

AVERAGE ANNUAL HOURS WORKED

	2000	2006
U.S.	1,841	1,804
Germany	1,473	1,436
Denmark	1,554	1,577
France	1,591	1,564
Netherlands	1,372	1,391
Switzerland	1,685	—

Source: EPI, OECD 2007 data.

Remember, you're looking not at a median but an "average." I stress that because, in the U.S., there is also huge inequality in hours. The people who survive in the U.S. are putting in far, far more than the "average"—lawyers like me, kids working three shifts at McDonald's. What's the big power of a U.S. employer? It's to decide which of us, dog-eat-dog, gets to work up to 2,300 hours.

The Europeans aren't doing this because their unions won't let them.

But for the sake of argument, let's take the numbers as being fair median-type comparisons. If the six weeks off for the Europeans has any cash value—if this shortfall in hours has a positive material benefit—then maybe, in light of the table on page 13, Europeans are "materially" better off, even apart from the higher quality of the public goods they receive.

Or maybe I mean this: Europe has a kind of invisible GDP, which we don't know how to count. The European who might *want* to work 2,300 hours over here may be the luckiest to escape his or her fate under the U.S. model. When that person has 700 more hours a year, to learn an extra language, to go to Sri Lanka, or just to read, it's that high achiever who may be best off under the European model. There is a new skepticism about GDP per capita, at least from a few economists. But we still need someone who can show us how to keep the books.

Long dead now is the one who might have done it: I mean John Maynard Keynes, who wrote the haunting essay "Economic Possibilities for Our Grandchildren." In that long-ago essay (1930), he talked of a world in which his grandchildren would not really have to work. Or not in the old way. We'd write. Read. We'd have long afternoons full of cigarettes and novels. "It was Keynes at his silliest," or so his biographer writes. But was he so silly? I am old enough to be one of Keynes's grandchildren. And of course, we have to work! I *want* to work. But maybe by now, we should be working at jobs that we consume, like long afternoons full of cigarettes and novels. We should not be at jobs that seem to be consuming us. Think of all the Bloomsbury-type jobs that higher taxes could provide: teacher, artist, the softer jobs Keynes wanted for us. In Europe, or in a social democracy, with more safety nets, I get work that slowly, over a lifetime, I consume. Over here, where they—or we—keep cutting the nets, I get work that ends up consuming me. Why do we keep cutting them? It's the inequality, even the rage, of red states against blue states: paradoxically, it's that veto at the national level that has blocked all of us from having a bit more of what Keynes promised.

So was I born on the wrong continent?

Yes. No. I don't know. I'm haunted by it. Of course, I'd die if I were a European. Think of all the choice and freedom I have. Think of what I can buy at a Whole Foods or a Trader Joe's. We have bigger, better supermarkets than they do.

"But look at all the garbage we toss out."

With fewer choices, you and I might be happier. We might be healthier, i.e., thinner.

We might also save the planet.

Still, I'd hate to pay more for gas. And I'd hate to give up other things that I have as an American—and it's more than just the French roast coffee I get for $11.99 a pound at Whole Foods.

What would I get if I gave all that up?

I'd get a public pension I could live on. In 2004, the OECD reported that the average public pension in the top twenty developed countries was 67 percent. In the U.S., it was 39 percent. And people at my income level get less than that.

As I get older, where will I be safe? Look at these rates of elderly below the poverty line (50 percent of median income) from the year 2000:

ELDERLY BELOW 50 PERCENT OF MEDIAN INCOME

U.S.	24.7
Germany	10.1
Denmark	6.6
France	9.8
Netherlands	2.4

Source: EPI.

Wait: in his first address to Congress in 2009, Barack Obama talked about the need to "strengthen" Social Security. So does that mean it's going up? No. Whenever people talk about "strengthening" Social Security, it means they want to cut it back. Sure, as long as the Democrats are in, I know I will get something. But Social Security just had a near-death experience under George Bush, who tried to privatize it just before the market crashed. How do I know the Republicans won't get back in again?

Now the Cato types would say: "Those Europeans put money into their pensions, and they don't think about the young." Look at what the young workers pay, etc. It's true that Europeans have had to cut back pensions to take some of the burden off the young. But even if they'd done nothing, the young in Europe would still be better off.

Look at the rates of children below the poverty line (50 percent of the median) from the year 2000:

CHILDREN BELOW 50 PERCENT OF MEDIAN INCOME

U.S.	21.9
Germany	9.0
Denmark	8.7
France	7.9
Netherlands	9.8

Source: EPI, Luxembourg Income Study.

Aside from ducking child poverty, look at the other things kids get: no college debt! In some of the German federal states, there's no tuition at all. Imagine. Even in the German states that do charge, the cost is a few hundred euros a year—about the cost of a day of class at some private American schools.

Yes, but what about the higher taxes? Well, it's odd: I think of Europe as a tax haven. After all, we pay up to four-fifths of what they pay in taxes. But we hardly get back four-fifths of a European-type welfare state.

Still, I went for years waiting for an explanation as to where I'd be better off. It seems the bookstores should groan with tomes that compare Europe v. the U.S. to tell me where I'm better off.

"Why are there no books like that?" I asked.

"Maybe," said a friend, "it's impossible to write such a book."

Still, for the record, I'd like to know for existential reasons: "Even if my life is over, where would I have been happier?"

After my coming down from the mountaintop in Zurich, I was frustrated. There is so little news about Europe. Sometimes I think it's just because out here, at least in the Midwest, we're too weighed down. In the heart of the heartland, the force of gravity, it's so heavy that it's amazing the planes can lift off from O'Hare. But there's a second reason for lack of curiosity: for decades everyone in America kept saying Europe's in collapse.

Ever since college I've been reading the same story: Europe is about to collapse. Or it's becoming more like us. If the right wins an election, that proves Europe-is-going-to-be-like-America. And if the socialist left wins, that also proves the same thing, too. Why?

Here was the chain of reasoning when Gerhard Schroeder became the German chancellor: (1) he's really just like Tony Blair, (2) Blair is really just like Clinton, (3) Clinton is really just like Bush (the first one).

And the first Bush was like Reagan. So when Schroeder was elected, it just showed Europe was going to the right, and they were all more or less like Reagan.

"Wait: isn't Schroeder a socialist?"

Yes. They're all socialists! That's why Europe is collapsing!

It's collapsing.

It's collapsed.

Everyone is unemployed.

It's becoming just like America anyway.

I knew a bit more than that. As a union-side labor lawyer, I wanted social democracy to succeed. The vision I had in Zurich was, like many a story about conversion experiences, one that I was unconsciously getting ready to have. Professionally, as a labor lawyer, isn't that what I was taunted here for secretly wanting? So I admit: I knew the names of the prime ministers. I had often opened up magazines such as *The Economist*. It's just that, after Zurich, I came back furious that I knew no Europeans. And when Europe seemed to struggle with unemployment in the 1990s, I found it hard to defend the EU at parties. All I could do was point to the travel section of the *Times*.

For years in the 1990s, I was in the dark, and was mad at myself: when I was young, I had gone to law school when I should have traveled. I had taken Latin without learning a spoken language.

Worst of all, I knew no Europeans. As a baby boomer, growing up, I didn't see much point in knowing them because:

1. They Were Out of History.

When I was in college, I remember feeling sorry for kids my age growing up in Europe. It seemed to me they'd been born, tragically, into these little tea shops and tourist traps. For them, it was over. I mean, what role, in History, did they have? None. Except to watch the Russians, the Americans. And it was really just us, the Americans. So for an Ohio kid like me, it'd have been better to have been born even in Indiana than to have been born in a country so out of it as France. At least a kid growing up in Indiana had a ball, and a bat, and a chance to dream. What dream could a kid have growing up in Paris? None!

And besides, there was another reason I didn't have much interest in Europeans:

2. We Were Way Ahead of Them.

Way, way, way ahead. Kids who went there told me: I'd get sick on the fumes of the cars. I'd have to use a slug to use the phones. In some places, they probably had to crank up the phones. And even while watching the French New Wave films, I could see how far ahead we were:

Masculin féminin
The 400 Blows
Breathless

Oh sure, I might think Europeans so hip, they're so cool. But my God, they were so *poor*. Trapped in these black-and-white Janus films, flickering in the fog, they seemed to be falling further behind. Didn't they care? In the Eric Rohmer films like *Claire's Knee*, I was aghast at the lack of urgency, all the idleness at dinner, or at a game of tennis, or the whole situation with Claire herself and her knee.

Well, I'm all for ennui. But do they have to be so idle?

I'd go nuts. I was an American. We had things to do. For one thing, I was going to law school. Even in the 1960s, and maybe *because* it was the 1960s, kids my age couldn't fool around. Go abroad? It seemed like goofing off. I once heard of a guy who won a Rhodes, did his two years at Oxford, then came back and started law school. When he applied for a job with some well-known asshole at a New York law firm, the lawyer looked down at the résumé, saw the Rhodes, the time at Oxford, and said, "Well? How are you going to make up for those two lost years?" Still, if I'd had time, I would have liked to go spend some time in Europe. The whole wreck of the twentieth century was over there. Europe! Two World Wars. Fifty million people dead. *Fifty million.*

Of course, this was in a strange way the appeal of the black-and-white Europe in the Janus films. It was an attraction not to Beauty but to the Sublime, to shiver with pity and fear at all the darkness of History Over There.

In the movies, it's so terrifying:

The "honk," "honk"-ing of the police sirens.

The click-click of high heels running on cobblestones.

The sense over there that it's always September 1, 1939, and maybe any minute the planes will be overhead.

Oh, I should have gone over for a year, but instead I went to law school. And while I did make a few trips to Paris later, I ended up, in my middle age, not knowing any Europeans. And that's strange, isn't it? It seems to me that once, in America, everyone who was educated knew a European or had a European friend. I think of Henry Adams. Or Henry Cabot Lodge, who was an isolationist. Any educated American had a European friend. Holmes had a Laski. FDR could look up Churchill. Even Billy the Kid probably had some pen pal to whom he wrote in French.

Maybe it was World War II. But after that, something changed. At least when I was young, it seemed to me the kind of American who once had European friends knew no one there at all. We weren't some two-bit country in need of Europe or European friends. We were America: let them make friends with us. Still, it seemed bizarre. It was easier to get over. We were moving to a global economy. How was it possible we have no European friends? Even now, at least for my generation, it seems hard to know them. I asked my old college roommate, Peter, who goes over to Europe on business all the time:

"Do you, well, make friends over there?"

"No," he said.

"Why not?" I asked.

"'Why not?' You take the red-eye, you fly in there for meetings. All they do is hate you. If you get in at six A.M., then they really hate you. Because they have to go out to the airport and meet you, and you've not had any sleep, and they've not had any sleep, and now everybody hates everybody, and all anybody wants is to go back to sleep."

And that's just with the British, who at least historically were those we were most likely to befriend.

To me, I think the real problem is that in the schools, even in the elite schools, we no longer learn foreign languages. Harvard. Yale. Michigan. Northwestern. I doubt if one in thirty graduates comes out able to speak a foreign language. Didn't I have to pass a language requirement? Sure. In fact, I did two. Latin. (Because

I learned it from the Jesuits.) And German. (Because if I got drafted, I'd play it as my last card for avoiding Vietnam.) Two? I could have done ten. Maybe even twenty. French. Italian. Chinese. Tagalog. And after passing the exams, I still couldn't speak a word. Oh, maybe: "My name is . . ." "What's yours . . . ?"

A few years ago, at the University of Chicago, a professor I know boasted to me that they did not need the language requirement other schools had. I expressed shock. He just gave me a look. "Oh, come on, everybody knew they were a joke. Instead, we'll say, You want to spend a year abroad? Here's what you have to do. Take a course, say, a history course, and join a section where it's taught in Russian. You, the student, you figure out how you're going to learn it."

And I said, "What a great idea! That's terrific. They should be doing that at every school in America."

Unfortunately, it appears that even at the University of Chicago, where the T-shirts say "Where fun goes to die," one can't just assume that these kids will pick up another language as a matter of pride. Even down there, it's too much to expect that our nerdiest, alone in the library on Saturday night, would really buckle down to live up to such a cosmopolitan ideal.

Even if our kids now do have more contact with European kids via video games, we are becoming more linguistically tongue-tied in this world than ever. More cut off. It was a shock to me a few years ago to read, in *The Education of Henry Adams*, in which Henry Adams whines and whines about his lack of education, that he actually does cough up a list of what you and I need to know to be educated. Four things:

Spanish
French

German

Mathematics.

My law partner Len, who just died at age 101 and grew up in Paris before the War (World War I), once told me with a shrug: "I know all four." It seemed no big deal to him. But I knew no other American who knew all four.

I blush to say: at the end of college, I didn't know a single one.

Still, I tried to go to France!

Ah, I remember my first trip, in May 1977, when I went over for a week with Jim. It's the same Jim who, lonely, ended up in Glasgow, and whose mother picked him up at Logan. So why, after that, did he go back? Because with two of us, we figured we wouldn't be lonely. We'd be like two mountain climbers roped together.

Going together, we wouldn't end up being picked up by our mothers at Logan Airport.

But our first day in Paris, Jim dropped me for a girl. I certainly remember her. She was an American, from a big family in publishing, and she had come to Paris that summer to learn how to be a mime. I suppose it was her way of getting out of learning French.

Yes, I figured I'd be lonely. To my shock, I did meet someone French—though not a girl, unfortunately. Also, I got in touch with an American—a classmate, Craig, who was working as a journalist. After Jim left, Craig came by and I got in his car, and the two of us drove around, and around, the great Arc de Triomphe. Craig popped in the Beach Boys. And pumped it up for "Barbara Ann." And there's nothing to beat being an American, and twenty-seven, and roaring around Paris—Notre Dame, all of it—with the Beach Boys smirking:

Ba ba ba ba Barbara Ann
Ba ba ba ba Barbara Ann
Ba ba ba ba Barbara Ann

And I was being a kind of Ba ba ba ba ba barian, but at that time we were pretty much running the world. And Craig at least was a sophisticate. I mean, he and his friends had started an English-language weekly in Paris: it was like the *Village Voice*, or the *Chicago Reader*, or the *Boston Phoenix*, with lots of listings, all the things to do in Paris.

"There must be," I said, "a lot of stuff to list."

"No," he said. "There's not much going on in Paris."

"How can that be?" I said.

"There's no rock scene here or anything. I mean, any given night, there's more going on in St. Louis!"

"St. Louis? I can't believe that!"

But of course Craig was the one who lived here. I looked out the window as French women drove by us, with the lights on in their cars.

"Why do they have the light on?" I said.

"Oh," he said, "it means they're prostitutes."

"Oh," I said. I stared at them, as they drove around and around the Arc, that monument to dead young men. I was sure I'd never see anything like this in St. Louis.

"What is there to do at night in Paris then?"

"What is there to do?"

"Yes."

"People just go out and eat."

To me, that now sounds great. But when I was young, it seemed as thrilling as a night out in St. Louis. "Okay, maybe there aren't a lot of listings," I said, trying to be upbeat. "But Paris doesn't need a listing. Paris *is* a listing, right?"

I had no idea what I meant, so I kept on.

"And of course, there are the women. There's no listing for that, is there?" I thought this sounded worldly.

"It's funny about the women," he said. "I went out with a woman here, you know, someone French. Physically, underneath, they're like other women, but . . ."

He stopped.

"What?" I said.

"I don't know. It's something they do with soap and water. It's something that their mothers tell them."

Craig, I should say, being an investigative journalist, tended to sound like an investigative journalist, even at these moments. And it turns out: his weekly was quite a hit. All the French political types read it, he said. Even if it was in English? Yes. Giscard, the French president, read it at his barber's.

Because it was in English, that's where a gentleman would read it.

At any rate, Giscard read it. Why? "We're the only ones doing investigative journalism here. In Europe they don't have anything like it."

"They have papers," I said. "They have lots of them."

"Yes, but the papers here are all connected to political parties. *Le Monde. Le Figaro.* Even *Libération* is connected to the Maoists." In other words, we Americans did Watergate, while the French papers followed the workers in the streets. Which, I wonder, is the bigger story? In the end, Craig's paper did not survive. Maybe Paris is really no place for ambitious young American journalists. I get the sense it's considered kind of a backwater by the *New York Times.* The young stars went to Pretoria in the 1980s, to Moscow in the 1990s, to the Middle East today. But Paris? It's no place now for a William Shirer, or an Edward Murrow, who went there in the 1930s. Of course the biggest story of our time may be unfolding in Paris: i.e., that the living standard is rising, and people are living longer and more gloriously than at any time in human history. Still: to a journalist, it's like watching paint dry. Even if it belongs on a canvas at the Louvre.

Here's what I'd hoped Craig might help me investigate: how could I meet someone like, oh, a girl? I tried to ask indirectly.

"I'm sure it's true there's more to do in St. Louis," I said. "But there's got to be something to do here."

"Yves Saint Laurent just opened up a club," he said.

What? Come on. But Craig seemed serious.

"There's a woman singing there . . . do you know Fassbinder?" he said. Fassbinder, the German director.

"Uh . . ."

"This is his leading lady."

She was not Hanna Schygulla, but she was blonde, and she was supposed to have an act in which she was sort of Marlene Dietrich. I became obsessed with the idea that I should go to the club. The next night at 7:30 P.M., while it was still light, I stood outside with my ticket. It was a bit early for cabaret, but I didn't know. It was a good thing I had brought a book to read. After a while, I decided to order a Scotch. It was SEVEN DOLLARS, which, in today's dollars, would be like THIRTY-FIVE DOLLARS. I sipped. Very, very slowly. When was she coming out?

I was in Europe. Relax. By the way, there didn't seem to be any French people here. Then, very late, very very late, the leading lady, blonde, white, stumbled onstage: and she tried to sing. But she stopped. Then she giggled. Then she laughed. Hysterically: on, and on, and on.

That was it. Show over.

I phoned up Craig the next morning to complain.

"Yeah, she's on coke, of course," he said.

"Oh." I reddened, because . . . well, of course. She was on coke! I knew that. And I was mad because for one Scotch I had paid SEVEN DOLLARS. And the worst of it: I was alone, with my book, while she was up there laughing hysterically.

That's Paris: that's the way it would always be.

I'd be there alone, with a German woman, laughing, giggling on cocaine, onstage. I think this was a sign I might do better meeting Germans.

Of course, even when we Americans had European friends, I don't think we had friends in France. It's strange about Hemingway and even Fitzgerald novels—I mean the ones set in Paris.

Never

Never

Never

Never does anyone in these novels seem to know anyone in France.

Oh yes. A maid. A bartender. But otherwise? Maybe that's why they were the Lost, etc.

Poor Hemingway: even in *A Moveable Feast*, his memoir of Paris, he seems to have no luck. And if he and Fitzgerald couldn't do it, and they were trying, professionally, to get stuff in their books, what chance did I have in six or seven days? None. But I think it was all timing. In 1929: no chance. In 1968: no chance. Unless it was May '68, and you were a kid, with an armband, and went out and threw rocks. In 1977, though, I think I had a chance. For two reasons: language and GDP per capita. At last, they were speaking English. (E.g., Giscard, at the barber.) And at last, in terms of GDP per capita, they were also closing in. Fast. On us. And yet, I saw, in 1977, how backward France still was. Remember, in 1977 we still had public pay phones. There were no cell phones, just as there had been no TV when I was born. But in Paris, the phones took these funny slugs, *jetons*. The first night, with Jim, in the rain, the two of us begged Frenchmen for jetons. We ran into restaurants: "S'il vous plaît, avez-vous un jeton?" Paris, that night, seemed like a shantytown. Then I blink, and in a few years, half of Paris is chatting on cell phones.

And it seems half, now, can do it in English.

It's too late for Hemingway. And I feel sorry for myself. If I were twenty-seven today, I might even meet some French people. I wouldn't be cut off. But now I'm too old.

Not just to meet a girl—that's out of the question—but to make any friend at all. My twenties are long over, and that's when we make our friends. Isn't it? If only I could be twenty-eight and go to Paris. Ah!

If only I had one more chance to meet the French!

Instead I'd go out alone and flip open *A Moveable Feast*, and I'd tell myself: "We'll always have Paris."

I mean just Hemingway and me: we didn't know anyone else.

Yes, it was a bitter thought in the one city where I most felt the presence of women as the governing class. At the kiosks, the fashion magazines have, in a way, a kind of political effect. And indeed, an American woman tells me, French editions of *Elle* really do have political essays, political arguments. It's a social democracy not just for men but perhaps even more for women. At first I just assumed women were really oppressed here because, well, it was all so recklessly feminine:

The kiosks, with the pealing of their *Elle*

The shock of all the skirts, even in the Metro

The black-and-white buildings that look like grand pianos.

But this turns out not to be true, at least compared to the U.S. First, Frenchwomen make more, in terms of their relative pay, than men. Second, they have all the same job rights of French workers, unknown to either sex in America. Finally, to one's surprise, Frenchwomen have only slightly lower birthrates than American women, thanks in large part to a cornucopia of socialist-type benefits for working women.

WOMEN'S PAY (PERCENT OF MALE PAY), 2007

France	88
U.S.	80

Source: Conference Board of Canada.

All this whining about social democracy, the way it guts the birthrate, etc. It's not true in France, where it's respectably near our own.

BIRTHS PER WOMAN, 2008

France	1.96
U.S.	2.10

Source: World Bank World Development Indicators.

France pays out, and has paid out, not just recently, but for decades, a lot of money for women to have those kids. No other country, for so long, has paid women to have babies. And the effect, paradoxically, seems to be: well, women have babies. France is now on its way to being the Continent's most populous country, overtaking Germany.

Except under Angela Merkel, the German chancellor, the Germans have added French-type benefits. Result? In 2007 and 2008, even the German birthrate has bumped up. Everyone now knows: to keep a workforce in place to support all the pensioners, all the women in Europe have to get what Frenchwomen get.

What do they get? Up to twenty-six weeks of paid maternity and (some) paternity leave. Free child care. A system of backup government-paid nannies.

It seems that "work" is such a good deal that women would hold off having babies. In a Darwinian sense, there is now an incentive not to have kids. A professor in Berlin made this point to me: "If you have our social security system, it takes away the incentive to have a child, to have children."

"Oh," I said, "I get it. If you've got welfare, you don't need a kid."

"Exactly," he said.

"But France, Germany, they pay a lot if you have a kid."

"Not enough," he said. "There are three types of costs. First, there are the direct, or, really, the housing costs." (Everything else is free.)

"Right."

"Then there are the lost income opportunities."

"If the mother stays at home." (But the French have nannies and free day care.)

"Then," he said, "there are the lost pension costs."

I had thought with all the benefits, it'd be easier for a German woman to drop out and have a kid.

"No, not at all," he said. "I look at my secretary. She's leaving. We had a party for her. I can see for her it is frightening to cut herself off from the world of work and go off and have a child. She may think: Why am I having a child? I should be making money to prepare for my old age."

But if the workforce declines, her pension is in jeopardy. So there is no way out.

At any rate, Europe is on top of this: they lower the tax rates for families, they throw in bonuses, incentives, etc. More than one European family can claim that they can make money by having children.

"Oh, but it's an Islamic thing." Is it? Half the kids are born outside wedlock.

And they need to build up the workforce because women—especially Frenchwomen—are living longer. Some of the statistics are frightening, such as how by 2050 the *average* life expectancy of a Frenchwoman will be *one hundred*.

That is far ahead of when the U.S. women hope to get there, in another century or so. And one can come up with factors other than French social democracy—even if they're eating cheese and foie gras, Frenchwomen and Frenchmen just eat less, because the portions are smaller.

Still, think of all the goose liver, the cheese, these women are ingesting, while they smoke like Simone de Beauvoir, and yet only Japanese women living on sushi are slightly ahead of them in life expectancy.

Where are women better off?

Maybe they can be more recklessly feminine with the promise of living for a century.

But what's in it for the men? Well, in terms of mating, it may be easier for us who are bourgeois with no money. With all the safety nets, a female considering mating may or may not inquire into a male's income. One night, at a bar in Chicago, U.S. Beer Company, I talked to a freelance journalist, a rock critic, and by the second beer, he was going on and on about how great the women were in France. Why? "Because," he said, "you know, the first thing an American woman does, she wants to check you out. It's like: 'How much do you make?' If you make enough, fine. If not, she walks away."

"Come on, women don't care in Europe?"

"Hey, it's not like it's their first question," he said.

Well, I'll defend American women. The questions they ask of

us middle-class guys—including working-class guys hanging out in the U.S. Beer Company—make a lot of sense.

How can I have the most kids, i.e., biological immortality?

Where will my kids be more likely to survive, i.e., be safer?

I would especially ask these questions of men who are free-lance rock critics or who still represent labor unions in America.

Yes, it's a brutal, Darwinian thing, but both sexes here know there aren't a lot of safety nets. A Darwinian would say: "In America, with mass poverty, a woman has to ask about income. She has to, to protect her young. Isn't there a one in four chance her child will be in poverty, etc.?"

On the other hand, at least in Darwinian theory, a French-woman has less reason to care, where the nesting instinct is a legal claim against the state. At least she can take a risk on a rock critic.

Why?

Better child support.

Better day care.

Tuition—it's free!

It gives the term "safe sex" a whole new meaning.

Do I think I would be married now, or at least a parent of a child, if I had met someone on those lonely trips to Paris?

Oh, I don't know.

Besides, I still would have been a risk to her, since I don't speak French. Since the public sector is huge in France, she might have expected me at least to get a job as a civil servant. How could I have passed the exam?

So I did what everyone warns you not to do: I went to Paris alone.

I figured it would not be so bad.

I had picked out a hotel, moderate, highly touted in my guide-book: Hemingway himself had stayed there. The bellhop took my bag. "Well," I said, after he got to my room. "Maybe Hemingway himself stayed here."

"Hemingway was in a double." He paused. "You, sir, are in a single."

How tactful of him to clarify it.

Later, I went out by myself. It was a Thursday, the night of gallery openings. I passed stores lit up with lawyers buying rugs from Ephesus or a first edition of *Pensées*. Ah! I'd go from gallery to gallery: but I knew no one. No lawyer. No journalist. No way to read *Le Monde* or anything on the left. Just *The Economist*, which can often seem like a branch of British intelligence, full of disinformation about the Continent. ("It's going to collapse, etc.") And yet, if I could talk to them, these French bankers and lawyers buying rugs from Ephesus could tell me the secrets of their socialism.

I stood there: afraid to go up to anyone who's not a woman, and afraid to go up to a woman most of all.

Giving up, I walked out. I looked in windows of the bookstores. Ah, I felt so cut off. But even not speaking French, I was amazed at the books I saw in the French bookstores, in the windows, by the cash registers:

Essays. I mean, *Essais*.

And years later, after this night, now that I have a friend, an American, who lives in Paris, she tells me that this is right. "In France, the bestsellers, what they put on display—they're just essays." Lee could add: and those who write them turn into celebrities. The local pols write *essais*, just as if they were Montaigne.

Imagine: no novels. Not even a narrative. As Lee said, "Look in the windows." Want a book on Islam? They have not one, or two, but maybe twenty-eight *new* books, serious, full of essays about Islam. Why do they read essays? "It's the schools," she said. She has a daughter in an Irish convent school, where it's not so

French, and the nuns are more forgiving. "I think it's very tough in the French schools," she said. "The kids are under a lot of pressure." There's tracking, etc. Which we have too, even more so, but it's much more by income, so there's less pressure on the kid. That's the one drawback of European-type social democracy: the kids have to perform. Because over there, relative to here, there's more circulation of the elites. But, at any rate, Lee was astonished when she arrived in France. "Not only do they learn argument, they have to put it in this French logical way. Thesis. Counter thesis. That's the French system."

Pause.

It's the only thing, apart from French food, she doesn't like. "I think when you're a child, you're in a state of terror."

I think; therefore, I tremble.

So in a way, they grow up logical, linear. Look at the paper they sell in bookstores. It's not lined, like my American notepad; it's chopped up, cubistically, in Cartesian charts. And so is it a shock that, even in middle age, when they go into bookstores, they want essays? And Lee told me a story she heard from an American, a friend who came to Paris as a consultant from Silicon Valley. For Oracle. Google. Apple. Someplace where people are hip, and in chinos. And in come the French. They sit in a row. Then, to the astonishment of the Americans: they take out their pencil boxes. Which they still have from school. Open the boxes. Take out the pencils.

Shall we begin the meeting?

Then: go into the Metro, and look at the kids, nuzzling. It's hard to reconcile the nuzzling with the notepads chopped up in cubic blocks.

Later, since I am locked out of French books, I dropped into an American bookstore. At least I could read the titles, and I saw a clerk tearing open a crate and pulling out books, in scoops, five or six at a time. The crate was full of books, but every one was the same book: Jack Kerouac, *On the Road*. The cover is a big photo of Jack, smiling, as if he were running for reelection.

Today he'd be pleading: Add to cart!

I bought my copy of *On the Road*, and then I crossed the street to the bar La Palette. In here I began to brood about the French, Europe, etc. The problem is, while it's all very nice to be French and have pencil boxes, everyone is the same, it's so regimented, and they aren't free, individualistic like we are.

Otherwise, they'd all be reading Jack Kerouac, *On the Road*.

That's the problem in Europe. That's what the Green Party is for, I think: to get people here to loosen up. To be spontaneous. that is, American. But it's hard in these small countries, with so many people slammed up against each other. Maybe that's why, in Europe, they have no choice but to treat each other well, i.e., to have a social democracy. But this means: Rules. Rules. Rules. Central planning. Regulation. Then the problem becomes: how, at the same time, to get the Europeans to be spontaneous, as we are?

I had a drink alone. I thought of Hemingway in his double.

For a moment, I thought a woman was staring at me. In a guidebook, a British one, which I had bought, the authors say, "It's quite typical that in Paris women stare directly at you. But they don't mean anything by it."

But what if they do?

Then I sank into brooding about French central planning.

After I finished my drink, I decided to go to one of the gallery openings outside on the street. I thought of how Craig had said, over fifteen years ago, "There's nothing to do, at night, in Paris." It still seemed to be true. And yet tonight, the stores, the boutiques, the galleries were full. In Chicago, I once asked a couple from

Paris about this. "Well," I said, "what do you all do at night over in Paris?" The two seemed astonished: "What do we do? It is Paris! We go to a bistro or café, and we eat, and drink, and we talk! And we talk for three hours! And we philosophize! Of course, we are all French, so we are pessimists, but we are in Paris and it is wonderful!"

Oh! All around me there were French couples, pessimistic, and how happy everyone was!

In despair, I got in line at a restaurant. "This is awful," I thought, and I turned to leave. But as I did so, the woman in line next to me was speaking in English. I stopped. I said, just to make a sound to a human being:

"Your English is very good."

She turned away from her friends. "It should be. I'm an American."

"Well, it's still very good." (What else could I say?)

With her was a boyfriend, who turned out actually to be her husband. He was French: not a rock critic, but a drummer in a band. Tonight, he had brought along his sister. Since he talked to the sister, I could talk to the wife. Soon, the four of us decided to sit together. Thank God! I had done it. I had talked, with a human being! My mother would not have to pick me up at the airport.

"So," said the American, who had told me she was an artist, "you were at the opening next door? So were we. It was so 'Paris,' wasn't it?"

"What do you mean?" I asked her.

"Oh," she said, "the way all those people, all of them so in style, but it's like they're frozen, they're petrified, they're all afraid to move. I'm sick of it, I'm sick of all of them. The French."

I liked her a lot for trashing everyone. But I looked at her husband, taking no note of her. "But," I wanted to say, "aren't you married to somebody French?"

She looked at me as if I had asked. "I *hate* Paris," she said. I nodded.

"I hate Paris, and France, and the French. I wish I could get out." She was getting louder. I looked at her husband, who was smiling. He seemed to be happy. "He's a pessimist," I thought. The four of us now had a table. She went on, blasting away at everyone in France: "Oh, *France!* At first I thought it was great. But now . . . oh, I'm trapped, I wish I could get out."

I felt a chill: if I'd married in Paris, I might be talking this way tonight.

"God, if only I could get out. Oh, the city's fine. It's the French. They're so narcissistic. Self-absorbed." A pause. "Especially the men."

I kept looking over at her husband, the rocker. He had this strange look of not just happiness, but joy. Did he hear what his wife was saying? Maybe, since he was a rocker, he was deaf. But no, he seemed to know. But he went on smiling, at all of us, and beaming: full of joy.

Well, I thought, at last I have one European friend, i.e., an American expat. Probably, if I lived here, I'd know only Americans. When our friends came over, we'd go out with them and hope they wouldn't ask: "Where are your French friends?" And I felt sorry for this woman, my "European friend." But I wondered: if she went back to America, how well would she do?

First, she'd have to get a job. We don't subsidize the arts. It might be as a cashier. She'd have no vacation. ("A vacation," says H., my barber, "has to be at least five days.") No health insurance. Second, what if she had a kid? No paid maternity leave. No cornucopia of subsidies. Third, she'd have to pay for school. Unless she threw the child into public schools. Fourth, no child care. No one to help her. Fifth, her rocker husband would have to work. We'd wipe that smile off his face real fast.

I wanted to say, "Do you know, really know, what it would be like back in the States?" As an employee, in Europe, she was living like Bambi protected in a deer park. La la la. No one is ever fired. But over in America, she'd be more like Bambi's mother because employers have guns.

Still, some argue that it's changing.

In the years since, I have read all sorts of op-eds and pieces by Atlanticists and academics saying how America and Europe are becoming more alike. Yes, we're all the same. It's a staple of many think tanks. For example: oh, in Europe they are cutting back entitlements too. Everybody's doing it.

I think they're completely wrong. Sure, in some years, European governments did reduce the entitlements. If you crop the years the right way, you can show a technical cutback in Germany or the Netherlands. But over the decades 1980 to 2000, or even one decade, 1990 to 2000, European states like France (1) kept adding more entitlements, and (2) expanded the ones they already have.

"We're becoming more and more alike." Nonsense. It's the opposite. While it may not go up in a smooth linear way, it goes up. Just as a random sample, I will list a few European-type "entitlements" that have been added or expanded at different times *since* 1990.

GOVERNMENT-PROVIDED BENEFITS AS OF 2009

	Sweden	France	Germany	U.S.
Paid maternity leave	Yes	Yes	Yes	No
Paid paternity leave	Yes	Yes	Yes	No
Expanded holidays	Yes	Yes	Yes	No
Shorter work weeks	Yes	Yes	Yes	No
Nursing-home benefits	Yes	Yes	Yes	No

Source: EPI.

Come on: is that convergence? I leave out the fact that Europeans are in unions, so their contractual entitlements to extra leave and sick days have also increased.

But let's now put aside all these benefits: don't the Europeans pay more in taxes? Sure, they are paying more in taxes, but they are getting a lot more back. Up to a certain point, it's rational to pay taxes if people are spending it on themselves.

Lady, that money is going back to you.

Over here, only some of our taxes come back to us. A lot of them go to the private market—not just evil private insurance companies and drug companies, but also all the multimillionaire doc-in-a-box doctors and hospital executives who profiteer off the distribution of what should be public goods. It's not just that the Europeans spend more; unlike us, they know how to spend the money effectively. Even the least efficient health care systems, like Germany's, take up only 11 percent of the GDP. In America, by contrast, health care takes up over 17 percent—and we still have to deny coverage not just to the uninsured but often even to our middle-class insured.

That's why they call it socialism: not hung up on the word, they have a competitive advantage in the efficient distribution of public goods.

Now it's true we spend much more on the military: for some on the left in America, that explains the difference. Whatever one may think of the military on moral grounds, it doesn't explain the serious disconnect between what we pay and what we get. For those who live off it, the military budget is as close as we come to a European social democracy, both in terms of health care and pensions. Besides, while I'm sorry to say it, without our insane commitment to armaments we would sell even less abroad. Yes, without the military, we'd run an even bigger trade deficit. We'd have fewer middle-class jobs and be even less competitive than the Europeans. And anyway, the whole military budget is roughly 4 percent of GDP, and even Europeans spend some money on defense—the over 17 percent of our GDP that goes just to health care alone dwarfs what goes into our military-industrial complex.

Of course over in Europe they can push taxes too high. Yet as I hope to show with the Germans later in the book, when Europeans sense they are becoming less competitive, they know how to cut back. Even so, it's only a nip and tuck, at least by our standards. When a European government cuts back on even one entitlement, it's news around the world. But in a little while, with little notice, the same government may be slipping in a new benefit of a different kind. And even the old benefits keep going up in value, like—well, a practically free college education. So even when there's a nip and tuck, the value of the total package, the net benefit of social democracy, keeps on going up.

Naturally, I did not think about all this as I talked to the American woman.

But I could tell she felt trapped here. For how could she ever go back now? If she went back to America, she'd have to work until she dropped.

She was miserable that night. But her husband, the drummer, went on looking seraphic.

Who knows, though, what drives people out of Paris? And here I should say, I really did come close, on my first trip, to getting, truly, "a European friend." Ah, I came so close! Here's how it happened:

When Jim and I found a *jeton*, we telephoned a girl (not the mime, but a Frenchwoman he already knew) whose brother was in Cannes. The idea was that I would house-sit while the brother was at the film festival. The *jeton* worked. We met. We got the key. We climbed the stairs, and approached the door, and—

She forgot to tell us: her brother had a roommate.

And Jim fiddled with the lock. "Will you relax?" he said. Then he banged open the door. Oh. We found the roommate. His arm around a young woman.

He gasped.

She gasped.

We gasped. There was nothing to make me think I was about to have a European friend. Yet he did not scowl. He didn't throw a fit. He smiled! (I wouldn't have, at that moment.) He shook my hand: he made me feel welcome. He had a smile like the smile on the rocker.

And didn't he like people from America? Indeed, he had his arm around one. And over the next few days, I came to like him, and her too. She was, by the way, smart. Even better: she was just nice. And it was fun to be around the two of them.

So, I have to confess: while I had some bad moments on this first trip, like at the nightclub, I mostly had a great time. Why? For once in my life, I had a "European friend."

In the first few minutes Didi and I talked, we found out we had two things in common:

1. We liked essays.
2. We loved the French Revolution.

Indeed, the first night, we almost embraced when I said, "Yes, of course I've read George Lefebvre." *The Coming of the French Revolution.* "You've read him, really?" "Yes, of course!" For years after this, Jim would say to me, "Did you ever drop the right name! I'll never forget the look on his face!" But Jim, who'd have guessed?

Anyway, the next day, Didi woke us up. He had made dark roast coffee. Brought it out in big cups. Did I want to see the French Revolution? Fine. He'd show me the French Revolution.

The first one.

The later ones, 1848, 1871, etc.

The May '68 one, which he'd been in.

And, finally, the French revolution that is always going on.

For two days, he gave me a tour of Paris such as no one from America has any right to see. I kept thinking: my God, was this guy ever made for Paris! But he also had time. Time! Is this not true of all grad students? No. Not of me. What I remember of law school was—"I have no time!" Didi had time. And because he could take for granted the European classical order, he was more up than I was on the new and the avant-garde. We did much more "May '68" than "July 1789." We went to odd streets to see the bricks that, during May '68, the students had dug up.

I often tell how, on the first day, he'd say of block after block:

"This used to be a red-light district."

"This used to be a red-light district."

"This used to be a red-light district."

Except for certain other blocks, of which he'd say:

"Here is where the cops chased us."

"Here is where the cops chased us."

"Here is where the cops chased us."

Anyway, he was an insider: instead of Notre Dame, we poked into St. Eustache. Or instead of the Bibliothèque nationale, we crashed the Bibliothèque Mazarine, off-limits to non-Francophones. If they knew I was an American, the alarm would ring. And as I followed him around, I began to think: *Oh, he's living the life that I should have led.* I know—I was like some twelve-year-old girl in Cincinnati who thinks somehow she was meant to be Princess Grace of Monaco. Yet consider this guy: already, at my age, he'd written a book! Okay, it was a book of photos: old photos from the 1830s, 1840s, of the French working class. But he had been in May '68, and soon he'd occupy some academic chair. His friends read essays. He had all this classical order around him. In his life there was: Logic. Argument. History.

The problem, of course: how does one keep and value all this intellectual architecture, but also at the same time be a free spirit? That's what the Generation of '68, people like D., have to figure out. In a way, here's the problem: how to be Europeans, and Americans too. And D., though I didn't know it, was a prototype of a Green, a leftist like the younger Daniel Cohn-Bendit, and one day he'd be like . . .

The older Daniel Cohn-Bendit: still way on the left but too free a spirit to be in a labor-type party.

All I knew was that this is what I wanted to be. True, I was already a union-side labor lawyer, but I could see the hipness of being a European-type Green. Or let's just say I wanted to be like D. He's into essays. He's into things like the French Academy. The Bibliothèque Mazarine.

Of course he was into pop culture too, for out of pop culture comes the avant-garde. For example, I'm sure ordinary French people think more about the Hegelian implications of hip-hop than we do over here.

That's the difference: sure, at Yale, or Princeton, we have elite who are into that, too. But our elite lack the nerve of Europeans, to bring both the high culture and the pop culture together.

Or maybe we do hip-hop and not Hegel because we don't know how to do Hegel. It's similar to speaking English: we can do a language, but we can do only one.

And I learned something about legal culture. Too often I have told my friends how D. took me to the courts. I was mesmerized by the young left-wing lawyers defending Tunisian and Algerian kids about to be deported. The way they raged, I was sure they were declaiming from the Declaration of the Rights of Man.

Here in Chicago, I'm a moderate liberal, at least by D.'s standards. My favorite paper is the *Financial Times*. But over there, if I had stayed, I might have gone native, and learned to read *Libération* and drink a lot of dark roast coffee, without any milk. I say this because my friend Bill asked for milk in his coffee and the French waiter said, "Monsieur misses his mother?"

Yes, that's how I might have lived: reading *Libération* and taking every holiday they gave me. With all this extra time, I'd experience it more slowly. Maybe I'd be like D. and write a book. And at the same time, I'd learn not to work: I'd live in Paris, eternally, with a whole new sense of time.

Maybe I'd start thinking about Hegel and hip-hop.

Well, it didn't happen. Yet at the end of these ten days, I was sure I'd be coming back to Paris over and over in the years to come. For here, at the very start of my adult life, I had a European friend. But it turns out I never saw him again. Never. I think I know what happened to D.: that he left for a while but ended up back in Paris. Or at least, via Google, I found someone with the name. But is it him? Or not him? Now I wouldn't know.

Well, I forgot to write. And the next time I went to Paris, he was not in the phone book. And my next trip? Still not in the phone book. And so the years went by. Sometimes I think the D. I knew ended up in Kansas. Yes, seriously. Kansas. Right before I left, we had a talk about it. He was thinking of taking a year off and going to the University of Kansas in Lawrence. "Kansas? Why would you want to go way out there?"

Maybe he went there, fell in love with a Kansan. Maybe he went native. Just couldn't leave. Maybe he got to like coaching Little League.

It sounds impossible, but maybe he, D., who read *Libération* and drank the darkest of dark coffee, awoke one day and decided he was born on the wrong continent.

Maybe right now he's listening to Rush Limbaugh. Who knows? Our hearts are so restless.

One night at a dinner at the German consulate in Chicago, I met a German who was an artist. In a way, he was from Paris. Or at least he told me how, in his little German town, the kids would drink until 2 A.M. Then, blasted, somebody would say, Okay, let's go to Paris for breakfast. "We'd drive a few hours. We'd see the sun coming up, just about 6 A.M." But he left it all. He had given up Paris for—Chicago. "I am living in the single best place I have ever lived in my entire life."

"And where's that?" I said.

"Archer and Halsted," he said.

"Archer and Halsted? That's like a bus yard, isn't it? Nobody's there." And I stopped myself from saying, "It's incredibly dangerous."

"Precisely," he said. "No one is there! See, you are an American. You do not know what it is like in Europe. The houses are small, and there are so many people—there are people dropping in, they are next to you, on top of you. They come into your room, without knocking."

"But . . ."

"Yes," he said. "But now, as you say, I am at 'Archer and Halsted.' And there is nothing . . . but no one will come in, without knocking."

I'd worry someone would blow it open with a gun.

That night, as he gushed over Archer and Halsted, I was about to weep how I'd be happier in Europe. But then I remembered the waitress at the S & G.

That's where, in 1991, I'd gone for coffee while I was getting my car washed across the street. It's hard to believe that, even in 1991, I could still get a buzz from a plain old cup of coffee that didn't come from Starbucks.

Well, up came a waitress, obviously European, of a heartbreaking, Janus-film type of beauty. I swallowed, and tried to say, "Could I . . . could I have a piece of toast?"

She paused.

"With jelly?"

"Uh . . . ," I couldn't get my breath.

"It comes with it."

"Yes, jelly . . ." She had no wedding ring, and I dared to ask: "Where . . . where in Poland are you from?"

Silence. Finally, she said, "Northern Poland." She wasn't giving out her address.

"So . . . when did you come here?"

"Last year."

"Really? You came in 1989? When Poland was, like, in the midst of a revolution?"

She stared, and without reason, I went on: "If it had been my country, I'd have stayed, with everyone in a struggle like that."

Now she was awake! If you want to get a woman's attention, try accusing her of treason. "Oh!" she said. "I, I have no regrets! I was out of the university, and . . . and I wanted to come . . ."

Okay! But she had more to say:

"And personally, it was hard! And anyway, I don't like it here! I'm leaving, in two months, and then I will be back in Paris, with *my husband*."

"Husband?" Like a tree surgeon with a saw, she had sawed me to the ground.

Now I was just annoyed. "Well," I said, "I wouldn't mind living in Paris. . . ." I tried to imply, you know, only during a year that my country didn't need me.

"No," she snapped. "I'm sure you wouldn't like to live there."

"Oh? But I'm sure I'd like to live in Paris." (Did she think it was just for her?)

"Oh, you are an American, you would not be happy."

"Sure I would," I said.

"No." She shook her head. "No, you see, in Paris, my husband and I, we had a friend, and he was American, and he was an architect." She dropped her voice, as only a woman from central Europe can. "And he was not happy in Paris! Can you believe this? And we said, 'This is Paris! How can you not be happy in Paris?' But he was not happy in Paris because all he wanted to do was work."

"It's not true of *all* of us," I said.

"No," she said, still shaking her head. "You are an American. All you want to do is work."

She looked down at my legal pad, which I tried to pull away. Come on! It was just by accident I'd brought it in here.

Sure, I could be happy in Paris, or anywhere in Europe for two or three months. But I wonder if I'd last. Perhaps I'd wake at night, and hear footsteps under the window, or the click-click of high heels running down the street, or the roar of the planes flying overhead; and far away in America, at S & G, I'd hear the voices crying out:

"Two months! Two months! What about your practice?"

2

Where You'd Be Happier—
Or, the Story of Isabel and Barbara

Yes, I'd better give an answer, since some readers may be groaning: "Do we have to hear all his travels to find out where we're better off?" Others may be flipping to the back of the book. Some may be wondering: "Are you saying you don't want to be an American?"

No. And let's settle that right here. If I had to choose (or even if I didn't), I'd always choose America, always, forever. For one thing, I'm a lawyer. I've known ever since law school I was born on the right continent.

Besides, Americans are great! Once I met a German woman who worked in Washington, D.C., where she did little projects for IG Metall, a big German union that is somewhat like, but dwarfs, our own United Auto Workers. "Well," I said, "aren't you, like, this European-type socialist?"

"I am," she said.

"So why are you living in America?"

She was startled. "Oh, uh . . . but here the people are so great."

She lived in Virginia. I said, "Even in Virginia?"

"Yes." She paused. "I mean, if you know the right ones."

That's it, precisely. You just have to "know the right ones," and it's the vastness here that lets you pick and choose. Out in suburbia, we've still got big enough lawns to keep a distance from the "wrong ones," even if they live next door.

In Europe, people have their mitts on you. It's the problem with a social democracy: other people have a claim on you. Here, thank God, you're able to shut the door.

In that sense, we have more "mobility." It's not income or "vertical" mobility, the studies now say. Germany, France, and even Denmark have more income mobility, i.e., the chance for kids to move up. But aren't we still ahead in "horizontal" mobility? It's still easier in this country to hit the road, i.e., to put space between me and people I don't like. In Europe, I tell myself, I'd always have felt cornered.

But is that true? Let's just take rail: I can get from Paris to Brussels in eighty minutes. In Chicago, it can take me over an hour and a half just to reach O'Hare, on the same side of the city. It is thirty-five minutes by bus on Addison Street, and then I'm on the El, the Blue Line, broken down, 10 mph in the slow zones, if it comes at all. To get up to Brussels, I puff along on air. To get to O'Hare, I jolt along by stagecoach.

And I'm one of the lucky few: only 5 percent of the country can even use public transport. The rest are sick with road rage when they're not on Xanax. Here's the 2009 report card from the American Society of Civil Engineers: aviation D, bridges C (but the bridge that collapsed in Minneapolis would get an F), drinking water D minus (and sinking fast), rail C minus, roads D minus, schools D (they mean the buildings may collapse). Twenty years ago, in 1988, when we thought the infrastructure was collapsing, the grades were higher.

I wish the Whig Party—Henry Clay, the young Lincoln—

would come back to re-create the nation. Thanks to what Clay would call "internal improvements," Europe is unifying. Thanks to Ryanair and faster rail, Europe is becoming a single nation. By Eurostar, it's two hours, that's all, London to Paris. This is more important, for EU unity, than adopting or not adopting the new EU Constitution. They're voting in a new constitution with their feet. Yes, in the twenty-first century, thanks to cheap travel, on top of e-mails, cell phones, the EU is becoming not just a single nation but a single mall. A Spanish kid can do a "start-up" in Dublin. An Irish kid can have his wedding in Madrid. If Europe is uniting "constitutionally," if Europeans are voting in a new constitution with their feet via high-speed rail and the like, the U.S. is disuniting "constitutionally" when we're sitting in gridlock, when it gets harder and harder to get from here to St. Louis. Our constitutional scholars should pay more attention to what army people call the "facts on the ground." With no Henry Clay pushing a U.S.-type Eurostar, when the Obama stimulus just goes toward resurfacing the clogged roads, it's harder each year to get from A to B, from Chicago to St. Louis, or from Chicago to Milwaukee. Or even from Chicago to Chicago: I am in terror of getting into the traffic here on a Saturday. Like more and more Americans, I sit here at home, since I'm more or less trapped. Yes, it's good that "no one can drop in," but hey, I'd like to get out. Even on a Sunday, it's getting bad. Once, on a Sunday night, I had dinner with a friend who came in from DuPage, and when she pulled up at the restaurant, she was sobbing, in tears. She'd been in the car an hour and a half!

And as the state gets weaker, and there's still no real land-use planning, the Bastille-like entrapment of Americans will get worse. In Chicago, there are commuters who now live out on the banks of the Mississippi River. They drive to the Loop—two and a half hours each way. Why? "It's for the kids." This is a happy-talk way of saying that our infrastructure is collapsing. Yes, it's "for the kids," because even in the inner suburbs, especially on the south and west sides, the public schools are in shambles. That's why parents move farther out. Their kids will go to college and take out crushing loans, and they in turn will move farther out. Is it really so far from here to the Mississippi River? It won't seem that way when Chicago commuters start driving into work from the Dakotas. The U.S. is the land of faux mobility; for the more "mobile" we become, the more we're really trapped.

It's because I'm now trapped here at home, thanks to the Saturday traffic, that I can write this book at all.

Sure, in the 1960s, when I was in college, I thought I was better off in America. Not only did Truffaut and Godard make Europe seem bleak, but I sniffed at all those countries for not being melting pots. Back then I remember an Irishwoman saying, "The problem with England is—too many English. The problem with France is—too many French. And the problem with Germany— too many Germans." In America, we mixed it up. America was great! And of course, in terms of this great national diversity, it's still great, or even greater. By 2050 or sooner, thanks to Latino immigration, the U.S. may be majority nonwhite. So yes, I still have an experience here that is not available to a European—or I would if I could list a few blacks beyond a couple of guys I know in the Loop. By the way, I wonder if the U.S. would seem so "diverse" to a black male locked up in a ghetto—not to mention how "diverse" it would seem to one locked up in a prison.

But how far ahead are we? For now, country by country, Europe, too, seems more diverse, less insufferably monocultural, at least in the cities. In a certain way, in the new mix of European civilizations (partly due to Ryanair), it seems more diverse, and surely more multilingual, just within Europe, and they get the rest of Eurasia crashing in as a bonus. True, the Muslim population is still just 4 percent, and yes, as Muslim birthrates fall, Muslims may end up no more than 10 percent of Europe's population. (Yes, that's all, according to some demographers.) My real point is: Europe's now part of Europe, i.e., the British are in Paris, the French are in Berlin, etc. For Europeans, it seems more of a flat world in that they seem readier to roll from place to place. In the big global companies, it's the European who's more likely to spend a year in Hong Kong, or Africa, or even parts of Latin America. For one thing, Europeans live and die by how much they export, while we do not. They're likelier to have been to dicey places, like Sri Lanka, or just weird ones like Timbuktu. Also, to paraphrase what a Belgian once said to me, in Europe, every baby knows when it's born it's got to speak another language. Just look at the readers of the *FT* v. the *Wall Street Journal*: which readers are more likely to be stuck in the rut of a single English-speaking civilization?

Besides, if we really were such hotshots at diversity, we'd be less Bush-like when we go abroad. Aren't we like him? We use first names. We slap their backs. We act like George W. Bush at a G-8 dinner: "Yo, Blair!" He starts to give Angela Merkel a back rub before they're on a first-name basis. Well, we've got to loosen up these Europeans. This artifice of being natural, it might work if we were less Bush-like and more Barack-like, but we're not. And at least Bush speaks rudiments of a second language, Spanish, which is more than you can say for Barack Obama and many other liberals, including me.

How many who bash Bush are more Bush-like than he?

Still, the issue here is not where you and I are more civilized. The issue is: where are we, ourselves, *materially* better off?

Let's imagine the lives of two women I'll call Barbara and Isabel. I'll put Barbara in Chicago, in a good manager-type job, a graduate of Northwestern. As for Isabel, I can say she's also at the top, though I hate to put her in a particular country. If I say she's German, people who hate Germany will hate her. If I say she's French, people who hate France will hate her. To shield this poor girl, let's just call her European.

I don't ask if Isabel is happier. God knows where we'd be happier! As Kant says in *Groundwork of the Metaphysics of Morals*, this is a matter for divine omniscience. It would require foreknowledge of every single circumstance in the lives of these two women. No, I just mean: where is it more likely that Barbara or Isabel will be materially better off? Now, for the people I represent, i.e., hourly workers, I know where they're better off. People in the bottom half of the U.S. (by income) would be better off, by far, in a European-type social democracy. I speak here as their labor lawyer—and yes, I do think I know what's best for my clients. So let us suppose it is true that half of America, the bottom half, would be better off in Europe. Some would not even think this was a flaw of the American model. What if it were true of the bottom three-quarters? Some would still wonder: "Is that a criticism?" etc. But suppose I could show that Barbara, who is in the bottom 90 percent, is better off in Europe. Even readers of *Town and Country* would perk up: "Okay, we're listening, tell us more."

"But isn't our GDP per capita so much higher?"

I said "likely" to be better off.

But can you show even that?

Well, I think I can.

Although I admit the higher GDP per capita is a stumbling block.

PER CAPITA GDP, 2006

U.S.	44,155
Germany	35,270
Denmark	40,702
France	36,546
Netherlands	40,167

Source: OECD.

Come on, Barbara beats Isabel by $4,000 per capita—a lot more if we stick her in the former East Germany.

But assuming Isabel's either in France or West Germany instead, I'm here to say: no way. Now, I could just keep beating how much inequality skews this number—how, if the U.S. is made up of one Bill Gates and six starving Bengali beggars, then the six beggars are doing "better" than Danish civil engineers. Of course, that's an old point, made long before the U.S. had such an explosion of inequality. See chapter 1 of *How to Lie with Statistics* by Darrell Huff (1954).

Still, for our purposes here, I don't care about "unfairness." Indeed, the unfairness of the U.S. is really a point against me here, since I'm comparing the lives of Barbara and Isabel, people at the top. The worse the inequality, the better off Barbara will be, or should be, if we assume she's highly educated.

"Yes, that makes your case harder still."

Good. That's what I want you to think.

No, I want to focus on whether this extra GDP is making *anyone* better off, and even whether it might even be making *everyone* worse off.

(Then, after that, we can focus on Barbara and Isabel in their respectively well-off but not superrich lifestyles.)

Okay—first let's start squeezing some of the "fat" out of Bar-

bara's GDP per capita. We have to put our GDP on a diet, or de-
flate some of the bloat in it, before we can decide which woman
is better off.

Let's take a nonpolitical thing, like the weather. Robert Gordon, one of our leading economists, a professor at Northwestern,
makes the point about heat and air-conditioning in the U.S.: the
extremes in our weather help pump up our GDP. We spend more
on oil, coal, even water. Like Sherman's army, the whole U.S.
population is moving to the South, where it's ever hotter. Like the
Mormons, the population also is heading into the West, deeper
into the desert without water to drink. At any rate, Gordon's point
is: while it builds up our GDP to go to extremes, are we truly
wealthier by living in places where the air-conditioning has to
be on?

Is Amsterdam worse off because it's not 98 degrees Fahrenheit?

Now let's forget the weather and go to a true political or insti-
tutional difference—our lack of any land-use planning. The U.S.
model as it now exists would be impossible without suburban
sprawl. If we were efficient, we'd collapse economically. We depend on sprawl, waste, and the bonfire of the malls. People move
farther out. Why? "It's for the kids." "We do it for the schools."
But one might say, "We do it for the sprawl." Without the increase
in inefficiency, our economy would stall. The more I sit in traffic,
the bigger our GDP. In terms of GDP, if we aren't stuck in traffic,
we can't keep ahead of France. Yes, it takes me half an hour to
drive each way to the mall to get an aspirin, and without all the
spending generated by all this chaos and inefficiency, our GDP
would be much lower than it is. Don't we end up earning more?
Maybe—but many of us end up lowering our real standard of living or going deeper into debt. In this respect, the neocons are
right: weak government and low taxes really do help "growth."
With all our lack of planning and infrastructure, we have to spend

and spend. Let's say Barbara spends two hours in a car commuting every day. Why? She's paying lower taxes. So the schools collapse. So she has to go farther out. Then *those* schools collapse. And now she's even farther out. Thanks to low taxes, we get chaos, poor planning, etc., which drives up our GDP per capita. We can't move, we're in a rage, but we're roaring past the Europeans. We're backed up, idling, in snarls, just to drive to the store to get an aspirin. The more stuck-in-traffic kind of GDP we have, the worse off Barbara is, though she looks better than Isabel in GDP per capita.

But this is too obvious, isn't it? With more disposable personal income, we have more ways to drive each other nuts and get in each other's way. With lower taxes and inefficient planning, we may pay a higher material cost in lost leisure, stress, even obesity, and not to mention road rage. In Europe, on a total mileage basis, people use public transit ten times more frequently than we Americans do; and in Germany and France specifically, that figure is higher.

I leave out the fact that Isabel can even ride her bike.

If the U.S. were more efficiently planned, our GDP per capita would fall. Yes, the lower we keep taxes, the more our "bad" GDP goes up and "good GDP," i.e., going out and having fun, goes down. The lower we keep taxes, the worse the infrastructure, i.e., mass transit, schools, etc. In turn, we pack up and move. As a result, as our GDP per capita rises, we become more like the Joads in *The Grapes of Wrath*, even if they're now just moving from the suburbs to the exurbs. It's crucial to our "lead" in GDP per capita to go on creating dust bowls that keep us on the move. Barbara gets type 2 diabetes and hypertension, but her GDP per capita is going up. A big reason we're number one in GDP is that, being sicker at every income level than Europeans are, we're creating more jobs—or at least we are in health care. It's not so much that we're working longer—as some would argue—but it's the weakness of government, our lack of planning, which sucks the life out of us.

And our GDP per capita goes right up with our blood pressure.

But lower taxes don't just undermine public health; they also take away our fun. If laissez-faire really let me live in the fast lane, I could see being a libertarian. The weaker the state is, the more I've got a ball and chain. By the time Barbara fights her way home—exhausted, out of gas, she pulls into the drive—she's in for the night. She watches more TV and has to find her dates online. If that's happening in a big U.S. city like Chicago, life way out there must be even bleaker. I'd hate to say of Isabel: "Because she pays higher taxes, it's easier for her to party." Still, there's a certain truth. At least she gets out. Isabel benefits from planning, efficient movement of people, EU limits on working time. Home before 6 P.M., she can rest up, redo her makeup and head out to the bars. All of this efficiency means Isabel has a lower GDP per capita but a hotter social life.

There's a puzzle here: wouldn't our GDP per capita go down if we're stuck at home? I think it does; on the other hand, if Barbara is stuck, she is more likely to supersize her home. She may opt to buy an even bigger house, and turn it into a Home Entertainment Center. So, GDP-wise, it's good if we're stuck at home. Poor Barbara, lonely in her cage at night, spends all that more to gild it. Isabel, in Amsterdam or Berlin, would just, well, move into a place and not do much to it. Why sink earnings into a money pit if going out is much more fun?

Barbara is also worse off from that increment of her GDP per capita that really comes from holding back our poverty and inequality. For example, think of all her GDP per capita that comes from the fact that we have a standing army—no, not in Iraq, but in cities like Cleveland and Chicago. Let's just start with guns. With ninety guns now for every hundred Americans, we better have an army. We need not just millions of cops, deputies, sheriffs, private security guards, public prison guards, private prison guards, but also the prosecutors, the public defenders, the janitors, the cafeteria workers to cook the prison food, and the rest of the baggage train. The Founders feared a standing army at home. Well, we have it, but it adds to Barbara edging out Isabel in GDP per capita. Only an editorial writer on the *Wall Street Journal* would think this makes Barbara better off. She has fewer places she can live. She moves farther out. A lot of her GDP per capita comes from her efforts to save her life.

Inequality is a tax on her in still other ways, e.g., from the existence of a plutocracy. The plutocracy just above her head can opt out of the way of life that she leads. That shrinks the kind of market for the "goods that would do her the most good." The more people who are at Barbara's income level, the better off she is. For example, it's simply cheaper in Europe to find a sophisticated European-type hotel, because there are more well-educated, modestly affluent people like Barbara to demand it. There are fewer rich who can spend $500 a night, and there are fewer poor who can spend only $5. It's why so many things are better. Products are less likely to be shoddy, because there are more people like Isabel who are demanding better quality. This was essentially Michael Porter's argument in his book *The Competitive Advantage of Nations* (1990), but it applies especially to egalitarian countries. With fewer poor or fewer rich, these countries are more likely to demand quality at low cost from things pitched to the level that Isabel and Barbara enjoy. That's why the better cars tend to come out of countries that are more egalitarian. I admit it's not an exact analogy, but it explains the success of Southwest Airlines. It doesn't try to serve everyone. It doesn't try to fly every type of plane. They just fly a particular plane, the 737, and don't try to do everything, and so do better than their competitors. The end result is that, over here, it costs Barbara more to live "like a European," to live the life of good taste that Isabel can. Too much of our productive capacity goes into catering to the hyper rich, and that interferes with an efficient delivery to Barbara of a bourgeois-type lifestyle. But aside from interfering with economies of scale, a U.S.-type plutocracy has other costs for Barbara. She also has to pay more to get her kids in the "right" schools, as the hyper rich keep bidding up the tuitions to keep out the riffraff like Barbara and her ilk.

A plutocracy shifts costs not just onto the poor but onto the Barbara-types a few rungs below the hyper rich. The richer the rich get and the more gated communities there are—and "gated" prep schools and colleges for the kids—the more Barbara has to pay to break her way in. It's not an accident but a crucial part of the U.S. model. When there is such a U.S.-type plutocracy, it's the near elite like Barbara who also pay a higher price. Barbara may have a higher GDP per capita, but a lot of this higher GDP—i.e., "bad" GDP, which comes from (1) crumbling infrastructure, (2) our "standing army" of prison guards, cops, and all the private security now blanketing America, and (3) the spending of the hyper rich to keep people like her at a distance—is a drag on her lifestyle. The "bad" GDP crowds out the "good" or "fun" GDP that an Isabel in a social democracy can get.

Worse, more of our GDP is just coming from gambling, from Wall Street, from the Merc. Take out the stocks, the commodities, the derivatives, not to mention real estate (until recently, that is), and there'd be no local economy in Chicago or New York. "Oh, that's all over." Well, thanks to the bailout, it's even bigger than before. Indeed, as I write, our banks are doing even less lending to the "real" economy and more lending back and forth to each other. Our two biggest cities in terms of "GDP output," namely, Chicago and New York, now basically exist for making bets, i.e., gambling. That's a major change from fifty years ago, when it was just New York alone that made big bets; even back then, in the time of DiMaggio, New York had a local economy with other things to do. Let's not consider what it does to our moral character. We can leave that to the Christian right, which seems to love electing a gambling-oriented plutocracy. The question is: what does all this gambling do for Barbara? If she's at the table, okay; but she may not have the chips or the instinct to gamble.

If that's so, then she has to work longer hours to keep up. Next to gambling, that's what pushes up our lead in GDP per capita. After all, we lost our lead in productivity. If we look just at productivity or GDP per hour of work, Europe is roughly in a tie, a bit ahead, or a bit behind:

GDP PER HOUR WORKED, 2007

U.S.	100
Germany	95
Denmark	85
France	99
Netherlands	100

Source: EPI/OECD.

Indeed, I bet that true GDP per hour of work is higher than ours in the four European countries in the table above. How do I know when the experts don't? Simple: as a U.S. labor lawyer, I'm dead sure that with all our wage theft, and people working off the clock at Walmart, we get a cumulative undercounting of U.S. hours. In terms of that table, we cheat. Meanwhile, countries like Germany also cheat, the other way—Germans take off early. They overstate how long they work. Even if I'm wrong, the table still shows that what's driving up Barbara's GDP per capita is the simple serflike fact that she works longer hours.

Or at least she did until the meltdown in 2008.

Long ago a private-sector economist now working for our government said to me: "I can't stand these stories about how 'last month' average income in the U.S. went up. Then two years later, you look at the numbers, and all of it's gone to the top 1 percent." He's right. Page through the editions of the oft-updated *State of Working America*, put out by the Economic Policy Institute in Washington, D.C. Still, won't I admit that even in the U.S., total family income has gone up? Of course! But it's not that any breadwinner is winning more bread per hour, but that we are working longer hours or finding more family members to go to work. So let's assume the worst—that Barbara is a single mom. Then she has two choices: she can work longer, or she can gamble. She can get an "extreme" job, e.g., a 24/7 job finding oil in Alaska, or she can work longer as a PR-type at Leo Burnett. Or she can gamble: i.e., she can stay home with her child, get online, and be a day trader. George Soros started out this way—why not her? Alas, whether she works an "extreme" job or is a day trader, she is unlikely to be keeping up. Still, it's possible—the great thing about America is that anything can happen.

Of course, other things drive Barbara to keep working longer hours. There's no social contract anymore, so if she doesn't work longer hours, she has to worry she'll be fired. This is how some labor economists, like Linda Bell and Richard Freeman, explain why Americans "choose" to work longer hours while Europeans do not. See "Incentive for Working Hard" (Conference Board, May 2001). If she doesn't, she's out, because there are others like Barbara who will work the extra hours. As an economist once explained to me: who's got the power at a McDonald's? Whoever assigns the hours. It's the same in the big corporate firms. We all have internalized "Chainsaw Al," even when he's not around. It's the fear of being zapped, like a lab rat; Barbara is much more likely to develop a little twitch than Isabel, who may have to look harder for a job but is much less likely to be fired. I think here of my client Joan, a real-life Barbara, a middle manager, now forty-seven, who's been "downsized" or laid off four times in four Chainsaw-Al "restructurings." She just gave up and now lives downstate on a family farm. (I think she grows her own food.) In a lab-rat way, she had learned that she has to work more than the person in the next cubicle or she will get a Chainsaw Al–type shock again. If millions of Barbara-types keep calculating their hours in this way, "x plus one more than yours," it means that, in a one-upmanship way, everyone's hours keep going up. So if we work 2,300 hours a year now, we'll soon be working 2,400 hours a year. There's no way collectively for people to stop.

Meanwhile, over in Europe, the hours of work really are collective decisions, made by unions or works councils. Isabel may be downsized, but it's not going to happen to her three or four times. Besides, she's under a state law or contract that puts some real constraint on her hours, whether she likes it or not. The bigger point is, unlike Barbara, she does not have to keep up with a whole class of people who gamble and make bets. So there is no reason for her to work the extra hours. It's the stock market that keeps driving the companies to downsize, something they would never have done fifty years ago. It's financial people who get rid of the production people, etc. In Europe, there's not just a labor movement to protect people like Isabel; perhaps just as important, within a particular company, there is a real balance of power between—oh, call it what you will: production people v. financial people, or managers v. bondholders, or what we once would quaintly call Chicago v. New York. Now, of course, it's all New

York. Even Chicago is New York. It's all financial people who keep cutting costs so that the short-term bets they make in the market keep paying off. That means people like Barbara have to work longer hours and there is a kind of "faux" productivity, i.e., it *looks* like the companies are more productive, but it's a degraded kind of output. In journalism, for example, the paper now is leaner, meaner, but they've cut out half the news. As Louis Uchitelle points out in his book *The Disposable American* (2006), this hollowing out keeps going until the company collapses. As the company is hollowed out, Barbara is hollowed out. Of course, there used to be a way out—to wake at 5 A.M. and start day-trading before going to work.

Still, bad as it is, the longer U.S. hours helped pump up GDP. After the financial meltdown of 2008, our gurus like Paul Volcker said, "We have too much consumption," as if we should be producing more, like the Europeans. The irony is, the more time we spend at work, the more we have to be consumers—just because we are all such worker bees. As Barbara stays later, she has to "outsource" her life for various vendors to handle. Why? She has no time to cook, so she has to eat out. She can't scrub the toilet, so she hires a housecleaner. She has no time to fix or repair, so she throws stuff away. To Europeans, it's a shock to see whole families in America eat out at McDonald's: on a weeknight! A lucky family of four may boast three members each working 2,300 hours a year, at least if times are good. Never mind shopping, or cooking, or cleaning up: who's got time to eat? Who's got time for McDonald's? People now eat when they gas up at BP. The more supersized Coke we slurp down, the more the GDP per capita bubbles up. The less time there is to consume, the more money we have to spend.

We have not so much "consumer" as "producer" wants. Long ago in *The Affluent Society* (1958) John Kenneth Galbraith made fun of our imaginary "consumer wants." To him these were just the "wants" that Madison Avenue wanted us to want. Who needed the "Veg-O-Matic"? Yes, maybe they were spurious, but at least they were genuinely *consumer* wants. Back then, when we worked shorter hours, we had "world enough and time" to consume. Maybe, in unionized America, we had too much time. We had pensions, health insurance, and lifetime jobs. Why did people even know they could order the "Veg-O-Matic"? They could stay up *after* Jack Paar to see the commercials on TV. Now we're in bed before Letterman comes onstage. Back then, in 1958–59, the highly unionized U.S. (at least in the North and Midwest) was in danger of turning into a European social democracy. With shorter hours of work and a rising standard of living, we needed madder Mad Men to keep us busy buying crap.

Now, in the new age, the wants we want are not spurious at all. As we work longer hours, we really do need to eat out, bring in housecleaners, and in general contract out our lives. As I say, these are not so much "consumer" but "producer" wants. We need computers so that we can work at home, i.e., on weekends, late at night, etc. We build our little private gyms so we can stay in shape. We need day care to raise the kids. These are "wants" we "want" so we can go on working longer hours. These are the "wants" we need to free ourselves to work. We are not so much "consuming" as we are "investing" in ourselves as human capital. "Come on, let's bear down." We contract out more things to free up our time to work in order to be less vulnerable to layoffs. We skill ourselves up to keep producing. We have to buff our bodies to keep up our stamina. One day, a Barbara-type may ask of every purchase: "Does it help me bear down at work?" Of course, Isabel also has to bear down at work. But she does not need to spend four hundred or more extra hours working a year, so she's safe from Chainsaw Al. She doesn't have to keep pouring money into herself, like a Volvo, so she doesn't break down on the road.

Yes, Isabel may get older, but Barbara depreciates. In terms of "human capital," Isabel is more the "human," and Barbara more the "capital."

That's why I think Daniel Bell and other social critics get it wrong when they say that our "hedonistic" consumer ethic is at odds with the "ascetic" producer ethic that fired up capitalism at the start. Their point is: "What would Max Weber say if he looked around and saw all the people like Barbara at health clubs and trattorias?" Okay, but what Bell and others miss is that, unlike the 1700s, people today have to invest in themselves as human capital. Barbara and her type are the ascetics now, partly because they do "consume" (i.e., invest in themselves) rather than "save." For many people at the top, to be in debt may even be a mark of self-discipline. On the other hand, Isabel et al. are relatively "hedonistic," and the proof of Isabel's hedonism is that she has a higher savings rate. All her money in the bank is proof of her profligacy. If she worked like Barbara, she'd be contracting out her life to vendors as she went deeper into debt.

Here's what Keynes and Galbraith never saw coming: a dystopia-type economy in which "consumer" wants would be "producer" wants, so people could buy computers, join gyms, hire other people to live their lives. In order to produce efficiently, we need to have a whole team of people to raise our kids: day care, counselors, tutors. With the kids, it's not just to help us be better producing machines at work. We also have to invest in babies as human capital. These investments, tiny in the 1950s, keep getting bigger every year for Barbara. They are flat or falling for Isabel. (Universities in Europe are free, etc.)

Still, it's really ourselves we invest in. If we need face-lifts and

Botox, it's not just to look younger, friskier, "sexy," as Europeans like to think. No, it may seem like it's all frivolous, but it can save us from downsizing. That's why Barbara does it, secretly. When they cherry-pick in a downsizing, it's helpful to look apple-cheeked. You don't want to end up in the glue factory, like Boxer in *Animal Farm*. It's Orwell I think of when I'm at the East Bank Club or Whole Foods and see people munching organic oats.

In a way, Americans really aren't a nation of consumers like Europeans are. You will say, "That's impossible!" Isn't our problem right now that we consume too much?

Yes. But the question is consumer choice. Sure, at Whole Foods, Barbara has got a lot of choices. But over in Europe, Isabel has more.

First, she has more choices in public or collective goods—the subsidized concerts, the swimming pools.

Second, she has the choice of not consuming—the one choice that no one in America seems to have. Unlike Barbara, for example, she doesn't have to keep moving out or pouring money into some new house.

Third, she has time to consume. Let me pause for this third point. It takes a certain amount of leisure to consume. In a certain sense, relative to Europeans, people in America suffer from a certain impotency. With respect to our private goods, we have the appetite but not the capacity for the "total" experience. Frustrated that I can't finish reading *Middlemarch*, I go out and buy more books. We buy boats but leave them in the harbor. We go to Majorca—for two days. We start—but we can't finish. And in a rage, we go out and buy more, and the GDP starts to count everything we don't have time to consume. In my own case, of course, it's books. Since I can't read any, or have no time, it makes a certain sense to go out and buy the biggest ones. Why leave around unread a book of ninety pages when I can buy Tony Judt's *Postwar* and leave unread nine hundred pages? Since I can't read either one, I might as well buy the book that will give the biggest boost to GDP. Incapable of consuming anything, even a book, I'm more likely to start writing one. At least then I can console myself that I'm really at work.

At any rate, the longer I work, the less capable I am of completing a single "*consummatory act*." I don't so much consume as buy the surrogates for what I might consume.

In short, Isabel is much better off as a consumer than Barbara is. Not only does she have fewer producer wants, but she has more time for her consumer wants. I admit, at Whole Foods, Barbara may have more choices. (As a European, Isabel may have the choice of an open-air market.) But the fact is, too many choices are exhausting. Do we need sixty-five varieties of organic juice? It's often liberating to have fewer. Also, as we work longer, we have no time for all these choices. The leisure to make the choices is declining as the complexity of the choices increases, as if the American economy is set up to mock us. "Look at the things in the window!" But who has time to go in?

I mean to say that, in Europe, Isabel's leisure adds value to what she buys. I doubt there is any way to measure what "freedom" adds to the value of goods and services. Over the years I have tried to come up with a graph. How could I show it? Let's take Barbara's GDP per capita and stack it up by Isabel's. What does freedom or leisure add in a material sense to the value of Isabel's per-capita stock of things?

I mean not just leisure, but freedom. It's her freedom from work. It's her freedom from the commute. Here's my thesis: if her material needs are otherwise satisfied, each hour of freedom is worth a lot. If they're not met, it's not worth a lot. But in a social democracy, everything is paid for. By "everything," I mean the pension, the health care, the education, etc. But Barbara is in debt. So every hour of leisure, while valuable to Barbara, has a cost. For Isabel, it does not. At a certain point, an extra hour of work makes her worse off. That's why Barbara's higher GDP per capita actually could be a measure of how much worse off she is than Isabel. It's just that our economic tools, at this early stage of the "science," are too crude to calculate the trade-off. After all, economics as a science is about two hundred years old. When it's as old as physics or astronomy, we'll get much better measures of standard of living.

Freedom or leisure is about as cosmically important as the dark matter, or dark energy, of the universe. It's just that our minds have been darkened by economists like Milton Friedman. Yet Friedman himself had half an idea as to who is better off (Barbara v. Isabel), even when he was writing libertarian-type tracts like *Free to Choose*. Friedman's very life was an indictment of the ideas in the book. As a professor with tenure, he lived like Isabel, not Barbara. He had tenure, and three months off, and no one could fire him. He had a big TIAA-CREF pension, which a teachers' union helped expand. It was a pretty nice life, even by Isabel's standards. To the extent Friedman was "free to choose," he chose to live like a European in a social democracy. I wish every one of us were free to live like Milton Friedman.

Friedman was free: being either in the government or academia, he had freedom from fear. Protected from the market, he was free to live a life that poor Barbara never will.

Really, Isabel is better off as a consumer because (1) she pays higher taxes, and (2) the state controls her spending. It's because she pays more in taxes that Isabel can save. While this sounds paradoxical, it's obvious in a way. A European-type social democracy is really a form of guided spending. The state taxes Isabel and spends her tax money on what Isabel really needs. Barbara, by contrast, is pretty much on her own. Think of what the state "buys" for Isabel:

Retirement
Health
Education
Transportation
Child care

The state buys for Isabel, in bulk, in the most efficient way. This leaves her plenty of money to spend on her own. Barbara can't buy these things for herself as cheaply and efficiently as the state can. It's like trying to beat the house. In the U.S., we all think we can beat the house. In an oddball study once lovingly cited on talk radio, 60 (!) percent of American men think they can support themselves from gambling—I mean real, Vegas-type gambling. Well, they can't. And likewise, Barbara can't beat the house. As a consumer, she can't go out and allocate her money for

Retirement
Health
Education
Transportation
Child care

as efficiently as the state can buy these things for Isabel.

Of course, Barbara can try. She has no choice. But to get the same level of what are really collective-type goods, she has to pay more. Worse, she has no guidance, so she makes mistakes, and she ends up spending in wild directions.

Then, when she realizes she doesn't have enough money for these public goods, she goes out and tries to console and/or sedate herself by buying a Toyota she doesn't need and ends up in worse debt than before. Maybe she does indulge a spurious consumer want. She may think: "I'm not going to have enough for Mom's nursing-home insurance. Why not blow it on building a new deck?"

The problem is quite different from the one Galbraith wrote about. He argued in the 1950s for higher taxes because he saw a gulf between our "private" affluence and our "public" squalor. The public park looks like crap, etc. In the 1950s, he believed, that's why we needed higher taxes.

Okay, it's still true. But we also need them now so we really do have "private" affluence, which is something that people even near the top cannot assume they have. We need higher taxes so people like Barbara can guide their spending more efficiently— for getting into a good school at a reasonable price, for getting health care, for getting child care—indeed, for getting a lot of things that a New Dealer like Galbraith in the 1950s took for granted. Galbraith was calling for something like the German "Green Party," when in fact the U.S. was about to lose its version of the German "SPD," or labor party, i.e., a strong pro-union Democratic Party.

The only drawback is: if we deliver public goods in the efficient way that many European countries do, we may hold down GDP. The availability of public goods can spoil the appetite for private goods. If all other universities are free, Bennington College isn't going to be charging $40,000 a year in tuition. Nor are parents going to be working longer hours to send their kids to this kind of school.

On the whole, citizens can't make decisions to get these public goods as efficiently as the state can. How much should go into buying the BMW and how much should go into a private 401(k)?

If Isabel wants a BMW, it's a lot simpler: she's already got the "basics," retirement, etc., so there's no trade-off to make.

Barbara's got too many choices, and it's easier to get it wrong. The more she has to buy what the state buys in bulk for Isabel, the easier it is for her to mess up at least *one* of these choices. Who of us can beat the house, over and over? And once I realize I've blown it, I become even more irrational. "It's too late to build up my 401(k). I'll just take this $5,000 and lease a new Ford."

Don't do it! (Think of the car payments!)

Why? Don't I deserve it for not having a 401(k)?

There is no CPA standing over me, the way the French or German government is standing over Isabel. But even a CPA doesn't always beat the house. One advantage of a social democracy: it does your financial counseling.

Even if you're smart enough to marry a CPA, as my brother did, you're better off in a social democracy.

It's the way to explain why Barbara is in debt while Isabel has savings, though on paper Barbara has higher GDP per capita. There are other ways that, in a social democracy, Isabel is better off.

1. Jobs

"In Europe, aren't they all unemployed?" Well, let's look at people near the top, like Isabel and Barbara. As a college graduate, Isabel is less likely to be unemployed than Barbara in terms of getting a college-type job.

Of course, at least before the meltdown in 2008, it seemed on paper that our college graduates had a slightly lower level of unemployment.

UNEMPLOYMENT RATE FOR COLLEGE
GRADUATES, 2006 (PERCENT)

U.S.	2.5
Germany	5.5
Denmark	3.7
France	7.0
Netherlands	2.8

Source: International Labor Organization.

Since the meltdown, even the slight advantage here probably shifted to Europe, since countries like Germany have a lower unemployment rate. But even from the table, we can't tell what kinds of jobs these American and European BAs were and weren't getting. In 1994, three economists at the U.S. Department of Labor (DOL) did a study (never to be repeated, shhh) as to whether college graduates in the U.S. were in college-graduate-type jobs. The study, which can still be found online, blew the lid on the darkest secret of the U.S. model, i.e., that the "real" unemployment rate of people with BAs is at least 20 percent. That means one in five is working in what DOL calls "a high school job." Though "Marian-who-wants-to-be-a-librarian" has an M.A. in library science, she now gives massages at a health club. Heck, I know such people. One in twenty, I'd have guessed—but no, it's one in five! Well, of course, it was suppressed. Why would DOL ever let out a study like this again?

Nor did I get to the bad part: it's not the "one in five" being in a "non-college" job, but what the DOL has tried to call a "college" job, like "claims adjuster," i.e., figuring what it costs to fix a fender. It seems a kind of fraud to push kids into student loans just to get these jobs.

Let's not even get on the subject of Phoenix and other surrogate colleges that solicit "customers" at "prices" of $20,000 or more a year.

Still, how do I know that, in Europe, kids with high-octane BAs aren't selling ties and giving massages too? At least, in a country like Germany, college graduates aren't taking blue-collar jobs as crane operators and ironworkers. The dual education system won't let them. In the U.S., though, college graduates really are taking these jobs. I know that not only from the 1994 DOL study but from my clients, ironworkers with college degrees.

As the DOL study made clear, college grads in the U.S. can hold a lead in income partly because we let them cream off the best-paying blue-collar jobs. In Europe it's much harder for a graduate of Humboldt University to break into a top blue-collar job held by an IG Metall member.

So in matching the U.S. BA with a real college job, i.e., not selling ties at Macy's, the true "unemployment" rate for U.S. college grads should be not 2.5 percent as recorded in the table on page 72 but 22.5 percent, or even higher.

But aren't I being unfair to the U.S. model?

"Yes, it should be easier for Isabel to get a job, since your friends the Europeans don't put as many people into college as we Americans do."

While that may have been true in the days of Woodstock Nation, it's not true anymore.

PERCENT OF ADULTS AGE 25 TO 34 HOLDING AN ASSOCIATE DEGREE

U.S.	39
Germany	22
Denmark	41
France	41
Netherlands	36

Source: OECD.

Germany is a weird case partly because of its strong dual-track education system, which has helped keep up high-tech skills without college BAs. But the U.S. is not just roughly even with most of Europe, it's behind France, Denmark, and many other countries. It's even farther behind Canada next door.

In part because of the crushing debt, 47 percent of American kids entering college now drop out without getting the degree.

Indeed, the fact that the unemployment rate is slightly higher in France may just show that, with the safety net of a social democracy, Isabel can be choosier. She can hold out for what I'd call "Bloomsbury-type" jobs. These are the jobs that Keynes could have had in mind for the "economic possibilities of his grand-children." Now I admit, in that same essay, which I keep touting, Keynes actually seems to argue that if the return to all invested capital would go up at a certain current rate, then one day none of "us" would have to work. We'd all live like Lytton Strachey and Virginia Woolf, or even like Keynes and his ballerina wife.

But of course, as we know, Keynes himself loved to work. He may have even killed himself with too much work. Surely, Keynes would be aghast at a country like Greece where no one really works, and no one really pays taxes. The whole Greek middle class is sitting in coffeehouses every afternoon. And poor Greece, which was a subprime social democracy anyway, did not live off its invested capital but let Goldman Sachs keep piling up more foreign debt.

Countries like France and Germany abhor running up such debt. And of course there is work—for Bloomsbury-type work, work with a sense of craftsmanship, may be the most golden good a real social democracy provides. Keynes, in his heart, must have known this; he would not want to live in a world where we'd be as idle as Lytton Strachey or Virginia Woolf but one where we'd get to do their kind of work. Yes, we should work less, but I feel sorry for the Greeks who don't get to do the work the French and Germans do. And I think Keynes was saying what a German labor attaché in Washington, D.C., who came out here to Chicago, once said to us: "The goal is that we should be working less and less, and our work should mean more and more to us." One day we might consume and even savor our jobs the way one might open and drink a good bottle of Bordeaux.

Then, here's how to decide if Barbara or Isabel is better off: on which continent will she find a Bloomsbury-type job? If that's the test, social democracy wins. Let's take a few examples:

Public Employee. European countries experiment with how they deliver welfare. Some countries do it with public-sector jobs. Others do it with income transfers. So Denmark or Sweden or even France, which have strong central states, may have far more civil servants than Germany, where the state is weaker. Here I have to confess my frustration in getting good comparative data on public employees: which country has more, etc.

At any rate, there is nothing Bloomsbury-like about some public-sector jobs. Who wants to be a cafeteria worker in a prison? Even the job of teacher can vary: in America, some teachers in Montgomery County, Maryland, are making $150,000 a year and others are struggling at $29,000 in a bog in Baton Rouge. But at least I can say this: in Europe, especially in the social democracies with strong states, like France and others, civil service has prestige; it is possible to imagine the best and brightest wanting to get into it. Here, civil service is ridiculed, and it's ironic that, since the Wall Street crack-up, the public sector is even less secure. Here's where we had the layoffs, which by the usual Keynesian multiplier effect went on to wipe out so many private-sector jobs. Nuttily, at this moment our politicians are arguing for even more cutbacks in public employment, as if they are determined to deepen the recession. And even the vaunted pensions of our public sector now seem at risk. Let's leave out the small fact that in the recent crack-up many of these funds lost 30 percent or more of their value. No, the problem in Illinois and many states is that taxpayers are not willing to pay the taxes to fund them. Is it likely that taxpayers who have nothing will cough up their last dime for public-sector pensions? That's why mayors are privatizing: there's nothing efficient or low cost about the private sector in America except the ability to bust the unions. Who in America would want to go into the public sector at this time?

But in Europe, at least in countries with the strongest states, the public sector is still a high-prestige place to be.

First, in Europe they will at least get their pensions. In America, that's now an open question.

Second, Europe at this time has been generating a lot of "fun" civil service jobs—think of all the glorious elite jobs that have been created in the EU. Isn't it great for the elite that they have a whole new central government, on top of all the old ones? And yes, they still have all the jobs that used to come with the old ones: with twenty-eight EU member countries, each one with its own central government, think how many more chances Isabel has compared to Barbara to be a diplomat, a scribe, or a hanger-on at court. For one thing, think of all the foreign ministries of the EU member states, all the consulates these little countries have to staff abroad. By being born in a tiny country like Denmark, doesn't Isabel have a better chance than Barbara of being an ambassador to China? Denmark has to send someone to Beijing—why not her?

It's true we have fifty states, so if Barbara is from North Dakota or Alaska, she could be a shoo-in for senator. Or governor, if she shoots a gun. Still, one has to admit, for Isabel, there are relatively more openings to be an emissary to Kublai Khan than to be a water and sewer commissioner. It may be unfair, but where the state is strong, and not under siege like in America, the public sector is richer in Bloomsbury-type jobs.

It's not that we lack public-sector jobs: we have more prison guards, for example. But certainly Europeans have more of these in culture, especially high culture. Think of all the Germans who spend their lives at the Goethe-Institute not just in Lagos, Nigeria, but in truly remote places, like San Francisco. I am thinking here of all the German civil servants who have washed up in Chicago, where they drink white wine at lunch at Shaw's and go out at night to hear the blues.

That's the social contract—that's the European deal. The high rollers like Isabel support the wonderful public pensions, free health care. In return, the majority let her have her little subsidy for the opera.

Or put another way: "We let you have your fun. You let us have our fun." Now, of course people in IG Metall also go to the opera, just like some in the elite are into heavy metal or blander forms of rock. But on the whole, everybody gets the kind of social justice they want.

Some, like Niall Ferguson, the economic historian, say: Why don't they just spend their own money, each on what he or she wants, instead of cross-subsidizing each other? In theory, to a Scottish economist, it makes no sense. But all these cross-subsidies ally people to each other in a kind of defense pact.

At any rate, over in the U.S., by paying so little in taxes, we starve ourselves of the most creative and rewarding jobs. Yes, we get a lot of support from private money, but at least in Chicago, it's often a one-shot thing, a new wing for an art museum, but nothing that ever turns into a steady paycheck.

While we do have our public universities, we are seeing furloughs of professors even there. Besides, I'm talking about Bloomsbury-type jobs in the government—with a little power. Wouldn't many of us in the private sector like to pull the rip cord and have such wonderful jobs open up for us? Long ago, Daniel Patrick Moynihan wrote that, as people become more educated, they get a taste for more government. For many people like me, it's just more interesting to do "policy." Instead of selling widgets, we'd rather save the whales. Why don't more people like Barbara do it? They think somehow they must make enormous amounts of money, even when, paradoxically, they would make more money in a public-sector job. Of course with the meltdown, more of us have opened our eyes. But it's too late for those my age! We could have started work at age twenty-four and retired about six years ago, and been out on the golf course every day. The other night at a White Sox game, I heard a man in the row below me tell his friend what a fool he was to have left the government. "Of course," he said, "I hated being in the IRS. On my evaluations they kept saying, 'You smile too much.' But once you're in the federal government, it's easy to move around." He paused, sipped his beer. "Next year, at age fifty-two, I'd have been gone with 80 percent of my pay."

I, too, would have hated the IRS. But I also, in my own city, might have hated being a teacher, even if I could have retired by now.

I keep thinking of my first German teacher at the Goethe-Institute, a young blonde who taught us after work. She herself had a big job in design and was making good money, but she was determined to teach at night. Halfway through the course, I found out why: she had been a teacher once in Berlin. She ended up in Chicago because she had met and married an American, and she simply assumed she would be a teacher in the public schools. Of course, she was aghast. "They were starting us out at only $27,000!" she said, when she came in the 1990s. By the way, she had been a teacher in the old GDR, the old East Germany.

Even someone who had grown up under Communism could come here and realize that being a teacher sucked. Now at night, with a broken heart, she came to us just to be in a classroom again.

Still, in the rich Illinois suburbs, she would have been happier. Why is it so rare that someone like Barbara would do it?

Because by the time she's got all the right degrees, she's just too deep in debt.

Artist. For a European, I could also put this under "public employee," but I thought I should break it out. Art is a public good, and Europeans get it far more efficiently than we do in the U.S. There's more of it, too, so there are economies of scale, i.e., three operas going every night in Berlin. In Europe, it costs me ten euros (about $13) to hear Daniel Barenboim conduct. In the U.S., it's more like eighty bucks.

One night in Berlin, I was laughing to a German friend: "I guess the only people here who don't get subsidies are the rock bands."

He looked at me in surprise. "But they do, of course." His rock band used to get a government grant. "It's not official, it's true. But every year the city sponsors a contest of rock bands for prize money. And in reality everybody wins." It was prize money, but they depended on it, like money from the Ford Foundation.

Only in a social democracy like Germany would they have safety nets even for rockers.

Big Business Employee. Doesn't America win? Oddly enough, there are more possibilities in Europe. As my friend Lee in Paris said, "There's no stigma in working for a utility or a gas company, as there is for the kind of people we know in America." Of course in a meltdown, people will take any job. Her point is: in France, there was never any stigma in the first place.

It's not necessary for half of the Princeton class to end up at Goldman Sachs.

Should I add that, even now, some of European "Big Business" is owned by the state? So Isabel has less worry of being downsized: the unions are too powerful.

"Wait—doesn't she have to worry about privatization?" Yes, but she's safe as an executive as long as the French workers keep marching in the streets.

Yes, in the U.S., the pay will be higher—the pay can be great! But it can lead to twitching, nervous disorders, and maybe pancreatic cancer. It may shorten one's life. Think of the risk to your health of making $2 *million a year*.

A friend who works at a big company told me: "What I can't understand is—people who make $5 *million* a year. Let's say I get $2 million. For that kind of money, I'm going to work very, very, very hard. But if I make $5 million a year, I'm not able, or just can't, really work all that much harder."

It's true that, in some ways, our Big Business is less stressful; we know the big banks are now supported by Washington, D.C. "In fact," the Europeans say, "the only place where there's real old-fashioned capitalism is in socialist countries like France." The Europeans mean that the central bank and the taxpayers have not bailed out their bankers on the scale we have. But even if it should be less stressful because of the safety nets under our bankers, there is just a certain amount of stress from making so much money.

Because in a real social democracy people can't make $5 million a year, life turns out to be healthier at the top.

Small Business Employee. Only a fool would start a Small Business in the U.S. That's why, contrary to the stereotype, Americans are much less likely than Europeans either to be self-employed or to go into small firms.

"That's impossible! We're so much more entrepreneurial."

"Yes, what about high tech?"

But according to a 2009 report from the Center for Economic and Policy Research (CEPR), using comparable data from the OECD, we're at the bottom in everything, including high tech.

PERCENT OF ADULTS SELF-EMPLOYED, 2009

U.S.	7.2
Germany	9.0
Denmark	8.9
France	12.0
Netherlands	12.4

Source: CEPR and OECD.

Also, U.S. business has close to the lowest share of employment in small businesses in manufacturing, say economists John Schmitt and Nathan Lane, who did the CEPR study. Only 11 percent of the U.S. manufacturing workforce is in companies with fewer than twenty employees. Rich European countries have a bigger share of employees in small manufacturing firms: for example, Germany is at 13 percent and France is at 18 percent.

Considering how many U.S. companies use day laborers to run the factories, this statistic is astonishing.

Yet why should we be surprised? I'm not. I'm one of those Americans who is an "entrepreneur," running a small business. Our firm has six employees. Do you know what health insurance costs? It would be much easier for me if we moved the firm to Europe.

I know people say, "Oh, to have your own business: it's so wonderful." I say, go see *Casablanca*. When I see it, I get choked up when Rick sells his café and goes off with Claude Rains. Not because he's going off to fight with the Free French, but because he's sold Rick's Café.

Think of it: now he can forget the health plan. He doesn't have to make payroll.

In Europe, Isabel would have more safety nets for her Small Business, and she would be more likely to survive.

In fact, in the U.S., there are very few like Rick who escape with their lives. In 2005, the last year I checked, Americans started over 573,000 small businesses and over 586,000 went bust—and those were the good years.

So if Small Business is so suicidal, why do Americans start so many anyway? That's easy: as bad as Small Business is, Big Business is even worse.

So if the jobs are better over there, I have to explain why so many of Europe's best and brightest end up in Cambridge and Palo Alto, not to mention Manhattan. Of course risk-taking type A's, alpha males and alpha females, are attracted to the high risk here. But that, too, is a reason why Isabel is better off. The U.S. siphons off the abrasive, hard-charging types who would make her life unpleasant over there. Or let's say the U.S. is a safety valve. We take in more of the plutocrats as well as those who arrive in sealed boxcars to park the plutocrats' BMWs. That is, in America, we take in the world's predators as well as the people they like to prey on.

So long as France and Germany can dump their predators over here, those countries are kinder and gentler to people at home. Isabel is safer and better off.

2. Retirement

I refer the reader to Teresa Ghilarducci's wonderful article "The End of Retirement," still available online (*Monthly Review*, May

2006). We've retired the notion of retirement. The defined-benefit pension plans of the 1950s—the plans that employers paid in entirety—are gone. They disappeared with the U.S. unions. The 401(k)s and other voluntary contributory plans are a shambles. In 2008, the average 401(k) plan held by Fidelity Investment lost 28 percent of its value—a quarter or more being typical. That means many Americans lost 30 to 50 percent of their entire 401(k)s. Over age fifty-five, about five out of ten of us have less than $50,000 in total for any kind of retirement—I mean, it's more like $20,000. That's it. You can fix a little gruel, like the widow who took in the prophet Ezekiel, and then lie down and die.

It's true, as some say, that the losses in 2008 wiped out the gains of only the last ten years. So people are back at 1998: that's not so bad, is it? But that fails to take account of the fact that people in 401(k)s typically pay much-too-large investor fees that, even in the good years, wipe out the few gains they make.

Some experts are astonished there has not been more cashing out of 401(k)s. That's because, for all but a few, there is hardly anything to cash out.

When one considers the lost tax revenue, the payout in investor fees, etc., the whole thing is a scandal, even without the collapse of the market in 2008. We all would have been better off taking all that money and using it to shore up Social Security.

Of course, the fallback was that at least we could sell the house. Now, unless you live in North Dakota, even that is gone.

That leaves Social Security, which pays 39 percent of working income. (There is some dispute about this "average" number, but it is no higher than 41 percent.) In 2005, the OECD did a comparative study that put the average payout of such public pensions at approximately 67 percent. That's the OECD average: in a study that, again, finds the rate of only 39 percent for our country. In other words, without our pitiful Social Security pulling down the average, the OECD figure would be higher than 67 percent.

It's true, in defense of the U.S. number, one can say that our Social Security is a bit more progressive. That is, elderly who had lower earnings may get a higher percentage. But that is bad news for upper-middle-class people like Barbara, whose 401(k) just got clobbered and now has to count more on Social Security.

Okay, but hasn't Europe cut back too?

Even in the big example, Germany, where the public pension is just over 50 percent of working income, most Germans still have big supplements from collective bargaining. Besides, unlike us, who are deep in debt, Germans have high savings rates for their own accounts, which are not tied in to the stock market. Let's assume that Alicia Munnell and other economists are correct and we should still get at least 67 percent of working income for retirement. That's still true in Germany. It's generally true in Europe. I can't see how most Americans could even get close to that number if they have $50,000 median in their 401(k) and top out at 40 percent of their working income from Social Security.

And remember, in America, unlike Europe, many of us head into retirement deeply in debt.

Throughout her life, Barbara will spend about a fifth of her income paying off banks. At least in 2007, U.S. households were paying over a fifth of their after-tax disposable income to the financial sector in debt services and financial fees. So reports Dirk Bezemer of the University of Groningen in the *Financial Times*.

Isabel will never have to pay that kind of money. It just makes me wonder: how can people live?

It's true that most European countries, like our country, have raised the official retirement age by a few years. But at least Europeans will get to retire; in fact, they usually do so before the official retirement age by taking "unemployment." Yes, by my age, one may hope to be laid off and draw down a nice unemployment benefit, which leads very nicely after a year or two into a very nice pension. Besides, since Western Europeans live a good two years longer than we do, they should raise the retirement age by two years or so, if only out of fairness to us. It's not just that retirement is a good deal; but, as shown by books like Richard Wilkinson's *Unhealthy Societies: The Affliction of Inequality* (1996), Europeans outlive us.

Of course one reason they outlive us is that retirement in Europe is still so good a deal.

3. Tuition

One day there will be two ways for American parents to send their kids to college: Enlist them in the army or ship them to a European country where the universities are free. Yes, one day, Barbara may have to leave her child like an oblate on the doorstep of the EU.

"Please educate my son."

I'm kidding.

For one thing, I doubt the EU will take them. That leaves the army. And it's true that state universities still cost less: practically free by our standards, at only $10,000 in tuition a year. But remember: in our U.S. economic model the whole goal is to get in the top 10 percent of income earners, and if that is the goal, one had better think seriously about sending one's child to a top-brand school, one that charges at least up to $50,000 in tuition.

Soon that may be true just to get in the top 20 percent.

But that's a lot of money. Let's look at the sunk costs here for Barbara and Isabel.

Prep school in Chicago (St. Ignatius): $47,200—four years.

Private college (New York University): $160,000—four years.

Law school (New York University Law School): $135,000—three years.

I put the raw tuition cost to Barbara at well over $340,000, and that's not counting books, travel, SAT tutors, LSAT tutors, the calculus tutor, summer school, and anything at all for K–12.

And that's not an unreasonable prep for getting in the top 10 to 20 percent.

How much for Isabel? She could have her child go beyond this regimen, so by the end of it all, the kid could have a PhD from Milan for a song.

The above example shows why a social democracy can have more cash value for people at the top like Barbara than it does for an assistant pastry chef in Lyon or a cleaning lady in Chicago. That is, a social democracy with "Free Georgetown" or "Free NYU" is worth more in a material sense to people at the top than it is to the assistant pastry chef who just gets a nicer pension in the end.

4. Child Care

Ask a European couple the big cost in coming to Chicago. "It's the nanny!"

Here's a report from S., a journalist in Berlin. "We are now paying for full-time child care that is as good as anything I have seen in Chicago." And her standard is the Lab School at the University of Chicago.

What's she paying?

In Berlin, she's paying five hundred euros a month (approximately $680) for two children. And she's expecting a third child. With three children, she will pay even less.

What did she pay at the Lab School? For two children, she was paying $15,000 a year. I asked about five years ago, and since then the gap has grown. In other words, even in 2005, she was paying two to three times as much in the U.S. Oh, and I forgot about the nanny after school. The nanny was another $25,000: that's what leaves a European couple gasping.

Meanwhile, the deal just keeps getting better in both France and Germany. In addition to all this day care, and extra money in France if the local day care is full, mothers get another five hundred euros a month, just for the heck of it, for having a third child.

That's why they all have three kids. At the very time I am writing this section, I think of the French couple I saw on the El yesterday.

"Only two kids," I thought. I was troubled and was thinking of redoing the fact check.

But then, behind her dad, I saw the third child peek out.

5. Parent Care

Apart from kids, it's cheaper to have an elderly parent. In many European countries, the state provides nursing-home benefits.

Isabel doesn't have to buy an insurance policy (which may not pay out) or put more money in her 401(k) (for her mom's retirement and not her own). Barbara does. Of course, I leave aside the fact that, by drinking red wine, Isabel's French or even her German mother is likely to be healthier.

Did I mention that, in Germany, Isabel could take in her mother and get paid by the government? Yes, in Europe, after they pay you for having a third child, they are willing to pay you for taking in Mom as a boarder, at least in some countries.

I stumbled on this bizarre deal when I met a deputy consul at the German consulate here in Chicago. She had her mother live with her, and she got a check every month.

"Wait, Germany is putting in a new benefit? How can you pay for this?"

"How do we pay? We are giving up one of our paid German holidays."

By the way, this benefit came in under Kohl: it's a characteristic of Germany that some of the nicest benefits have been put in place when the CDU, the conservative party, has been in power. Still, as a union-side lawyer, I'm always suspicious of them.

I mention that benefits are increasing, even though some are being cut back. As Europeans understand, the way to solve the problems of a social democracy is not just to cut back benefits but also to increase them. To pay for pensions like golden parachutes, the Europeans have to have more kids.

How to do it?

Give mothers golden parachutes.

Just as the answer to the problems of democracy is usually more democracy, so the answer to the problems of a social democracy is usually more social democracy. That's why Isabel is better off over there.

Now reader, I ask you: let's assume we're paying 41 percent of our GDP to the state, and Europeans are paying 48 percent, as *Newsweek* claims. Are we getting 41/48ths of what the Europeans get?

But I know that you don't really care about these safety nets. You don't care about Barbara or Isabel, or where they would be happier. Why should you? You're an American, and you just want to compete.

I feel the same way: I want America to be Number One. I want my country to be competitive. But even in terms of competitiveness, I can make a good case for the European model. Even a country with high wages and unions can thrive in a global economy.

Or I should say: *only* a country with high wages and unions can thrive in a global economy.

Now let me give you the bad news: against everyone's advice, I picked Germany as a model. "Germany!" Ugh. Why didn't I pick France? Don't I have Denmark up there in those tables?

Yes, it was a mistake. We are leaving the City of Light for the shadows of central Europe. I'm sorry I picked the Germans!

3

I'm Sorry I Picked the Germans

But I couldn't help picking them. How often in the last ten years have I thought: "What a mistake!"

As I look at my scraps of notes over the years, I can find exactly the spot where I was about to give up. Here's what I wrote in August 2004: "Look at the *FT*: thousands of unemployed marching in East Germany."

Merkel was about to win, and she was supposed to be the German Margaret Thatcher. She'd get rid of the German model. Why not? Unemployment was 5 million, or 12.7 percent.

As it turned out, she had to form a coalition with the Social Democratic Party, the SPD. And, at any rate, the German model perked up. By 2008, unemployment had dropped to 3 million, or 6.7 percent. And, as I write, unemployment in the U.S. is worse. In the past year it has been over 10 percent. Yet hasn't picking Germany still been a mistake? Ever since 1997, when I first went, the Germans have let me down—no spending, no "animal spirits," as Keynes would say, as if the whole country were a little girl playing with her food. What was the matter?

Back in 1997, when things were even worse, many people used to blow up at me when I touted the German model. Many in the elite just detest the German version of social democracy. I think here of a St. Patrick's Day party, March 1997, where there were a lot of Irish Catholic lawyers like me, except most were from big corporate firms. Since I was just back from Germany, one of the right-wingers began to needle me:

"The whole place is in collapse, isn't it?"

"No."

"That's not what you hear—it's all these union people, they can't compete."

"Well," I said, "they're running a trade *surplus*. In that sense, they're doing better than the U.S."

"And you know the only reason they're running a surplus? Tom, come on, they're selling off their capital stock," said a lawyer—let's call him "Pat."

"Wait, Pat, you think they're selling off, like, the plant and the equipment?"

"I'm saying it's not a 'real' surplus."

I wanted to say, "Do you know that for a fact, or did you read it in the *Wall Street Journal*?"

"Let's just say," he said, "people are disinvesting in Germany." He seemed about to scoff: "And it's all because of your 'unions.'"

"You don't know what you're talking about," I said.

"You don't know what *you're* talking about," he said.

We put down our Guinnesses and glared, the way Irish Catholic lawyers do. Other corporate lawyers were barreling in now, but of course they all took Pat's side, not mine. "Oh, it's not competitive." "It's collapsing."

Someone said, "You know the problem with Germans? They don't have any work ethic."

Others said, "Yes." "That's right." Now I let loose.

"You mean I come out here on St. Patrick's Day to hear a lot of Irish tell me how the Germans don't want to work? Give me a break."

"They don't want to work," said Pat. So I turned on him since he was the farthest to my right.

"You know what I think, Pat? You don't like Germany or Europe because right now people aren't being squashed—you like this inequality, don't you? I mean people in this room, we've got everybody waiting on us."

(That was awful, I shouldn't have said it!)

"Are you questioning my motives?"

"I am questioning your motives," I said.

"I could question *your* motives," he said. "Just to get to equality, you'd try to lower everyone's standard of living!"

Everyone supported Pat, and these were Democrats.

I drove home in a rage. Question *my* motives? Of course I could question *his* motives. Ah! I was childish. No, I was right. Thinking of that night, I have sometimes said to Europeans: "You know, in America, people really blow up over Germany." Some of them protest: "Oh no, they blow up over France." No, that's Sarah Palin. When I say "people blow up over Germany," I mean "people" in a different sense. I mean the people who run the hedge funds. I mean the 47 or so percent of Harvard College grads who, in the glory year of 2007, were going into consulting and financial services; of course, they're Democrats and on the left, but they go off and read the *Wall Street Journal* because it gives "the other side." Those are the "people" who blow up over Germany, as they never do over Denmark, or even France, because Germany being bigger is just a bigger threat. And, in at least one big way, it's less "capitalist" than Denmark or France. If only because worker representatives have half the seats on the German corporate boards, it would be the "most left" of the European forms of capitalism. With the collapse of the USSR, it's the country with the greatest degree of shop-floor worker control. And I'm counting China and Cuba. Or at least, it's the place where the employee has the most privileged position in the firm. Aside from the boards, one can make the case that the works councils are more like Soviets than the Soviets in the Soviet Union were, at least after 1917. (By the way, during the entire Cold War, never once can I remember ever getting into an argument about the USSR. I get into arguments about Europe all the time, but I can't recall the subject of the USSR ever coming up. Why did no one ever discuss it?)

The USSR model was never a serious threat to anyone's bottom line. People blow up over Germany because, for all its left-wing bent, it may be a more plausible form of capitalism than ours.

Still, just because some wealthy corporate lawyers in a Chicago suburb can get all worked up over Germany, why should *you* be interested at all? You don't work at Goldman Sachs. You're not going to live there. You don't know German. You'd never dream of blowing $1.50 on a single issue of the *Financial Times*. One or two of you might even think: "I bet you're just writing this because you're part German on your mother's side."

Do you think I'd do that?

Let's say you're a non-European, nonwhite American. Why is it crucial for your whole life to read a book not even about France but about a dreary place like Germany, even if the baked goods are just as delectable?

Well, maybe you have a mild form of celiac disease and can't stop eating bread. But maybe you're exhausted as an American, and while you want to be competitive, you also want a life.

Maybe you're like me and long to hear "The Bells."

The Bells

Even now, on this Saturday night, as I sit here at my desk—I love to think back to that other Saturday night, my first night in Frankfurt, my first night in Europe, oh, that wonderful night when I first heard "The Bells." I'd just landed in Frankfurt to start my two months in Europe. (See page 1, supra.) And I was on a cinder path, jogging, when, at 6 P.M. on a Saturday night, with no warning, "The Bells" of the Dom—the great cathedral—all began to bong. They bonged, in the dark, from the cathedral, the Dom, and they bonged as if later, at midnight, Charlemagne would be crowned. *Bong!* I had to stop. *Bong!* Ah, I couldn't hear myself jog. The Bells: they seemed to bong not just from the Dom, but from everywhere, as if the lights were about to go out in every store in Europe. They were bonging out:

Stop!

Stop running!

Stop competing with each other!

Stop buying and selling, for God's sake!

Everybody has to rest!

It's a kind of a medieval air-raid alert. Stop all this capitalism. And I felt a chill, as I stood there in my running shorts, on that first night in Frankfurt: yes, the stores were being shuttered all over Europe, and they would not be open again in my lifetime, or at least till Monday morning.

I'd have no one to compete with for over a day.

Of course I was exhausted, jet-lagged, but I wasn't ready for a day of rest. It's odd that, here of all places, even for a day or so, capitalism would stop. After all, isn't this the very place that capitalism had its start?

Yes, I was in the Rhineland, the home of what economists call "Rhineland capitalism," as opposed to "Anglo-American capitalism."

But didn't modern capitalism start here, or at least the line of it that has come down to us?

Yes, right here, in Frankfurt. Yes, it started here, they say, on the very path I was jogging: on this little footpath, where the men in the Middle Ages used to pull the little barges up and down the little rivers, the little European rivers that run north and south. Since 1000 A.D., toll free, little barges had been going up and down the river Main and the other little rivers. Jared Diamond, Norman Davies, et al., argue that, thanks to these little European rivers, running up and down, capitalism in the West got its start. Yes, just as I shivered when I heard The Bells, I shivered when I saw The Boats.

The Boats: I also got a kick that, as I jogged along, jet-lagged, on this towpath, I could outrun them on foot.

Anyway, this is where the real European capitalism had its birth, in 1000 A.D. And maybe it was where a new capitalism would be born again, in 2000 A.D.

I'd come, for the first time, on this night, January 4, 1997, to see what the new European Union was going to be. And in this part of western Germany, around Frankfurt, one is not really so much in Germany, or really so much in France, as in a place that is both, all at once: it's the Kingdom of the Franks. So it is with "Rhineland" capitalism: it's part French, part German. And it's this Europe, the Frankish Europe, which is not Bismarck's Europe, or Adam Smith's Europe, but which is partly France, partly Germany, and which is, in sum, the Europe of Jean Monnet, that is, the native place of the only Western form of capitalism that can challenge ours right now.

It's the capitalism that's got Catholicism, solidarity, and social

justice, and it's also the capitalism that has The Bells. When The
Bells began to bong in the Middle Ages, they were saying:

The week is over.

Feudalism is over.

Stop clubbing each other.

The Sabbath is about to start.

Now, of course, even if no one is in the churches, people listen
to The Bells the way woodsmen in the woods may listen to The
Birds. They still go on bonging, telling people to stop:

The week is over.

Capitalism is over.

Stop clubbing each other.

And head out to the clubs.

That other life that's ticking away for us? These Bells, by their
bonging, seem to be telling us to live it. That's why, when I come
to Europe, I love to start in Frankfurt. To me, Frankfurt is the
most exciting and mysterious city in the world.

"Frankfurt?"

"I hate Frankfurt," my friends say.

"Frankfurt? It's boring."

"It's so 'American'-looking. It's just a business town. What's
there?"

Well, I have two reasons for loving Frankfurt: first, it's the nativity of First World capitalism, and it may be the nativity of social
democracy, too. And, as a sort of subreason (not the second actual
reason), it's the home of the two most distinctive institutions of
the EU: the European Central Bank, which sets the cost of capital, and IG Metall, Germany's most powerful labor union. So one
could say the bank sets the cost of capital, one of the great inputs
of capitalism, and IG Metall sets the cost of labor, which is the
other. The Big Bank and the Big Union: all week, they check and
balance each other. And then, on Saturday, someone rings The

Bells. Anyway, that's the first reason I tell people, "You have to see Frankfurt." To understand the EU, and to understand this new Rhineland kind of capitalism, the one that is the real rival to our own, one ought to start in Frankfurt, the place where it was born. This is based on the theory, set out in Vico's *The New Science*, that to understand any nation or supernation like the new European Union, one has to go to the place where it was born.

Then there's the second reason: Frankfurt *is* boring, like "America." But that is the allure—to me, it's like Tibet. I feel like I've wandered into the pages of James Hilton's *Lost Horizon*. Set in the 1930s, that is the book where the hero crash-lands in Tibet and is taken in by monks. The monks are—well, just monks, ordinary enough. Then the shock in the book comes when Hilton's hero finds out about their secret lives. By some trick (or "miracle"?) or another, these monks don't burn out in sixty or seventy years, but go on living for centuries; under the surface of looking like the rest of us, they get these double or triple lives. People say, "What's in Frankfurt but a bunch of bankers?" And yes, they look like us. But I get a chill when I see them. Like the monks in *Lost Horizon*, they have a different sense of time. The years go by more slowly, because they can stop, put little markers in their work lives, to slow down their heartbeats—so different from the felt experience of every American working 2,300 hours a year to avoid a layoff: "I don't have the time!"

Isn't it frightening to think that, once a year, for six weeks, maybe up in a cabin in Norway if not Nepal, the Frankfurt banker next to me lets go of the sense of time that I have in exchange for that of a Tibetan monk's?

That's why in Frankfurt, my favorite of all cities, I love the Dom Café. Why? I love to look at bankers. I walk in: "Oh my God, there they are." This place is near the Dom, but it seems to be for young Germans only, and they sit around in big communal tables.

Look at the waitstaff, who're all Danskin-ed in black and nico-tined. Look at the backpacking bankers back from faraway Cush and Seba. When I'm in here, I may be next to the Dom, but I don't need to hear The Bells.

I just look at them, hanging out: Bong.

Bong

Bong

It's a mellow Buddhist bong. They could be wearing saffron robes.

One of the boring Frankfurters leans over and says to me: "What is an American like you doing in the Dom Café? How did you ever find it?" I could say: Come on! It is right next to the Dom Cathedral, which may be the biggest tourist spot in Frank-furt. Yet—

He's right to be astonished. I've crash-landed in the Himalayas.

The Six Reasons: Forget France, and Sweden, and the little coun-tries. There are six reasons why I decided to pick the Germans:

1. Germany Is Big!

It's the real Europe, in a way. Maybe you think I should have writ-ten about France. In some ways, it is more civilized. I think of my friend Lee's comment: "I had cancer. I thought I'd go back to New York. Then I realized I'd get so much better care in France! What's it like? Here's what it's like. When I went to an appointment with my oncologist, he, the nurses, the whole staff, they were *waiting* for me when I walked in. 'Oh, we've been waiting for you.'"

Yes, France is so civilized! So why not pick the French? Well, there are things I don't like. For example:

Sex. It may sound odd for me to say—but all the sex in France upsets me. It's too overt. I guess, in the Second Empire, it was even worse, in a brothel version, rampant with disease. Syphilis did more than Prussia to bring down Louis Napoleon. Think how many great French writers it killed. It's too much on people's minds. It would be too much on mine.

Labor. I like German labor law. In France, the way to do things is to go out in the streets. The German unions may not strike enough. But I don't like locking the boss in the office, as French workers tend to do. Just as France has too much sex, it also has too much violence. In the U.S., we don't have enough conflict: they have too much. They can't understand why we file all these lawsuits; we can't understand why they have all these strikes. In 2005, when the French-Arab kids began to riot, I kept hearing Americans say, "See, the French aren't integrating the Muslim kids into the system." How do they know? If the French were integrating them into the system, it would follow that the Muslim kids would be rioting in the streets.

As I will try to show, Germans have more conflict than Americans do, but they handle it a lot better than the French.

The State. Compared to France, the state in Germany is weak. After all, the Allies wanted it to be weak. So in this respect Germany is quite different from the other social democracies that Tony Judt and others like to write about. It pushed social democracy in a different direction. The check on the private corporation could not come externally, through regulation, or even public ownership, which requires a strong state. As a result, the check on the private corporation had to be built into the structure of the firm.

By that I mean: co-determination and works councils, as discussed below.

In a sense, the impulse for social democracy that in other European countries came out in the form of a socialist-friendly state here went into shaping a socialist-friendly firm.

Size. France isn't the biggest. For us Americans, "size" really does matter. It's how we blow off the Nordic countries, or the Dutch. Still, as I noted before, the French birthrate is going up.

But the real question is whether the European model will be more like Germany or more like France. And there is a way in which the unification of Europe has to connect up or run parallel to the unification of Germany and the spread of the German model.

First of all, even if France were one day to overtake it, Germany is still, for now, the biggest country in Europe: 83 million people. And it's the real Europe: really, east of Brussels, Germany is just another name for Europe. It's Europe without the glitz. Staying relatively out of the imagination, it's the biggest, most businesslike, and most boring part of Europe. It's the Europe for adults. It's the Europe that people skip.

Sure, France is sexy, France is fun. (See above.) But it's here in this heart of Europe that we can get to the heart of the European model.

Besides, with the unification of East and West Germany, Germany has become a kind of paradigm for the unification of Europe itself. That's true in one sense, just because Germany is bigger. The more Germany unifies, the more Germany *is* Europe. But it's also true that the more Europe unifies, the more Europe is Germany, trying to bring its western and eastern selves together.

The fascinating thing is to keep in one's mind all the unifications that are now going on at once. Yes, Germany as a nation is unifying, as it has been trying to do ever since 1000 A.D., when the popes were dismembering the Holy Roman Empire. And Europe is unifying as the EU, as it has also been trying to do since

1000 A.D. The history of trying to unify Europe is a history of trying to unify Germany as well. So it's no coincidence that as Germany unites, Europe does as well. It is doubtful that it could happen any other way—one unification requires the other.

For more than 1,500 years, Germany has been trying to figure out one way or another of turning itself into Europe. At one time, it was going to be the Kingdom of the Franks. Then it was going to be the Holy Roman Empire. It has tried to turn itself into Europe via the west, as a Carolingian empire. Frustrated, it has tried to do it from the east, as a Prussian one. In one century, it's trying to stage it all from Frankfurt. In another century, it's trying to do it from Vienna. Then Prussia takes a shot under Frederick the Great. Then it tries again a bit later, under Bismarck, who sets up a German Empire, and then that becomes a German Reich. Then that one blows up, and Hitler's Reich comes in. And all through the centuries, everyone in Europe seems to be involved in how big Germany is going to get. In one era, it's the German Emperor v. the pope: Henry IV v. Gregory VII, etc., etc. Then it's Bismarck v. Louis Napoleon, then the Triple Alliance v. the Triple Entente, then the Axis against the world. And, later, in a vastly more benign form, it was a little tiff between Kohl and Major, squabbling at Maastricht over the extension of social democracy in the German model.

It may seem strange, in writing about the European model, not to write about what happens in Brussels. Obviously, it would make a certain sense. But the premise of this book is that the future of the European model, whether it can compete or maybe even overcome the U.S. model, depends on what happens to this German model, the German version of social democracy. The creation of a new "unified" Europe, the new EU, is a big story distracting from an even bigger story—namely, that there is a double-barreled unification going on. Europe, as a kind of "greater Germany," unifies in Brussels, while Germany, as a European state, unifies in Berlin. In the first case, "Europe" is unifying itself, in Brussels, with German leadership and money. In the second case, "Germany" is unifying itself, in Berlin, with a centralizing push from European Union law.

And in this second case, the unification of Germany proper, there are two kinds of "unifications" going on. Of course, West and East Germany are uniting *horizontally* as a single nation-state. But also Germany is trying to unite *vertically* as a stronger "federal" state, against the various *Länder* state governments. The central government in Berlin is trying to claw back some of the power held by the German *Länder* in education, taxes, and other areas. Bavaria, Germans like to tell the tourists, has never even technically signed to the German constitution. The Germans are dealing with issues that go back to the breakup of the German Empire by the princes and the medieval popes.

So if all these unifications are going on, all at once, and if a thousand or so years of European history are coming to a head in our lifetimes, aren't we curious about what is going to happen?

Also, I'm leaving out a lot of other things, such as the linguistic unification—how everyone in Europe is becoming European by speaking English. To be a European is to speak English, which is the unifying language, yet the unifying idea of Europe is to be even with us linguistically without being like us at all.

Yet over here people say, "Germany's boring." "Nothing's happening there." Imagine if, in our own country, we attempted anything as wrenching as one of these unifications. Just trying one, we'd have everyone screaming on talk radio. As it is, perhaps because our country attempts nothing, we do have everyone screaming on talk radio.

For social democracy to survive, this unification of the state, at the German level, at the European level, is crucial. It's not because the social democracy I like in Germany is rooted in a strong centralized state, with a lot of public ownership. Rather, in Germany, where the state is weak, social democracy is more about letting people have a bit of control over their lives.

The result is not just a certain limited form of socialism, but a capitalism that works. After all—

2. Germany Is Industry!

Yes, arguably, it's the world's leading industrial power: right up there with China, except it's green, and getting greener all the time. Come on, is the West really in such decline? Yes, we can sit here on our island continent and gloom about the rise of China, as our elite like to do. But look at the Germans! For here's a strange fact: since 2003, it's not China but Germany, that colossus of "European socialism," that has either led the world in export sales or tied more or less for first place with China. (Each has about $1.2 trillion in export sales.) It's a net creditor, not a net debtor, like the feckless U.S. According to the *Financial Times* in December 2009, the U.S. had over $3 trillion in *net* external debt to the world at large. Worse, we are running up this dangerous net external debt at the rate of $1 trillion a year. While we are in the clutches of our foreign creditors, Germany—at least in terms of this net external debt—is completely debt free. That's what comes from being the champion exporter in the world.

Sure, at this moment, in late 2009, it seems China will edge ahead of Germany in export sales. But that's not only because of the recession but also because the euro has soared far more than any other currency. Even so, the European Union as a whole—or just the "socialist" kingpins, namely, Germany *and* France—still sell far more than China. Meanwhile, though the drop in the dollar was supposed to set off an export boom, America still lags behind Germany and China with a bronze, in third. So for most of the recent past, it's not been China, with 1.3 billion people, or the U.S., with 300 million, but Germany, with 82 million, that has led the world. But in China and the U.S., we have to work till we drop. The Germans take six weeks off: in a sense, they have been outcompeting us with one hand tied behind their backs.

Surprised? None of this is supposed to be true, according to the business books. Pick up Thomas Friedman's *The World Is Flat*. We're all competing with each other, and we're competing on cost. Everyone says, "Labor markets have to be flexible." But at least by our standards, the German labor market is anything but flexible. Even in the big firms, they have half the corporate boards made up of workers. So how can they be so competitive? Far from rigging anything, the euro exposes them to fiercer competition than the U.S. and China get. And Dean Baker and other economists have told me, "Their tariffs are no different from our tariffs."

How can they do it?

Simple: it's socialism, as I will try to explain below.

At any rate, especially in the last ten years, after everyone wrote it off, the German model has thrived. The recent past may turn out to be the true "German miracle." When historians write of the "German miracle" they mean the long-ago recovery of its economy under economics minister Ludwig Erhard, after World War II. It was the time Germany became known as "Germany, Inc." In a way, that older German miracle is far from miraculous. Or it's open to a rational, not a supernatural, explanation. It's plausible that postwar Germany, used to being bombed, could get up and going again, just as it did through the war itself. It's a "miracle" one can explain. But why, in our own time, is high-cost Germany so competitive globally? In a "flat world" where we compete on labor cost, how can it keep doing better than ever?

Some say, "Well, they are competing on cost—at least recently, German wages have been 'moderating.'" Come on! Let's put aside that nonwage costs—like health—keep climbing. It's still one of the highest cost producers in the world. If it's such a flat world, the Germans should be toast. Instead they're breaking out champagne. Why?

Now, in the *FT* and in *The Economist*, which keep predicting the German model's doom, the excuse they give is: "Remember the labor reform we said they weren't doing? Well, you see, they are doing it, so that's why they're on top. Wages have moderated," etc. Sure, that may have helped. But even as a half truth, this so-called wage moderation isn't very credible.

First, in manufacturing, wages are an ever smaller cost of the finished product. The plants are automated. The "wage cost" is a tinier and tinier part of the total cost of the finished product. Wage moderation? Two percent v. four percent, it doesn't matter.

Second, the wage moderation explains even less when one considers the rising value of the euro. Especially outside the eurozone, where it's the euro v. the dollar v. the renminbi, it's even weirder to claim that wage moderation explains Germany's competitive success. While German unions held the line on wages, the value of the euro soared. It's soared against the dollar. It soared even more against the renminbi and other East Asian currencies. Even if German firms did get a bit of an edge from "wage moderation," they lost it over and over in the run-up of the euro.

So what's the big deal about wage restraint?

The most that the right can argue is that the relative moderation of German labor may have had a certain psychological effect.

But in terms of competitiveness, German firms are successful because, unlike U.S. firms, they don't have any illusion they can compete on cost. (That's why they can survive the run-up of the euro.) They don't have the illusion that they can bust the unions, in the U.S. manner, as the prime way of competing with China and other countries. It's no accident that the social democracies, Sweden, France, and Germany, which kept on paying high wages, now have more industry than the U.S. or the UK. During the 1970s, 1980s, 1990s, the Anglo-Americans, the neoliberals, *The Economist*, the press generally, would taunt the social democrats in Europe: "You'd better break the unions." Yes, that's the way to save your industry. Indeed, that's what the U.S. and the UK did: they smashed the unions, in the belief that they had to compete on cost. The result? They quickly ended up wrecking their industrial base.

But Germany, Sweden, and France ignored the advice of the Anglo-Americans, the *FT*, the people in financial services: contrary to what we told them, they did not wreck their unions. And it was the high labor cost that pushed those countries into making higher "value-added" things. Where is Germany competitive? It's in high-end, precision machinery, made by people with the highest skills. It's in engineering services. People look at Germany and say, "What about the unemployment?" But no one in the U.S. ever says, "What about the labor shortages?" Even in 2008, precisely because of "globalization," Germany had a serious shortage of people able to fill high-skill, high-paying jobs, especially engineers. In the U.S., engineers complain they can't find work; many of them just end up in sales. In the union-free, lower-cost U.S., we don't create the kind of jobs engineers can do. Germany's problem? It has too many. It's our whole globalization thesis turned upside down.

That leads to a seeming paradox: higher labor costs can make a country more, not less, competitive. In many ways, the U.S. and the UK got out of manufacturing because their labor costs were too low. I have spent my life watching plants close in Milwaukee and Waukegan, where skilled labor was paid $26 an hour, only to reopen in Georgia and North Carolina, where it was paid only $8 an hour. While we're still fighting over severance two years later, we get the news: the whole company is bankrupt. The products are now crap.

A company that made money when wages were high went into bankruptcy when wages were low. In that respect, not enough cost was imposed on our employers. Slowly, investors moved away from widgets, where we could not compete with high-cost labor, and went into stocks and bonds.

On the other hand, some labor costs are destructive. Paying twice per capita what the Germans do for health care doesn't make us any more competitive. The point is that labor costs can be good just as they can be bad. It's like good and bad cholesterol.

But what about China? It's not in Germany but in the U.S. where the elite sound relatively more Spenglerian. "The West is in decline." "Asia's on the rise." It's true enough that China is on the rise, though the way it rigs its currency to keep it from rising against a falling dollar is unfair. But even if the East is on the rise, the West can still do well.

In part, it's because China is booming that a country like Germany can do well. Even a few in the business press cite this as a factor: "It's perked up with growing demand in the developing world." They want German engineering, the high-end specialty goods that their own companies can't offer. Who's got this market?

When we groan about foreign rivalry, we think of the U.S. v. China. Why not think more about the U.S. v. Germany? At first this seems preposterous. Yes, we run a big trade deficit with Germany too, as we do with Canada and other high-wage union countries, but it's not nearly as big as the one we run with China or with other parts of Asia. But, in a way, Germany is our real rival. Germany is knocking us out of markets we should have in

China and East Asia and many other countries. Social democracies steal our sales. Compared to Germany, we have a "hidden deficit," the business we lose because we don't make the high-quality precision goods that social democracies tend to manufacture. That's why, in the U.S., we tend to lose elite high-skill jobs, while in a social democracy, like Germany, they tend to have too many to fill.

Does it begin to make sense why we might want to copy what Germany, and not China, is doing? Shouldn't we be copying this particular foreign model, i.e., the German one, the way Asian countries once copied the West? We go around hectoring our kids: "We have to compete with China." And the more we cut their wages, health care, and pensions, the less competitive we get. I'd tell kids to read about Germany just to see how a social democracy (which we don't have) would push our productive capacity into highly skilled jobs and also keep business from disinvesting in such jobs. After all, things could and probably will get even worse in the U.S., in terms of job loss. Our great economists who used to laud free trade (Paul Samuelson, Alan Blinder) are right to think that things are tanking here. But one good thing about a high-cost social democracy like Germany (or France or Sweden) is that it penalizes business when it disinvests. To shut down a plant is easy in the U.S. It's a big pain in a social democracy, though. The employer has to come up with a "closing plan." There has to be a plan for taking care of people, paying severance, etc. In subtle ways, it's easier just to keep going. That's why over there so much industry survives. And that's why over here so much industry is gone.

In other words, in the U.S. and the UK, we got out of manufacturing because the labor costs were too low. We took the path of least resistance, competing on the basis of labor costs. Then, when that didn't work, it was so much easier to shut down.

But there's an even bigger reason why social democracy tends to keep its industry: the high level of public spending tends to hold down private consumer spending. Sometimes, as Paul Volcker recently said, there can be too much consumption.

Let me paraphrase what I take to be the argument of a well-known economist, Ronald McKinnon, and others of similar views: If we spend and don't save, or if we consume more than we produce, the extra 'output' has to come from somewhere, i.e., outside the U.S. And what form will the 'extra' output take? It won't take the form of a free tan at a tanning parlor or a yoga lesson in Manchuria. It will take the form of an object, probably a cheap plastic one, that can be imported. That is, it will take the form of a Manufactured Good. So it follows that the more we run up our debt to the rest of the world, the fewer things we make.

That's our plea now to Germany and just about every other European socialist country: "Run up a big debt, so you can buy things from us." Well, why should they? First, even if they did, it might not help us. We have shut down so many factories, we can't easily come up, even if the dollar falls. Second, why should they devour their middle class? By not running up their Visas, the middle class in Europe has stayed basically intact. That's in part because spending is more "guided." Or, put another way, because of the efficiency of higher taxes in delivering public goods, people are much less likely to spend. Year after year, the Germans never come close to spending more than they produce. And what's the result? They end up with more highly skilled, high-wage jobs than they can fill.

"Oh," some scoff, "the Germans, they're mostly making it off of high-end specialty items." If they're making $1.5 trillion in export sales, maybe we should be doing little industrial knick-knacks too.

I know, people still insist China is the real story. At the moment, though, in 2010, the combined total of exported goods of both France and Germany is $1.6 *trillion* v. China's $1.2 billion. And remember the disadvantage of the euro. Still, in terms of exports, a country like Germany with 82 million people, taking six-week vacations, is edging out a country with 1.3 billion who work around the clock. It hardly seems fair.

One may answer: "Yes, but this advantage is temporary. One day China et al. will catch up with the social democracies, France, Sweden, all of them. Then we'll all laugh." *Yes, China's the new story.*

But isn't China the *old* story? It's like Japan sixty years ago. It's like Germany a hundred years ago. It's the new kid on the global block. Yes, China is hot, now. But China may cool off. The population, by the way, is aging as fast as Europe's. They can't keep working that hard. Germany's lead may even grow. "Yes, but isn't Germany selling the engineering and machine goods that will let China demolish them?" Also, there's no proof yet that China can compete as well on a higher value-added plane without . . . well, without becoming more like Germany.

That's hardly an argument against the German model.

Anyway, so what? There are a lot of countries on the make, in Asia, Latin America, and Africa. In the next fifty years, they may want the things that China's buying from Germany, too. The more the developing world develops, the better the "inflexible" social democracies will probably do, especially compared to the "flexible" U.S.

Besides, in moral terms, it's even a good thing if more low-wage, U.S-type industry goes abroad, while the developing countries in turn need more high-end German- or French-type manufactured goods. There is a term, "virtuous growth," i.e., growth without inflation, which is a nice thing but has little to do with moral virtue.

But the competitiveness of high-cost unionized social democracies really is "virtuous," in a moral sense. Think of the developing world:

Africa

Parts of the Middle East

Chunks of South Asia.

They're the poor of the world, on Europe's doorstep. What if they start buying? We have very little stake in wiping out global poverty. The social democracies do.

Anyway, Germany is industry. Yes, of course, globalization has rocked it. A German used to have just one job for life. Now he or she may have two, or even three. "Aren't you ignoring the unemployment?" Yes, the term "globalization," which is a term that partly means "the rise of Asia," does take away jobs from people at the bottom. That's the crisis in Germany: "What are these people going to do?" Yes, I will agonize about this, a lot, in the chapters to come. "Come on, you have to take the problem seriously." I do!

But at least it's not a crisis for the German middle class. It does not threaten the German way of life. "Germany, Inc.," is still standing, when the neoliberals in the U.S. and the UK said it wouldn't survive.

And at least Germans have jobs to fill. Over there, it makes sense to educate, to skill people up, while over here, there's no point. We already have things for people to do, like cleaning urinals and parking cars.

Here's a trickier point, but one I believe with all my heart. It's simply this: without an industrial base, a democracy dies. An industrial base makes it easier to organize a labor movement. And a labor movement makes it easier to keep a social democracy in which people have a stake. Look at the voting rate in both the UK and the U.S., which wrecked their middle-class industrial bases.

Then compare it with that of France and Germany, which did not. The more manufacturing there is, the more truly specialized skills people have. They're "numerically" literate, not just facile with words.

Why is that good for democracy? When people get numerical-type skills, they have in effect assets or stakes to protect. They are "experts," in a way, with a sense of self-worth. That's why at least they will go out and vote. Besides, so long as there is industry, at least there will be a labor movement, to pull them into civic life. You don't care about industry? Fine. You don't care about labor? I understand. But what about "character"? The existence of an industrial base and a labor movement may determine what that will be. Will people be independent and skill oriented, the way highly skilled industrial workers tend to be? Or will they be like our college grads: service oriented, dependent, trying to please, seducing us, giving us big smiles, "Hi, I'm Bob, I'm your waiter for this evening," and never registering to vote? Industry is destiny. It shapes the character of a country in a certain way. That point leads into point no. 3:

3. Germany Is Socialism!

But of course this is not your father's socialism, i.e., *state* socialism. It's not even like that of France. But it's why people blow up over Germany. It's the way, internally, like a watch, the corporation is engineered.

In the end, it's socialism that is the reason Germany is competitive. Because German workers are at the table when the big decisions are made, and elect people who still watch and sometimes check the businessmen; they have hung on to—well, a highly skilled tool-making culture.

The irony is: we helped set it up. Sure, the idea of works councils, of worker control, had its conception in the Weimar Republic. But when our New Dealer Americans occupied Germany after 1945, and in the time they were in charge, they and the British Labour Party (also in power) helped midwife what became the German form of "European socialism." Our own generals blessed the idea of putting workers on the board, even to the point that the Christian Democrats like Konrad Adenauer complained that what had been imposed on Germany was not "normal capitalism."

He was right. It is a rival form of capitalism, and it's helped Germany hang on to its industrial base.

So let me here roll out the three big building blocks of German social democracy: the works council, the co-determined board, and Germany's regional wage-setting institutions. Now I know: this is all hard to take in. If I came to the U.S. to teach the German model, I'd probably have to go over it all at the beginning of every class. "What do I mean by the German system? I'd like to see hands." I'd make someone stand up and say, "It's the works council, the co-determined board, and the wage-setting institutions."

Kids would look up from their texting and say, "Can you explain it again?"

Well, the works council is simple in theory, though hard for an American to take in. Let's say you work at Barnes & Noble, at Clybourn and Webster in Chicago. You may be just a clerk, and of course you have no training in being a bookseller. (In Germany, you'd have a certificate in bookstore clerking, but in the U.S., there's no need.) Still, you could be elected to a works council just at this store. That means you help manage the place. On layoffs and other issues, the employer has to reach an agreement with the works council. So you help decide when to open and close the store. You help decide what shift someone gets. You help decide if someone is fired. (No, I'm not kidding.) "The whole system leads to consensus," said a staff member at the Böckler Foundation, which is a tax-supported foundation promoting the "German model." So how did you effectively become a co-manager or business partner? Barnes & Noble had no say in it. You were elected by your fellow workers. You went out and campaigned: "Elect me." In effect, you are in politics, like Barack Obama or Hillary Clinton.

Just pause here: you are joining thousands of clerks and engineers and bus drivers who at this very moment in 2010 or just a few years back were also "elected officials," officeholders, wielders of power, with real responsibility for the welfare of your fellow workers. Think about it: management has to make an agreement with you. You help run the firm. What it amounts to is that, at the big firms, you really are in the country's governing class, its leadership class, even if you have only a high school degree. That's the point of social democracy: it's not just that working people get an extra chicken in the pot; more important, they get the right to stir the pot.

In America, by contrast, it's only the postgrads and guys at Goldman who get to stir the pot.

If that's a works council, what's a co-determined board? Well, it's less simple in theory, and even harder to believe. We now leave behind the little Barnes & Noble at Clybourn and Webster and try to imagine all of Barnes & Noble, the whole company, globally. Way at the top, on the board of directors, where you expect to bump into Warren Buffett or Robert Rubin, you, the clerks, get to elect half the board. That's right: it's not a fifth, not a third, but half, 50 percent of them, literally the same number of voting directors that the shareholders and hedge-fund hotshots get to elect.

I know some readers will throw down this book, in a rage. "That's impossible! The clerks get half the votes?"

I'm making it up, right? No.

Yes, but of course there's a catch! Under the German law of co-determination, if the directors elected by the clerks and the directors elected by the shareholders are deadlocked, 50–50, then the board's chair can cast a second vote, or a double vote, to "break the tie." And who picks the chair?

Just the shareholders: so, by a second tie-breaking vote, capitalism wins. Yes, in the end, the stockholders, the bankers, and the kids from Goldman Sachs—of course they "win," provided they vote in a single bloc. Now other readers may be fuming—"You said this was socialism!" Okay, I exaggerated, but the clerks still have a lot of clout. If the shareholders divide on whether "A" or "B" is the next CEO, the worker/clerk directors get to pick the king. Then "A" is CEO, but he owes his job to the clerks. By the way, the clerks have all this power without owning any shares! As in a socialist model, they only have to act on their interests as "the workers." There are other catches, though. *This* "board of directors" is a "supervisory board." Under it, there is a smaller "executive" board, which is more like a U.S. or UK board of directors. Also, this co-determination law applies only to the very big German companies, with over two thousand employees. So, in the U.S., clerks would not have this clout in the little independent bookstores, if any such things are left.

At any rate, everything in these firms gets discussed, so that it's not just a single CEO going up to a mountaintop to pull the plug on everyone, without ever having to look anyone in the eye. Can co-determination stop outsourcing? It can't stop globalization. But at the same time, through being on boards, the workers can cut deals. "Conditions, that's my motto," is how one worker-director put it in my favorite German magazine, *Mitbestimmung*. (It's an Oprah-type magazine for those who can't read enough about co-determination.) In the end, as the worker-director says, "We can only put up hurdles." Sure, that's the reality: it's a global economy. "But reality has a lot of nuances." In the U.S., people often don't even know there is a plant closing until all the employees are ushered out under an armed guard. But in Germany, the workers are Cato-like guardians, who are reading files, looking over the manager's shoulder: if they don't go along, they can make things harder. Maybe they can't stop a sale. But they can push for a different owner, with a deeper pocket to run the plant. They can raise questions; they can squawk. "We're bringing that in from China? Look at the shipping cost."

And they're everywhere—the guardians. Wouldn't your own behavior change if you thought at every moment Cato was watching you?

Okay, now that we've covered works councils and the co-determined boards, then what are the unions supposed to do? They do the bargaining over wages and pensions, but at a "macro" level, with an "employer federation." Let's say, in our example, it's made up of big bookstores like Barnes & Noble and Borders and of course Walmart. So they set the wage for everyone over a whole square-mile area. Though we used to bargain this way in the U.S. in the 1940s and 1950s, we do nothing like this anymore. I doubt if even one out of a thousand Americans even knows or has heard of the term "multi-employer " bargaining.

Basically I just mean that the German unions try to set the same wages for everyone across the board as much as possible. Yes, there's been very serious slippage, but that's still the ideal. Every Barnes & Noble, every Borders, everywhere in the covered area, would pay the same wage for the same type of work or job classification. Unlike in the U.S., it's not set store by store or shop by shop. It's not set city by city. It's the same, everywhere, as much as possible.

And it's public, "transparent." Who knows what Barnes & Noble pays in Chicago, or Borders in Joliet, and who knows who gets what in each store? But to the extent this part of the German model stays intact, everyone in theory is supposed to know. And it's not just transparent in the bookstore industry, but everywhere else in the country. If the IG Metall workers at ThyssenKrupp get a raise of 3 percent, then shouldn't the bookstore clerks also get 3 percent? That's now the weakest of the three building blocks we rolled out. But at least they're still trying.

The point is: no company should compete with another company based on wages.

That's the real socialism, the way everyone can stay in the same general world as everyone else. That's what can help keep a country relatively egalitarian (even now), even if inequality has increased. Yes, the German left may be in despair that the pilots at Lufthansa aren't bargaining in solidarity with the people who clean the planes, but at least they're still trying to keep this broader type of bargaining in place.

Well, I hope they can keep as much as they can. Because getting your wage set outside the firm—over your head—helps you get more power within the firm. Even if you're on the works council, you don't have to ask the boss for a raise. Even if you're on the supervisory board, you don't ask.

As Professor Martin Malin at Chicago-Kent College of Law once told me, "It takes the blood sport out of collective bargaining." Compared to all of that, it's not such a big deal who gets to set the closing hours.

But why aren't there huge nationwide strikes? They don't riot. They don't burn tires. It's not like France or Italy.

Well, think of the difference between the French and German model. In the French model, the workers are outside in the street and throwing rocks through the window. But in the German model, the workers are "inside," running the place. Of course, they're both "inside" and "outside," i.e., they get to have it both ways. It's hard for German businessmen to make war on the labor movement when the labor movement is wired into the structure of their firms. That may be why, in Germany, a labor movement is still intact.

But isn't this changing?

Yes and no. It's like everything in Germany. Something changes in business's favor. But then something changes in labor's favor. You hear about the former: "Wage bargaining is weaker." In the U.S., you never hear about the latter: say, how works councils in the last ten years have continued to spread. Or you may hear how the cutbacks known as Agenda 2010 make the welfare state weaker. But you don't hear how it actually raised the minimum payment and more people are now eligible for welfare than before. Suddenly, more people apply because it's big enough to be respectable. So as the welfare state is cut back, it's stronger than ever. Over here you only hear about the movement one way. It's not that simple! Yes, it's changing to the right, but it's also changing to the left.

But some may wonder how Germany got this strange, and even rival, form of capitalism. Let me offer just four of my favorite explanations:

1. "The U.S. Army did it." Yes, America put this German model in place. After World War II, as the occupying power, we had a problem: who would keep watch over all the German business-types who had supported Hitler? One way to do it was to set up "co-determined" boards. (Works councils came later.)

Back home, New Dealers who ran the U.S. war effort were used to pushing unions on businessmen. They did the same thing during the occupation. In a way, Germany of today is where the New Deal went on to live.

2. "The British Labour Party did it." The occupying authorities were not only New Dealers but British Labour Party socialists. Wary of class war, the young leftists wanted a way for workers and managers to cooperate and have less class war. "Yes," they said to German workers, "don't make our mistakes."

Of course the British went on making them.

3. "The Jesuits did it." Of course, as I have a Jesuit education, I'm sure it's true. But is there any other reason it might be true? And yes, in fact, in the Weimar era, it was a Jesuit, Father von Nell-Breuning, SJ, who argued for works councils in many of his dozens of books. He even got to ghostwrite a 1931 papal encyclical on labor, *Quadragesimo Anno*, which lays out his idea. In the shambles of the Weimar Republic, it was hard to try it out, but, after 1945, in largely Catholic West Germany, in came a version of papal social democracy, which even some of the Catholic right wing in Munich claim to respect.

Surely, I'm leaving out the obvious . . .

4. "German labor did it!" But it's not so obvious. At the start, the left-wing unions were suspicious, even hostile to works councils. There was a fear that German employers could use them to undercut the unions. "Oh, we signed a contract with our works council." But at least in the big industrial companies, it turned out the other way. The unions used the works councils to get more clout with the employers. It did not "divide" labor so much as result in a division of labor. The unions did the wages. The workers did the work rules.

Still, the "business party," the Christian Democrats, more or less went along with this. Being Jesuit educated, I have to fight the urge to make a big deal of this. I owe that to the reader. But someone else might make a bigger deal of it. What makes "German capitalism" so different is that there is this whiff of Catholicism about it all. It's not the worker control but the very existence of the CDU that may be the hardest thing for Americans to understand. The Christian *Democrats* began as a genuine European movement in 1906 when a young Belgian lawyer started a series of "discussion groups" on the pope's labor encyclical *Rerum Novarum*, which supported the right of workers to organize. Imagine if the Republican Party of Dick Cheney had started in 1906 as a series of discussion groups on the pope's encyclical on labor.

(It might have been fitting. The pope had come out in favor of unions in part because Cardinal James Gibbons of Baltimore, an American, came over to lobby him on behalf of all the Catholics in the coal mines. That's another way the European model was the work of Americans.)

At any rate, after World War II, with the defeat of the Nazis, and the division of Germany, the pro-Catholic Christian Democrats ended up by default in the West as the party of the business right. Though tainted by papal encyclicals on labor, they were the main pro-business types not tied to the Nazis. In the 1950s, the voters, who were mostly women (since so many of the men were dead), put in this Catholic, mildly pro-worker party, partly because it was the party of the Church. So most women tended to vote for a pro-worker right, while the men tended to vote for the pro-worker left.

In short, the "business" party in Germany is not a "business" party in the way the GOP is in America. Even today, at least a few of Merkel's allies will scoff at free-market capitalism. Of course, there are many strongly pro-business types in the party too, but it's not a solid front.

I don't want to overstate it, but without the Christian Democrats, this "socialism" I write of might have sputtered out.

Still, while it's easy to overstate, it's also easier to understate how really different the German model is. To go into the fine details of it all—well, do you want to hear them? No, of course not. And on each trip I've made to Germany, I've had to force myself to phone up one or two German labor people to remind myself what they're doing. Let me take as an example the version I got on a trip to Berlin in 2005.

I'd already picked up these points—on trips in 1997, then in 2001, then in 2004—but somehow they keep dropping out of my head. Being a lawyer, preparing a case, I am used to learning things in great detail, and then a year or so later not remembering anything at all.

Anyway, on this last trip, I phoned up a press person at that oddly named union, IG Metall, and asked her to set up an interview, just so I could go over it all again. After telling me I'm too late, the whole system has collapsed, and it's just awful in Germany now, she then said, "I have just the person. He advised our works councils in IT." She said he used to be a CEO of a high-tech company. Now he works as a full-time organizer for IG Metall.

"What?" I said. "You're saying this guy was a CEO like Bill Gates and now he's a union organizer?" But it turned out to be true.

His name was Wigand, and he had white hair, and he looked like the drummer for the Rolling Stones. He also looked like a U-boat commander, except he was in jeans and smoked more than they'd let you on (or "aboard") a submarine.

Right after we shook hands, I had to ask: "Were you really a CEO of a high-tech company?"

He gave me a kind of wolf smile, the smile of a commander of a U-boat: "Yes, but of course this was only for a few years." He had gone from being the president of the works council to being the CEO. That doesn't happen often, even in Germany. He lit another cigarette. "I can't talk too long," he said, smiling. "I have to pick up my son at soccer." (It's odd that he used the American word, "soccer.")

"Well, can you tell me, again, what the works councils do? I know of course, but . . ." I stopped before saying, "I keep forgetting . . ."

"You've seen this book?" he said. Then he handed me a book, put out by IG Metall, in English. It's called *Employment and the Law*. For two or so minutes, as Wigand talked, I flipped through it. Then I looked up at Wigand, whose hair was all white, and wreathed in all the cigarette smoke he was blowing. At times he reminded me of Andrew Jackson on a $20 bill. We went through some of the rights listed in the book. Here are some: "Can a works council set the time when people go to work?" Yes. "What about when people leave?" Yes. (I remember a reporter who was on a works council: "We try to make sure they get home early enough to get to the theater.") "What else can it do?" If there have to be pink slips, it can say who does or does not get one. It can set vacations. It can even set wages, but only if the wages are higher than the union sets. There are so many rights that I was ready to ask the question that is on page forty-one, namely: "What orders can a supervisor give?"

Yes. Is a supervisor allowed to do anything?

I asked Wigand, and he laughed. "Yes, there are a lot of rights. But it is not so easy. You must teach them how to use these rights." And when he trains his members to be on works councils, he teaches them about the rights that are not set out "in the books."

"What's an example of a right not in the book?"

"Four times a year, or every quarter, the works council has the right to call an all-day meeting." The whole place shuts down. They can talk about some related political issue, like Agenda 2010, or even something odder.

"Once," he said, "in our company we had an all-day meeting on the war in Iraq." I must have gasped, a little. Anyway, he laughed. "It's not quite as you think. It has to be related to the company in *some* way. In our company, we had a contract to do business with the U.S. Army."

Can management call a meeting on something like this?

"No, no," Wigand said. "It is our right only. It is the heritage of antifascism."

It's odd to think the U.S. Army helped put in co-determination, and now German workers can take holidays to rail about our occupations of foreign countries. Somehow it's not fair.

"Of course," he said, "it's very expensive for the company to have these days off, four of them every year. So let's say a company has three thousand employees in four cities, and we on the works council have a right to four meeting days. We may say, 'This year, we will not use all our meeting days, but in turn you must put 3 million euros in the workers' fund.'" This is the kind of trick he would teach the young workers who got on the works councils in IT. Basically, he helped organize people who were like Dilbert. That is, he would "train" them to bargain, even though the works councils are separate from the union, IG Metall, for which he worked.

Why does a union like IG Metall train them? It helps bring in the shop-floor activists. It teaches them—indoctrinates them. Besides, the company has to pay for the training.

"Wait," I said. "You mean the company pays you directly?"

Wigand seemed a little shocked. "Not me, but they pay the works councils to have the training."

But he pumps up these little Dilberts to do the duties of their elected office. Now think about this: they hold "elected office." They legislate. All over Germany, ordinary citizens have this totally un-American chance to govern. And this is real self-government, literally laying down the law for where they go to work. It now occurred to me to ask Wigand: "How many people, at this moment, right now, in Germany, are serving on a works council, fulfilling a term of office?"

After a pause, he said, "Half a million."

Half a million! With turnovers, it could be millions of people who could end up with this experience of being on a works council. I mean, there are only 83 million people in the entire country. Think of how this changes the ratio of "activist" to "passive" or couch-potato citizen. That's why Germany, Inc., is like another planet.

As if to head off my gushing, Wigand said, "But the works councils are not everywhere." Yes, I should have said so above. "They are in the big companies, over a thousand workers. They are everywhere in auto. But in IT, it is only about a third."

"It's a third? I'm surprised it's so high," I said.

"Yes, in auto, there is a tradition of solidarity, but in IT, people come straight in out of the army," he said. In other words, they're kids. They're barely out of puberty. They don't stand up to the boss. But still, nerdy or not, some kids do vote to put in works councils.

It had not occurred to me they come right out of the army. "Yes," he said, "they're in for nine months."

"All these kids get guns and everything?" Oh no, he said, it's only about 60 percent. The other 40 percent, they are the COs. They empty bedpans. Or they come to the U.S. and work in homeless shelters. Anyway, I wanted to get back on the subject. "So what's the big thing you try to teach?"

"We must be consulted," he said. "The works council has an *intense* right to be consulted."

"Intense?" (I wish, in America, our rights were "intense.")

"We must be consulted, about everything." He said this included the appointment of the supervisors. "I remember at our company, they wanted to promote a rightist. But we said no."

"A what—what's a rightist?"

"Political," he said. "He was not politically correct."

"And it was just because of his politics?"

He flicked an ash. "We could do it. Why not?"

Well, okay.

He usually slouched, but now he sat up. "Yes, you see, we have an intense right to be consulted. In IT, if they plan a new product, we have to be informed." Yes, they could go and see the business plan. Now I was surprised. Even when I bring lawsuits for workers, and I can subpoena documents, I can never get the business plans. Yet the way Wigand made it sound, they could rifle through the files. Do they know what they're looking at? "Yes," Wigand said. "For complicated things like mergers, we get lawyers for them." Who pays? It's the company, of course.

It was hard to believe any union opposed works councils. But there really would be a good reason if works councils ever bargained over the level of wages. In an hour of talk, this was the only thing that made Wigand lose his U-boat cool, or made him seem "intense."

The union has a role. The works council has a role. "Each one must respect the other," he said. "There must be this clear division." He paused. "It is all right: the union can set the 'total' wage, and the works council can say, 'But we want to have it paid in this way.'" For example, he said, if the union gets a billion euros, and splits it up 80–20 between wages and pension, the works council could say, "No, we want it 70–30." "And," said Wigand, "if they do, it is okay, it is fine."

But the works council can't reduce the total wage. If they did, that would be the end of union power. It's Wigand's great fear. In the B&N example, the big "global" Barnes & Noble could take a hammer to each little store. Corporate goliaths would now bargain not with a union for thirty thousand clerks, but just a works council for thirty. Sometimes in the *FT*, there will be an editorial praising "the admirable works council." The pious thought is: oh, they work so *well*, why not let them set wages, too?

Heh, heh, then that would get rid of socialism in Europe.

But of course it's not state socialism, is it? After all, in Berlin, there are still reminders of the real thing. For example, just after I spoke with Wigand, and felt the need to get out of all his cigarette smoke, which had worked its way into my skin, I went out to swim in Potsdam, at a big USSR-type pool, one built by the Communist regime. The train from Berlin to Potsdam got there like a rocket. Of course Potsdam is now too hip to mock. At the station, I went through a mall, past kids buying CDs in little stores like Coconuts; they could be kids in Chevy Chase, Maryland. That is, they seem like kids who will never have any nonelectronic interpersonal communication with each other. Yet in a few moments I will see them splashing, in a collectivist way, in a USSR-type pool.

The old state pool built by the GDR is way up on a hill, across the street from the mall, and in the dark of January, it's lit up by only a faint blue light. Of course it's dark at four in the afternoon. So even at that hour, it's like a haunted house on a hill. It seems like the paint is peeling, even if it's not.

It's too big, it's too open, and inside I feel weak, helpless. The first time I visited, I went into a locker room to change my clothes. As I started to disrobe in front of my locker, I looked up to see two adult women a few feet away chatting. (They didn't even look at me.) What? At first I thought, "Well, that figures; these Europeans, they've really got no morals." Then I saw what I was doing wrong: there are little cabana doors, like swinging doors in a barroom, and you're supposed to step behind the swinging locker door, to get in your trunks. But, my God, why just one locker room for both sexes? "It's to save money." "It's to shame people." "It's easier to spy." All of these may be reasons.

But it's not just the locker room. The pool itself is big, open, and you feel like, well, a swimmer-ant. The first time I saw it, I gasped. The damn thing was bigger than a Red Army latrine. Yikes: a lap was like a mile. The other side was France (Calais). Or maybe it was Russia. I'd have to swim around what seemed to be the Masses: I mean all the boys doing cannonballs, and all the girls who just went in circles doing the breaststroke.

There were all the kids from Coconuts, but now I saw just their heads, a hundred heads, and they all seemed to be bobbing, like the head of Chairman Mao, back in those grainy photos of him swimming in the Yellow River to prove he was still alive. Then I dived in, and began to swim: stroke, stroke, stroke, and . . . my God, I'll never make it.

Why is the Big Pool so Big? The Harvard economist Alexander Gerschenkron argued that under central planning, the planners want just One Big Pool, since they need just one of everything. So under state socialism, there is likely to be One Big Pool, One Big Department Store, just as when I went to Moscow in 1993, there was One Big McDonald's, the biggest McDonald's (six stories of Big Macs) that anyone had ever seen.

Is the Big Pool such a bad thing? "Under Communism, I'd have come here to go swimming every day." Is it so much worse than a supersized YMCA?

Years ago, just after 1989, my friend Inga in Moscow said, "In

Russia everything is big. The government is big. The department store is big. The McDonald's is big. Everything is big."

She paused. "Except the apartments."

Another pause. "And the salaries."

And, as she might have added, the people. The "old" state socialism, the so-called Second Way, with these leviathan public goods, had a way of making you feel small. I hate that. While it's good for us to be humble, we shouldn't feel small.

Is this "old" socialism anything like the world that Wigand just described? What hit me in the Big Pool is that in the old GDR, *that* "socialism" did not involve a whole lot of "civic trust," as Robert Putnam and other sociologists use the term. Indeed, no one trusted anyone. That is why family members ratted on each other to the Stasi, and why they had only One Big Pool and One Big McDonald's and One Big Locker Room for Both Sexes, so that everyone would be under state surveillance.

So the old socialism, the GDR kind, required no trust. But the works councils—and Wigand's world—require lots of it. First, there are all the elections on shop floors all across the country. That means people must have the nerve to run for office. Second, they then serve on these boards with others who may be total strangers. Then they have to fix rules that their bosses may not like; and they have to trust they will not be poleaxed if they do it. Finally, the CEOs and officers have to trust that their employees will use their "elected" power in a fair way. By the way, the union people like Wigand also have to trust that this will work to their advantage.

In other words, people can't feel that they're small, like Inga in the USSR, and they can't feel nervous, rattled, I-can-be-fired-any-minute, like so many in the U.S. feel. They have to feel like (1) they have a say in things, and (2) they can say it safely.

That's what's different. In the old socialism, things operated without trust. In the new kind, people have to trust each other, or the whole thing will collapse.

It's also the difference with U.S.-type capitalism. Over here, kids can have Britney Spears blasting out of their baby brains, and keep doing so until they die. But over there, the kids in Coconuts at some point have to take off their headphones. They have to have some nonelectronic form of interacting with each other, or the whole thing will collapse. They can't just consume or be consumed. They have to be responsible to each other.

Thanks to the European model, or at least the German version, some of them can have a different kind of life. At any moment, there are a half million Germans holding rotating office, so the number of people who get pumped up with civic trust is huge. Without this civic trust, I doubt that Germans or Europeans would ever vote these higher taxes. Unlike Barbara, Isabel has more trust she'll get her money back. Of course, that's also why this social democracy is not as open as our system is to newcomers. Okay, if you like, let's assume all Europeans are irrationally xenophobic, etc. My point is—even if they were utterly nonxenophobic, people in these European social democracies might be reluctant to trust strangers. It's the downside of a Wigand-like system that it requires so much trust.

Can I tell a story that gets at the difference between USSR-type socialism and Wigand's? It comes not from Wigand but from a young German who worked at a small but rising global bank. Hey, I asked, do you have a "co-determined" board? Oh yes, he said. How does it work? He grinned.

"It's causing some problems."

What kind of problems?

"We just elected a gardener to the board. In the bank now, we usually speak English. But the gardener does not speak English, so now at all the board meetings, everyone must speak German, so the gardener knows what is going on."

Ah, there's the answer to globalization! Put the gardener on the board and force all the best and brightest to slow down and talk to him in German. But consider the two different modes of surveillance: in the old state socialism, "Big Brother is watching." In Wigand's, the person who is watching is the guy who holds the watering can and is watering the flowers in the lobby.

Were the employees sending a message? It seems the bankers at the top have to step out of the fast lane of global English to tell the staff what's going on.

I know, it's hard for us Americans to believe this kind of thing can survive. Over the years, I've gone through three phases:

Phase One (1991–97): "It will survive!" I remember the Saturday in December 1991 when, at the laundromat, I first realized there was a rival system to ours, even after the collapse of Communism. I was reading a Saturday edition of the *New York Times* and, half-paying attention, I began to read a little squib about Kohl pressing Major over some kind of European "social charter." As the spin cycle started, I got to the end. "What is going on?" Now shook up, I read it again. It seems Kohl was risking the breakup of the European project. Why? He wanted the UK to sign a clause that required larger companies to "consult workers about basic decisions affecting the firm." Isn't Kohl the conservative? Later I realized why Kohl the conservative had to push for this provision. He either had to impose the German model on the British, or they would impose the Anglo-American model on him. Or so I thought in 1991: and even the so-called Treaty of Maastricht in 1991 came to something of a draw—with an opt-out for the British—but that would not be the end of it. As companies became more global, it seemed that they would have to pick one model or the other. Why would they pick the one where the gardener was on the board?

Phase Two (1997–2005): "It won't survive!" Actually, even before then, fascinated by this alternative capitalism, I started reading the *Financial Times*, to see what would happen next. Ah: I soon found out Germany was floundering. The UK-types were gloating. Soon there would be one "global form of capitalism," and it wouldn't be theirs. Even in Germany, the professors were writing Max Weber–like papers: "The Disintegration of Organized Capitalism in Germany." All the signs were bad. Even in Germany, the global bankers now spurned the old-line family firms. German firms were selling more shares, and shareholders wanted bigger Wall Street–type profits. By 2005, Angela Merkel was about to be elected and take down the whole thing like a Teutonic Margaret Thatcher. The *Financial Times* was thrilled. And I'd lost all hope—the German model was doomed.

Phase Three (2005–): "I guess it will survive!" Merkel did not win outright as predicted but had to form a coalition government with the SPD, the socialist left. That meant nothing could change. All the economists groaned. But all the ordinary people seemed happy. Now that it was assured that Merkel could do nothing without the approval of the socialists, her popularity went up. She herself began to defend co-determination. So did others in the CDU—that is, they actively defended it, as Kohl had.

Meanwhile, the German model perked up. Unemployment dropped—a lot. It's now lower than in the U.S. And people began to appreciate, at last: "Hey, we're taking more out of the global economy than it's taking out of us."

Now, some will scoff: "You talk about this co-determined workplace, but really, not everyone is in it." More companies are union free. Not everyone has a works council. Indeed, about 40 percent

of Germans work for companies which have this kind of "constitution" in place. "Ho, ho! Not everyone is in it." But so what?
Even when the U.S. has been its most democratic, whether in the
Jackson era or in the New Deal, not everyone was "in it." As the
historian Sean Wilentz has argued, in any democracy there are
boundaries. It was true in the age of Jackson: blacks, women, and
others were not "in" it. It was true in the New Deal: the South
was not "in" it. But Wilentz has argued that, in both cases, there
was a red-hot core of the democracy, and in that red-hot core, ordinary people had more political power. To him, the issue is: given
that there may be boundaries to this red-hot core, are these
boundaries contracting or expanding?

If that's the question to ask, I think there's no clear answer. But
there are at least two reasons to be hopeful. For one thing, since
I first read about Helmut Kohl v. John Major, more German companies have works councils. When the SPD and Green Party
were in power from 1998 to 2005, they passed a law increasing
the companies that could have works councils. As a result, just
the raw number of ordinary people making big decisions is going up.

It's true—the unions did not do this. At least in terms of wage
bargaining, the unions seem much weaker. IG Metall had to give
priority to fighting layoffs. But even if the expanded coverage happened by legal decree of the SPD-Green government, the boundaries of this core are still expanding.

Also, the boundaries are expanding in another way—outside
Germany, to the rest of Europe. The EU is pushing the model, or
at least the works councils. There are works councils in the
Netherlands. They even have some in France. Is it possible that
one day the clerks, the cleaning crews, the electricians, and, yes,
the gardeners in companies all over the world will have a chance
to stir the pot?

But I'm tired of the Labor Question. I'd like to move on to a reason where people really will blow up at me.

4. Germany Is Print (Sort of, Still)!

Or, I should say: Germany is Newspapers, and Germany is Books. It's here, in this country, where it may be decided whether reading will survive in the West. Do I exaggerate?

Here's the reason I get goose bumps in Frankfurt: it's not when I hear The Bells, or even when I see The Boats, going up and down the Main. It's when, on my first day in Europe, I go to see—

The Trains.

Now it's true that the cities on the board can goose up a bump or two: four hours to Paris, four to Amsterdam, one to Cologne, four to Berlin, and so on. When I stand there and see all the cities of the world, I know I never want to die.

Let me live, O Lord.

But I really get the goose bumps in this station when I look at all the papers: I mean the big, thick German dailies, like the *FAZ* (*Frankfurter Allgemeine Zeitung*), and *Suddeutsche Zeitung*, and *Berliner Tagesspiegel*—and I could name a lot of others—big, thick newspapers with few if any pictures on the front page.

And then I look at all the racks of books. Though it's changing, it used to be the books had no pictures on the covers. Nothing. One chose a book just for the sake of words! Words, words, words, and no pictures. Do we realize how relatively untelevised Europe has to be to have so many papers with so few pictures, to have books that just have words? Sure, the Germans watch a lot of TV, and have even started to bloat up the way we Americans do. Yet even so, the U.S.-Europe gap is growing. It's gone up over 4.6 hours per day in the U.S., while it's dropped under 3.5 hours for

Germany, and it's now just 2.7 hours in ultra-left Sweden. While German tube time is dropping, U.S. time is going up. In that extra hour and ten minutes, a Gutenberg form of literacy has survived.

Also, they have all that time to read on these trains to and from Frankfurt, while on the U.S. highways we can only text our friends.

I could sit on the ground and weep. I'd forgotten what it was like to be in a country where people read.

Now I know the arguments about the newspapers, the big, thick German dailies. "Circulation is declining in Germany. Fewer people are reading these papers that have no eye candy. They're also on the Internet over there," etc. In other words, it's just like here.

I also know the arguments about reading books. "Oh, no one's reading anymore. Besides, go to a Barnes & Noble. They still have books. How can you say Germany is the last place where reading will survive?"

Here is my reply: it's true paid circulation of papers is in decline in Germany, as it is in France and the UK. It's hardly surprising, given that some of these daily editions, like *FAZ*, have enough heft to last a whole week. Some German dailies have four or five sections, each one of which could last a reader a good part of the day. It makes sense to me that Germans might pass around these big dailies the way we might lend out a book. I'd be ashamed to "lend" my scrawny U.S. papers even to the poor. Also, Europeans now have a lot of free subsidized newspapers. So a spokesman for the Paris-based World News Association could claim in 2007 that, digital age or not, "in many developed nations the industry is increasing or maintaining sales" of old-fashioned papers. If one counts the free dailies, newspaper reading is even rising. According to *Facts About Germany*, the official government publication, 78 percent of Germans read a newspaper every day for an average of twenty-eight minutes. And while paid circulation has wafted gently down in Germany, it has plummeted in the U.S. Germany has 23 million in paid circulation, while the vastly larger U.S. has only 34 million. And most of those U.S. papers have the news content of a "shopper" that I could find on the floor of a Safeway or a Jewel. So this leads to the Einstein-relativity point about the observers who are going at different speeds. I will state it as follows: "Even if Germany and the U.S. both have dropping circulations of big dailies, the drop is much faster in the U.S. Accordingly, to us American observers teleported to the Frankfurt station, it seems that the Germans we see in front of us are reading more than ever. This is true, in the Einsteinian sense, even if they are reading less than in the past."

Furthermore, the situation with reading may be similar to the situation with manufacturing. Germans have gone through a downsizing and/or restructuring of their manufacturing. Likewise, Germans have gone through a corresponding downsizing of their civic life—just not on the scale that we have. Fewer people are working in the manufacturing sector, where worker engagement in firms is the most pronounced. But for those who are still in industry, there are the new forms of worker control, described by Wigand. For high school grads with no skills living outside this unionized Germany, Inc., they have less of a stake in acting politically to protect the system. So they have less of a stake in reading political news. For those outside Germany, Inc., vacation, retirement, and the rest are not being decided collectively. But for those who are still part of Germany, Inc., there is as much reason to read as ever.

In the U.S., the UK, and even parts of the EU, the manufacturing sector is gone, and people see no point in acting collectively to protect their skills. They're right. It's hopeless. There's no political payoff to them in keeping up with the news. Why bother? But in Germany, because the basic system is intact, and because

people can see very clearly how collective action is a good investment, there is a built-in brake on how fast and how far the decline
in civic life can go. In the U.S. and the UK, the reading of print is
in free fall, except for pictures of celebrities. There is no payoff in
reading except to Google the stars.

So more and more, in the U.S. and to some extent in the UK,
everything is in pictures. The kids get on the Internet and zap
their photos to each other. They put on these headphones that
suck out their little brains. "Oh no," a friend has said to me, "people are starting to watch less TV." Okay, despite the surveys,
maybe they do watch it less, but that may be just because they
don't have the attention span to get through an entire episode of
Grey's Anatomy.

The defenders of the Internet give me a hard time indeed. "Oh,
how do you know? We're reading online. We're as engaged as ever."

Sure we are: we're all texting each other about the latest Paul
Krugman column during the commercial breaks for *Grey's Anatomy*.

Well, that's possible. Without my knowing, people in the U.S.
may be reading just as intently as Europeans. We may be in a
golden age.

But it always comes down to this argument: "Just because you
can't see it, doesn't mean it isn't happening."

It's invisible.

Just believe. I'm ready to shut my eyes.

But in Germany, I can see people reading, on the trains, on
the buses, in cafés, in restaurants, everywhere. They seem just as
young and hip as Americans, but they are reading *print*.

Except in parts of New York and Washington, D.C., I know of
no equivalent, and I do not see as much reading even in Manhattan, on the 1 train, as I do in an S-Bahn in Berlin.

Besides, when I see people reading on the 1 or on the Red Line
in D.C., I have to wonder whether some of them are Europeans.

Chicago? Cincinnati? Milwaukee? Anywhere in the Midwest? I see nothing: nada, not one person on the El or the bus reading a paper.

In Frankfurt, Hamburg, Munich, Berlin, I might as well be on another planet.

But it's true, secretly, without my knowing, people on the El who are staring at nothing for the entire half-hour ride—never mind that they have graduate and postgraduate degrees—may be engaged in reading, somewhere, out of sight.

Reading on the Internet is like having a light flash in your eyes. So maybe that's why they sit gaga on the El cars and stare out the window.

It could be that I'm just a reactionary.

That's why I go to Frankfurt: just to see The Trains. Of course, I can't "prove" anything, but I have a theory as to why Germans read more than we in the U.S. do.

First, we don't have their socialism. We don't give ordinary people any real power, while the Germans at least partly do. What's the result? It makes it even harder for our literati to read. When people at every income level are more engaged and reading heftier papers, then in a competitive way people at the top read even more to keep ahead of them. So the whole country starts dumbing down, right up to the top. Doesn't that ring true for the U.S.? The language of the elite in the U.S., especially, is shaped by the language of the street. The talk in the most bad-ass public schools in Chicago can change the way math majors at the University of Chicago think and speak. So if high school grads or even dropouts were more interested in politics, even more postgrads would put down their iPods and read the *Times*. It would be a form of competition, as well as a sense of civic duty.

Okay, but why would people in Europe read more? Well, if the economic decisions on wages or vacations are taken collectively, in a transparent way, then it's in people's self-interest to read the paper to find out what's going on. What will the unions do this year, etc.? Will I keep my pension? Will I get more vacation? They have to know—someday, via the works council, they may be in "elected life" themselves. It is logical they would read the paper: "Yes, I'm just the gardener, but next year I could be on the board of a global bank. Don't I want to know the latest from Bahrain?"

Occasionally in the U.S., our economists like to sniff: "We invest more in human capital than Europeans do." More go to college, etc. But this is both technically true and also nonsense. Our universities may be better. But "formal" education in the U.S. stops for good by age twenty-five. But in Europe, far more high school grads go on reading the daily paper their entire lives. How can we in America continue our adult education except by reading the paper?

Second, in Europe people have the time not to watch TV. As I said about Barbara and Isabel, the latter is less likely to be trapped in her home. To the extent we can create an infrastructure that gets people out of the house, the better the chance they'll keep their wits about them to read, even if it's only on a tram to a club.

Third, it's just too hard to read German online. In the eighteenth century, they made the language difficult, on purpose. But that means on the Internet, where people flinch because it's like a flashlight shining in your eyes, you find yourself involuntarily turning away from a thick, clunky German abstraction a nanosecond before you had the time to absorb it. The way German makes a car wreck of three or four abstract nouns, you have to see the damn thing in print, and stare at the word longer than the digital world will let you.

At any rate, I see more people reading cold, hard print—the kind that pulls the light into its dark matter without flashing any back—in Germany. And maybe it's because people can stare at a sentence and think about it a little longer when it's in print that it seems to me I can get into the kind of long and thoughtful political conversations over there that I never seem to have here.

I should be clear: we can be thoughtful. We just can't do it for an hour and fifteen minutes.

On this point, since I'm now done with Wigand as a witness, I have to call on "Tom." How else can I explain that over there I have conversations that I could never have in America?

I just have to show you how it goes.

Once again, this was another "first-day-in-Europe," on a trip in 2005. Jet-lagged and over-caffeinated, I had just landed in Frankfurt and was headed to see The Trains. Yes, I had the same shivers, and had seen all the dailies, etc. But the train was full, and I realized that this time, on this train, I would not have any great "European conversations." The only seat vacant was next to a kid, who, yes, like a U.S. kid, was wearing a video-game type of T-shirt and headphones and was clearly tuning out. I went to sleep next to him, and then awoke in a half hour, and saw that he was doing homework. I started reading over his shoulder. To my shock, I could understand most of what I was reading. "Wow, my German must be getting better." Then I realized why it was so easy. He was actually reading English. In fact, he was on page 475 of *The Decline and Fall of the Roman Empire* by Edward Gibbon. (I remember the page number precisely.) I was so surprised I blurted out, without thinking: "Are you reading that for school?"

The kid, about twenty or so, looked at me: "I'm in engineering. No, no . . . I just thought I should know some Roman history." His name? "Tom, it's just Tom. Not Thomas." He was at the Technical University, which I thought of as a lower-class type of school—a notch below a really elite school like Humboldt or Freie.

I told Tom I was trying to write a book about Europe. "I'm especially interested in Germans and their education system."

He laughed. "Why write about the Germans? You should be writing about the French." He thought the French were ahead.

"I can't write about the French," I said.

"Why not?"

"Have you ever seen *Saturday Night Live?* Well, they used to have a skit about these aliens, the 'Coneheads,' and when they were asked where they were from, they'd say, 'Oh, we're from France.' And the point is, it would be like writing about the Coneheads. You see, no one has ever seen French people. They don't have ethnic neighborhoods. I mean, who are they? It's like no one knows."

"I see," he said. "I don't understand, though, why Americans are so against them." He paused. "Yes, but the French . . . I think they are much better at reading than the Germans. Do you know about the PISA test?"

I knew it was an international test given in Europe to fifteen-year-olds, and the kids in Finland always come in first. But this year it was a scandal because the Germans had not done well in reading.

"People are upset, aren't they?" I said.

"Yes," he said, laughing, "we Germans want to be perfect. We want to be number one!"

"Ah," I said, "that's why people are upset about the British, and how well they are doing. I mean, economically, isn't that the real rivalry?"

Tom nodded. "Yes, that goes back a long time."

"They're 'The Enemy' now, aren't they?"

He laughed and put up his hands. "No, no," he said. "Please, no enemies! We Germans have learned that! We don't want any 'enemies!'"

"Well, you tell me . . . what should I say in this book to Americans about Germany?"

He was thoughtful. "I think you should make this point: there is not one Germany but two Germanys."

"You mean, East and West?"

"No, I mean . . . Mercedes and BMW!" He laughed. "Those are the two Germanys. Mercedes in Stuttgart and BMW in Munich. That's really all you have to know."

"What about, oh, Hamburg, or Berlin, or . . . ?"

"That is all *Kleines*," he said. "It is all 'small stuff.'"

And now for an hour we went into German politics, literature, and the single biggest thing (he thought) to know about Germany, namely, that everything is Green. If I didn't get that, I wouldn't get what was happening in the country. We talked about works councils, pensions, the future of social democracy. As for the German character, he told me I had to read Heine.

"But he wrote in 1840!"

"Yes, but nothing has changed."

And I'm ashamed to say that I kept looking at his techie T-shirt and spiked hair and thought of his low-rent university and wondered: "In American terms, how can this kid exist?" I even asked about the Technical University. "Do you know the joke?" he said. It goes like this: someone asks a kid from Humboldt and a kid from Technical: "What is rubber?" And the Humboldt kid goes into the history, the composition, the industrial process, and talks for forty-five minutes. Then it's the other kid's turn, the one from Technical. And he goes up to this person who asks the question and takes out a piece of rubber and puts it in his hand—

"'Here!'"

And Tom imitated the kid slapping down a piece of rubber. *Here*.

Tom identified with this kid of course. But here he was, reading Gibbon and also telling me about politics, cars, and how I had to read Heinrich Heine. And clearly he had read the papers, as I could demonstrate from a thousand things he said. But I'll just mention the very end.

"Hey, this has been great. But maybe you have some questions about America? Do you?"

"Yes, really . . . there are two things."

"Go ahead."

"Cheney, who is the vice president—how can he . . . how can he be the vice president when he has all these ties to Halliburton?"

"That's your question?"

"Yes."

"What's your next question?"

"The Bulls—I am curious about this—do people in Chicago still support the Bulls?"

"You mean, now that Michael Jordan's gone?"

"Yes."

"Not so much."

A look of great sadness came over Tom's face. "I was afraid of this," he said. As we got off the train, he told me I was the first American he had ever met, not counting a girl from Florida he'd run into late at night at a big dorm party.

Certainly I was the first American he'd ever met since he'd picked up Edward Gibbon.

Anyway, Germany is Print. And what's the proof that they really read more? As we talked, I noticed nearly everyone around us was reading a paper, not a tiny U.S. one but a big, thick German one.

What's stunning about this: in front of my eyes, people are reading big, thick newspapers in Germany, but if the OECD numbers are right, most of these readers do not have college degrees. But they continue to read long after our BAs have stopped. That's why, in terms of literacy, it is more important to be a social democracy than to give out a lot of BAs.

But let me turn now to Tom's point that Germany is Green.

5. Germany Is Green!

Even though Germany has been beating out China in shipping global hardware, it wants to hug every tree, stop all the carbon, and be the planetary model of how we all should live. What other country has a Green Party that is such a major player in its politics? And really, the CDU and SPD are just about as Green as the Green Party. Only in Germany would the government buy up enough DVDs of Al Gore's *An Inconvenient Truth* to play in every classroom. At this point, it would be easy for me to say "Germany is Green," and move on to something else. "Now let's talk about something serious." I am sure people in the U.S. will nod and say, "That's nice," or "Let's pat Germany on the head."

But I think the world is furious that Germany is Green.

No one would put it that way. Instead people blow up and say, "The economy isn't growing." Or, "There's no consumer demand." Or, "If they start spending, they might do something about their unemployment." When people talk about the problem of German consumer demand, or tut-tut how it is the sick man of Europe, it never occurs to us to say, "Well, Germany is Green!"

When I say Germany is Green, it's almost like an act of war. Perhaps the country is like the little drummer boy who keeps beating the drum in Günter Grass's famous novel, *The Tin Drum*. In that book, the little boy who keeps beating the drum doesn't want to grow. Isn't that what Germany as a whole is doing? To the fury of people in London and New York, the world's greatest industrial power doesn't want to grow! With global warming, with dangerous new toxics, with the coming depletion of our oil stocks, people in Germany simply aren't consuming enough to get up their GDP. They seem to be all beating on their little drums, as if warning all the rest of us.

Yes, as a labor lawyer I want to urge people to go over because "Germany is socialist." But as a human being on this planet, I also urge it just because "Germany is Green." Of course the two things are connected. Our environmental types in the U.S. don't really understand this. It's because Germany is a social democracy with high taxes that it can do things so efficiently, and it's this very efficiency that holds down our kind of wild consumer spending. Without a social democracy it would be harder to have limits. Yes, because it's socialist, with high taxes, Germany is Green.

Even in winter, it's green, dark green, as I could see when I looked out the train as I chatted with Tom. It's surprising enough that Germany, with a fourth of our population, fits inside the state of Montana. But it's even more surprising to take the train and look out the window. Germany is empty! It's empty in a way that no place in the U.S. east of the Mississippi is.

Empty

Empty

Empty

Then suddenly, all at once, I'm in the middle of a big city like Berlin. And in the old GDR, or East Germany, or the old Prussia, it's even emptier. Sometimes, when I have driven through it or been on the train, it's like looking out at the hills in *The Sound of Music*, except you don't even see Julie Andrews. There's no Trapp family, or really anything at all.

Indeed, Germany compares pretty well with Montana. In his 2005 book, *Collapse*, the anthropologist Jared Diamond has a long section on Montana. He goes into the toxic waste, the runoff, and all the other environmental evils. Ecologically, Montana is a candidate for "collapse," a place like Easter Island or Greenland that people one day may evacuate.

Why is Germany so much less likely a candidate for collapse? I think in part it's because it went through a version of an Easter

Island–type collapse, namely, the destruction of World War II. Arguably, they had it coming, but its collapse was still fairly gruesome. In some way or other, there is an unconscious memory of this trauma, which now comes out as a horror of "Collapse," or as a fanatic determination to be "Green."

Of course there are many other factors, as we like to say in the essay part of our College Board exams. One reason Germany is so green, literally, is that Germans unfairly subsidize so many farms. Maybe all those fields look nice as the train rolls by, but it's dreadful for agriculture in Africa and elsewhere. In one way, the EU is shamefully antiglobal—keeping high-cost European farmers in business. Indeed, propping up Europe's agriculture at the expense of the poor is one of the shameful reasons we have starvation in the world.

So it's "green" outside the train window for some bad reasons, but mostly Germany is trying to show how a consumer-based democracy can live within some limits. And all our knocks on Germany—the failure to spend, the refusal to grow, even the subsidized unemployment—are the very things that in a planetary sense may end up saving us. Americans may dislike it, but whether or not the "German model" works could decide the future of the human race.

Something about this model has people cutting back voluntarily. Maybe it's the German character, which is "neat" and "orderly," so we should look at the institutions that shape this character. One can see this character in Norway, the Netherlands, other countries. Why are people in a social democracy likely to internalize these controls? Or, put another way, why are they more likely to save money with a high tax rate (leaving less net disposable income) when in our country, with a lower tax rate (leaving us with more such income), we go much deeper into debt?

Even Tom thought it was just character. How so?

"It's the inflation after the war," he said. "The currency became worthless."

It took me a moment to grasp that when Tom referred to "the war," he was talking about World War I.

"Wait a second," I said. "That's why you and the other kids aren't spending? Come on, that was, like, 1923 and you're just twenty-two. Give me a break!"

"But why not?" he said. "My grandmother was alive. She is still very frugal. And she passed it on to my father, and he passed it on to me."

"I don't believe it," I said.

"You should see my father. If he thinks he can get gas cheaper, he will drive to another town."

Another *town*? Not even my cheapest cheapskate friend goes that far.

They're frugal. They do their own ironing. They don't send out their shirts.

Well, I don't blame World War I, but it could be World War II. And of course the memory of this last "collapse," which is the mother of all collapses, may explain some strange and tangled motive for why Germany is Green.

6. Germany Is Dark!

Now let's get to what we all think.

"After India," my old college teacher S. said, "Germany is the most mysterious country in the world."

"Why?" I asked.

"Because how can you go on 'being German' and 'rational' and so on, and still explain to yourself the whole fact of Hitler?"

I feel the way that S. does. I'd hate to be German and have to explain it to myself. Of course, in every country we should have some crime upon our conscience. "Okay, I'm from Japan, and up to now I have followed your argument. But we're responsible for Pearl Harbor. What about the rape of Nanking?" Or a kid from China could say, "What about Mao? He murdered in the millions." Or look at the genocides in Africa, not just in the recent past but even now. Or what about the U.S., and slavery, and the extermination of the Native Americans? At the moment, we're running the biggest prison system in the world. Yes, I would still argue that Hitler was unique, and the Holocaust was the central event to the understanding of evil in the twentieth century.

Even if every country has its history of murder, the history in this case is so much worse. The thing I can find most easily in the good bookstores of Berlin are books that are more or less histories of evil. There's Eric Hobsbawm, Niall Ferguson, Mark Mazower, or just Herodotus, and you walk around Berlin and think of all the evil. And the odd thing is, out of this history of evil some good things may have come—for example, this sense of impending ecological catastrophe that Germans seem to possess. But then I forget about the evil. I tell friends: "After a while, it's just a place to live."

But then there are moments when I realize a certain amount of trauma is still encoded in the body politic. One of these came a day or two before I met with Wigand. It was on New Year's Eve, when I went to Miranda's party. At first I thought it would be pretty mellow. That whole weekend, I had been saying, "Guten Rutsch!" It's what hipster-type Germans say at New Year's. It more or less means: "Have a *good* 'slide.'" And if I said this to a deliveryman or taxi driver, the guy would pump his fist and go: "Hoo! Ja! Guten Rutsch!" He'd rock on his heels: "Guten Rutsch!" In a few hours, I'm sure he'd be sliding under some table. I'd get looks from girls who walk around Berlin with black balloons. "Guten Rutsch!" So I thought New Year's would be pretty mellow, with a lot of guys sliding like base runners into bars and then just passing out.

At our quiet little dinner party it was mentioned there'd be fireworks. "We'll go up on the roof." Someone said that Joschka Fischer said that there should not be fireworks this year and people should give that money for victims of the tsunami instead. Others began to argue about the fireworks. As it grew late, people seemed to tense. Why? At Sox Park, I see fireworks every time a shortstop hits a homer. Why were people so excited?

At midnight, Miranda and the others climbed a ladder to the roof. "Are you coming with us?" Sure, I'll be up. Bored, not wanting to do this, I climbed up to the roof and looked out over Berlin, and what I saw was—

Well, it was like a night raid on Berlin, as in a war. I'd expected the government or a civic body to shoot them off, but instead I saw people pouring in the streets and hurling—what? I could only call them "rockets." In the streets below, kids were firing genuine missiles. Some whizzed right by my head. In half of the blocks that I could see from the roof, there were now plumes of purple smoke, lit up, with streaks of fire, and I was certain in the streets below people must be dead.

Then it hit me what was going on: the whole city was trying to reenact a firestorm. The bombing, the rockets going past my ear, all of this continued for two hours. At 2 A.M., I wanted to climb down from the roof. But how? Miranda said, "You can't go out on the street! You need someone to escort you." She was right. Some of the guests went with me, in a little detachment, to the tram. When we came out on the street, there were kids, about fourteen, still throwing firebombs at each other. But by now there was too much smoke for me to see.

It's hard to say how self-conscious this reenactment of a firestorm was supposed to be. I remember a line from a lecture by a German historian: "It's true: in the end, every nation is a kind of death pact." Perhaps in that sense Germany used to be a "death pact," but no longer—not now, in this era of the EU. Still, the sense of being a death pact hasn't completely died out.

After all, in Berlin on this night, there are some old people who still remember the firestorms of before. They remember the wet towels, trying to get oxygen. Maybe the day after they went through the city and looked for signs on the walls: "Miranda, I'm still alive. Call me on my cell phone. Tom."

This nation was not just a death pact but a pact to commit murder. In all the evil of the twentieth century, it was the single most evil thing. And of course it's a mystery how people deal with it, what they are thinking. Yes, Germany is socialist. Yes, Germany is Green. Yes—it's disturbing—Germany might be enlightened because Germany is dark.

Of course the social democracy may collapse. What is enlightened may collapse. The argument of this book may collapse. For what I argue depends on a country that not so long ago had a government based on murder.

PART TWO

Berlin Diary

Preface

Though I could go on arguing for Europe, I get bored wearing my angel wings and opining from above. I . . . I wanted, well, not to be a European, but to fight for the European model, as Orwell volunteered for Spain. Stop opining about Barbara v. Isabel and just get in the trenches for Europe. But I'd want to do it on the side, without giving up being an American or having my American-type job. Maybe I could save the European model by living a second life, on the sly, with my new European friends.

With e-mail, and all that, no one in America would even know I was gone.

O, Europe! How little I did for you. While Orwell got a gun and went to Spain, all I could do was to take my Visa card to Berlin. In Our Time, this seemed to be the best thing I could do to defend the European model—to go over there, spend, and give a push to the GDP. Was that so wrong?

O, America! How much more I spent on you. For you, my own country, I went much deeper into debt.

We all went so deeply into debt that we brought our country down.

It is true that on many of my days in Europe I spent very little: like, in the Bible, a penny for two sparrows. It seemed some days I could practically live on a song. Back in the U.S., I was often shocked by how much I had to spend just to go to work. How is it I'm spending more over here when I've no time to buy?

At any rate, in trying to start this second life as a European, I really took just two big trips, one in 1997 and then a second in 2001, each of them over two months long. Since then, I've been back on many short trips to Berlin, from 2003 through 2008, to see if the German model would survive.

From the first trip I despaired. What I found when I got there was—

4

Germany *Is* Dark

January 1997. I came to love the German model when things were at their darkest. When I arrived that winter, the number of jobless had reached over 4.7 million: "worse than Weimar," everyone said. As I wandered cold and sick around Germany that winter, stumbling in the dark, running a high fever, I kept seeing before me the face of Larry Summers, Gorgon-like, mocking me, because the German model I'd come to praise had turned out to be a dud. I was too late: it was all over. As if he were glowing in the dark, I kept seeing Summers, whispering in Clinton's ear (now Obama's), soon to be our secretary of the treasury and already our man-in-Davos talking to the global moguls and crowing that the U.S. model had triumphed, we had to deregulate Wall Street, the high-unemployment German model was through. I admit that, in the Bush years afterward, I began to think of him as on my side, my "friend," but back then at global gatherings, he seemed to be the one banging his shoe, the way that, terrified as a child, I had seen Nikita Khrushchev bang his shoe and say, "We will bury you." Now Summers was saying, "We will bury Europe," and the sclerotic German model with its worker control would go into the deepest pit of all. And as I went through Germany in the dark that winter, reading the pink pages of the *FT*, it was Summers who seemed to be taking off his shoe just to bang it on my head. He seemed to be so right about the U.S. model: it was not just our lower unemployment but our growth rate, our productivity, at least on paper, that was exploding, though I knew the hourly wage of U.S. workers was not going up but dropping. But how could I argue? He knew a lot more math. In college, he was crunching numbers while I was just an English major working out the meters of lines with the kind of unscientific kids Summers would write off as girls. Well, some of them *were* girls. And as I got sicker that winter, I felt all the worse because Summers was up on stage with the world business leaders at Davos not just as a Democrat but as *the* Democrat setting the economic policies of—well, the party of the left, or really the center left. By helping junk the Glass-Steagall Act and blessing all sorts of deregulation, Phil Gramm, Robert Rubin, Alan Greenspan, and Summers made London and New York the places where all the big go-go global finance was happening, while over in Frankfurt, cut out of the action, the Europeans could pound sand. In the U.S. and the UK, we were coming up with new financial products, while the poor Germans were still making things like widgets; it seemed shameful to defend a country where people still made things with their hands. So in going over for two months on a German Marshall grant (for which I became too demoralized to turn in my report), I dreaded in a certain Lincolnian way that I was about to see democracy, or at least social democracy, which is the only true version of it, perish from the Earth.

Why did I care so much?

I cared so much because Germany is the country, of all countries, with the greatest amount of worker control.

It's astonishing, in fact. And what astonishes me is that no one comes back to the U.S. to talk about it. Dare I give out this breathtaking fact, the experts leap up to chide me at once:

"I hope you take their problems seriously."

Others said, "I hope you take their problems seriously."

And yet others said, "I hope you take their problems seriously."

In other words, don't come back here and let ordinary working people know how much better off they would be. I wouldn't be taken seriously anyway: "Oh, he's just a union-side lawyer. What do you expect him to say?"

Germans gloom about their problems, too. As I later came to find, no one can outcompete the Germans in believing the German model is doomed.

Well, I was determined not to take their problems seriously, and that's why I held off for so long in turning in my report to the German Marshall folks. I know what people would say: "Wait! You didn't take their problems seriously!" Okay! Even now, in 2010, I despair of getting away with defending the German model, though if there will ever be a time, it is surely now. Of course I went back in 2001, and 2003, and 2004, and 2005, and in 2009, to find out if the German model will survive.

It's still there; and in fact, Larry Summers is still in charge of U.S. economic policy. But a lot of things have happened since 1997.

This first trip was the darkest: and what was darkest was just to stop—stop—going into work. For an American like me, what's terrifying is to lose the reassuring daily terror of being at work. For two months—and I still find it hard to grasp this—I was away from my desk. Oh yes, I'd often taken Christmas off, and when I go to D.C. for work, I try to stay the weekend if I don't have to get back. And it would be wrong to say that even in 1997, many lawyers were unfamiliar with the idea of "vacation," at least as a concept. But to be off for more than ten days can bring on shock or trauma. My coping strategy was to tell myself that I was headed, in the dark, not to Club Med but to Bonn; *Bonn* not in the sense of "good," but in the sense of bondage, to yet another losing cause. It's crucial in getting away to keep telling yourself: "I hate this, it's awful, I want to go back home." For it's crucial to have something to replace the stress of not going to your jobs. In that sense it was also helpful that I was so unprepared. I had written people to set up interviews, but no one had written back. I didn't want to go. I had a small grant from the German Marshall Fund, where someone had thought it would be fun to send a U.S. union-side labor lawyer to the country that had more bottom-up worker control than any other country on the planet. But it was— well, I just couldn't leave. I was supposed to fly out on January 3. But on New Year's Eve, I got a break when I was packed in on an El car and could feel two little punks lift my wallet with my Visa inside. When the doors opened, they popped out and ran. I ran flying up the stairs after them, and I like to think I would have caught them, but since they were only twelve or so, they probably carried guns. Let them go! With no Visa, which is the crucial visa that I needed, I really could not go to Europe: I had an excuse, thank God, to blow off Bonn and stay and work. I'd miss the flight, and then a week later, when at last I got my Visa card, I'd be in the middle of some case, etc.

Besides, going over without my Visa would be like volunteering to go to Spain in 1937 and not bringing a gun.

But at 7 A.M., less than six hours later, the morning of New Year's Day, a "special messenger" was knocking on my door to give me, as I stumbled out of bed, a "temporary replacement" Visa, explaining they would mail the permanent one to Bonn. Ah! Two days later my friend Tony was driving me to O'Hare. "Two months in Europe, why are you so glum?" he said.

"Tony, I can't cut out of here for two months."

My practice will collapse. I looked out the window: I'd end up with nothing. He tried to cheer me up: come on, come on. What's your first appointment?

"I have no appointments."

He didn't believe me.

"I wrote all these Germans to set up interviews, and no one wrote back."

"Well, then, what's the first thing on the schedule?"

"I don't have any schedule. I don't know where I'm going. I'm just going over there all alone, in the dark, for two months, and, I don't know . . . to just walk around. I have no 'schedule,' I have nothing   nothing."

Being a salesman and therefore trained to hold off all forms of darkness, he said, very upbeat: "It's perfect."

"What is?"

"'No schedule.' This is just the way to do it."

"It's because no one wants to meet with me."

"Do you realize how lucky you are? NO SCHEDULE! That's exactly the way to start."

Anyway, by putting one foot in front of the other, I got on the plane, Lufthansa, and wondered yet again why no one had written back. Dick Longworth at the *Tribune* had given me some names, but none had written back. Dick had told me that, because of the oddity of being a labor lawyer from America, "the Germans will be more curious about you than you will be about them." And for a moment I had a vision of myself as Benjamin Franklin dressed up as an Indian at Versailles and surrounded by rouged-up courtesans coming up to goggle at me as a kind of zoological curiosity from the New World; indeed, I think that's what the German Marshall Fund had in mind. But no one had written back.

There was no point to this trip.

Besides, I already knew what I was going to think. Ever since I'd graduated from college in 1971, I'd read in *BusinessWeek* and even the *Washington Post* and the *New York Times* how the European model was "collapsing," so the coming collapse of the German model certainly did not deter me. I already knew I was going to defend it. I'd already told that to Martha, a friend who had been a stringer for *Newsweek*. She was aghast. "It must be something about men," she said. "Men: they go to all these places and they already know what they're going to think. When I go, I just have these . . . impressions. It's like I'm waving grass." Well, if I was waving grass on the subject of Europe, the Republicans would trample me, so I better know what I'm going to think. I intended not to have impressions: save that kind of stuff for novels. Indeed, flying across the ocean, I began to lecture the woman next to me. I had complimented her on her English. "Well," she said, "I'm an American." She was teaching English in Nuremberg, and she put down her magazine, *Bild*, and pointed to a photo of a man. "I'm teaching English to his wife." The man in the photo was a German businessman trying to get rid of the German model. "So, what do you think about that?" I said.

"They have too many benefits, social security. I guess it started with Weimar. . . ." And then the Nazis.

I was starting to hate her. I said it had started with Bismarck, and I went on about the gift of the Germans for taking care of illness and old age, the two great evils of industrial society.

I could see she was squirming. "Perhaps this doesn't interest you."

"No, I'm interested," she said. "Excuse me." She got up and got in the line for the bathroom.

Meanwhile, outside the window, something eerie was happening—or not happening. Normally, as we come over Ireland, or at least France, there is a pink glow in the east . . . dawn, or something. But this time, as we came near the airport, 7:30 and then 8:30 A.M. Frankfurt time, there was . . . not so much "light" as a milky substance that I came to know as "less dark," or "day dark," the dark of an hour before dawn, except over here it came a good two or three hours after dawn.

What was I doing here?

We landed in the dark. It was a long taxi: the planes in the dark glided by like coffins. I stumbled to the exit, and the flight attendants, who looked like coeds, were smiling, waving to each of us:

Bye

Bye

Bye.

Like everything was sunshine and we'd landed in Hawaii.

Then I took the subway to the Hauptbahnhof, and checked into the Hotel K., surrounded by sex kinos and tiny little storefronts where Turkish workers smoked. And I was horrified to be in Europe and not at my desk at work. Then I decided to do what I had promised not to do, at least on my first day: call the only two people I knew in Europe and ask if they wanted to have dinner. They were two graduate students, Germans, whom I knew from a year they had spent at Northwestern: they were in other cities, but, Europe being Europe, that meant they were only about a half hour or so away. Desperate, I called, and, sleep in her voice, H. picked up the phone. At first she thought I was calling from Chicago. "No, I'm here, in Frankfurt." Thank God, she and her fiancé, S., said they would drive down that night to see me.

Would we do this in America? I am only asking.

Later, before they arrived, I had my "Rocky moment," when I went jogging and heard The Bells and crossed over the Windmill Bridge and looked over all of Europe and raised my arms in the air. Sure, despite the unemployment, I was here to make the case, in 1997, for European social democracy. Back home, I had met academics and economists who would roll their eyes: "You have to take their problems seriously."

That's all I ever heard: "You have to take their problems seriously."

Well, the question I was going to raise was: "Why should we take only their *problems* seriously?" After all, every year they get to take six weeks off. Why not take that "seriously?" And besides, the very fact that they had "problems" that one had to take "seriously" was, in a paradoxical way, the very appeal of the place. By that I mean, at least they try. I mean that the social market economy is a human creation, and not an impersonal machine, inhuman, cold, barking out commands, the way Americans such as Alan Greenspan conceive of it. The very constitutions of these countries, like the German Basic Law, make clear the purpose of the state is to protect people from the "excesses of capitalism." Law professors actually state this in their lectures. In the Basic Law there is literally a provision to protect the family, and yes, it's right wing and Catholic, but they're serious about protecting the family against laissez-faire capitalism. In that sense, laissez-faire is unconstitutional. In defending the Gothic against the Classical, John Ruskin argued that, however flawed and imperfect the Gothic style might be, at least it was human and, because of that, greater and closer to the divine than the cold, impersonal Classical style could ever be. And so it is with the European model: however flawed, when compared to the "perfect" but impersonal Anglo-American model, at least it is a work of human beings and not machines. Sure, European politicians make mistakes; yes, they screw things up. Yes, I would find out the Germans have made all sorts of blunders that U.S. government leaders would never make simply because they are afraid to touch or interfere with our more impersonal and colder version of capitalism in any way at all. But

human intervention is a sign of Europe's vitality. And it's why ulti-
mately, in a globalized world, Europe, for all its problems, will have
a middle class that will survive better than ours will.

Still, because it is so human a thing, it's hard to write about the
European model as such: every incarnation of it has its own
DNA. Every welfare state in Europe has its own unique human
expression, even as they all try to merge into a single European
Union. Burckhardt described the Renaissance city-state as "a
work of art," and in a certain way, the European welfare state is
also "a work of art." And, like any work of art, each is trying to
solve a problem—in this case, keeping a capitalism that protects
the middle class. Yet because they all hang in the same European
gallery, one can see there are different approaches to the problem.
And while I could have stopped at any picture, I wanted to go to
the one that would appeal most to me as a labor lawyer.

And that's what I was about to do.

That night, when they drove up to my hotel, my grad student
friends H. and S. gasped. "It's so seedy."

"I'm trying to make the grant money last."

But I sat in the back, feeling like I was the grad student.

We got lost as we drove around the city. "We never come here,"
H. said. Yes, she and S. had been to Mexico and Sri Lanka and
China: but Frankfurt, which is about half an hour away, is the
kind of place, being European, they had never been. Nor had they
been to Bonn or Berlin. Of course, they were students. We went
to one of the Frankfurt taverns and had the famous apple wine,
and all around me these delicate-looking European women were
filling up on sausage, just as they had wolfed down baloney at
breakfast, and probably moose and squirrel. Once, I had asked a
friend in the U.S.: "What is it about Europeans that make them
look so fragile, with high cheekbones?" "It must be the diet, my
friend." "But how can it be the diet when these fragile, high-

cheekbone young women eat so much sausage?" No, it must be some vapor coming out of the ground, some chemical reaction with that European mud. I know, as the novelist Diane Johnson writes in *Le Divorce*, Germans are supposed to look like Americans, by which I think she means fleshier, Midwestern, but to me, as a Midwestener, they look porcelain, delicate. I heard once that German women tell each other not to use washing machines in America, because they'll tear apart their clothes. Yes, it's a puzzle. But I was not given a grant to write about why Europeans look so fragile, or the character of the mud, or what they eat for breakfast. I was not even sure that H. and S. had gotten up for breakfast. And later S. told me a little joke about grad students: "Why is it that, in Germany, graduate students have to get up at five?"

"I don't know."

"Because the stores all close at six!"

It's an old joke, since now the stores stay open till eight o'clock at night. So the kids can sleep in.

But this first night in Europe I wanted to talk about politics, and sure enough I did in a way I can't do over here. It annoys me whenever I hear Americans say, "The Germans aren't really very political." An American reporter in Bonn told me: "I have to call our embassy in Bonn to find out what's going on, because no one here talks politics." Lady, I wanted to say, we're the ones who don't talk politics: we talk celebrities. That night, drinking apple wine in the tavern, H. and S. and I had a political talk such as I have never had even once in the U.S. We talked about things that people talk about only when they live in a country with a labor movement, where they decide the "big things" collectively: my wage, my pension, my health benefit, my retirement age, my vacation, and everything that people in America never talk about as "politics" because we have no control over any of these things at all through "politics." It's not that it's impossible for these subjects

to come up in the U.S. in a political context—they do—but if it
happens, it's usually smothered in *People* magazine chatter or
nasty talk-radio attacks. Here, it's whether Obama or Pelosi or
Reid is "winning" or "losing," without all that much interest as to
what exactly is being won or lost. Here I could talk politics with
H. and S. and many others without anyone ever mentioning the
name of "Schroeder" or "Kohl." Ah, I wish I could explain it. Well,
let me try an example from that first night. We were talking about
the *Mittelstand*, the middle-sized manufacturers. "They're being
cut out by the government," S. said.

"Cut out of what?" I said.

"Research. Basic research. Now the global companies get it all."

"Do the two of you—do you really think this will affect your
lives?"

"Of course," S. said, and looked annoyed. "The problem is,
Germany is not interested in research—"

"Who is?"

"The French are; they're more interested in basic research—"
S. said.

"Why is that?"

He paused. "I think it's because of their socialist tendencies. . . ."

And that's an example of how people talk politics: it's about
these collective decisions.

Or for a long time we talked about the retirement age. Of
course that's political: it's a decision made not just individually
but—to some extent—collectively as a country. With both H. and
S., their parents, though younger than I am now, were already
traveling the world and gardening. So what is the retirement age?
Is it really sixty-two? "It can be fifty-eight."

Yes, at fifty-eight, some voluntarily went on unemployment,
even before "normal" retirement age, to start the good life even
earlier.

H. and S. wanted their elders to hurry up and retire, especially in the universities, where the Generation of '68 was still holed up: the rebels, the Greens, Joschka Fischer, people my age. "Yes, the young rebels get in and they kick everyone else down and try to hang on." S. laughed. "Of course this is what we are hoping to do."

At last I gave out: jet lag, sitting at a bench with no back. The two of them said, "Oh, we have to get you back."

No! Don't go. I'm in a social democracy. Keep talking!

But the next day when I awoke, Germany was in ashes. It was dark again, and I was alone. And in the breakfast room by the window, I saw evil-clown types strung out on drugs come up and press their faces on the window, and a woman at the table next to me screamed. The evil-clown types and the dwarfs laughed at us, and one of them stuck her tongue out at me as if to say, "Here's what I think about your Social Contract—BLLLEEEEEEHHH!" And then rolled her eyes and spat a big wet raspberry splat on the window as the diners fled the room.

But I stayed and went on reading about German unemployment.

Later I walked along the street, away from the sex kinos and up to "the Dom," where Polish-looking men in motor caps came out of Mass and not a single person smiled. Everything was closed: in this whole global crossroads of a city, there was no place I could go and buy a cheap electric razor. By 3 P.M., it was night again, and, depressed, I walked into a café called the Hoechst. At a table, there was a woman my age who looked like Veronica Lake; it could have been a movie except she was reading *The Essays of Ralph Waldo Emerson* and doodling. I sat near her—not so much to meet her as to get away from all the other Germans sitting there with dogs. I was so lonely that I tried to make small talk about Ralph Waldo Emerson, and she looked up, unsmiling: "How did you, an American, find the Hoechst?"

Why did she think I was an American?

"Your yellow legal pad," she said. "You only get those in America."

I explained I was here to study the Germany model.

"Model? I would not hold Germany up as a model. We have so many problems." She paused and went on: "We used to think of Scandinavia as a model, but now they're no model either." She said that because Sweden happened at that moment to be having a bad year.

Okay, I said, I know there's unemployment in Germany, but at least there is no poverty: I would cling to this point for years.

"But there is poverty!" she said.

Well, I did not see poverty, I said.

"Oh," she said, "I just saw a TV program about the homeless, and some of them were businessmen." I must have given her a look, because she repeated: "Yes, some of them were businessmen. They got used to the good life, and they ran up a lot of debt, and that's how they became homeless."

I wanted to laugh at her—really, how "German" of her. I suppose they had used credit cards. How many German businessmen, I said, are homeless?

She frowned: "I admit, I don't know the exact numbers." I could see she was wildly on the left; indeed, she turned out to be a professor of philosophy. But she was in utter despair about the German model.

I later decided that this despair is a kind of permanent, built-in aftershock from the good years of the 1970s, just like there is a built-in aftershock to the inflation of the 1920s: there's a numbness that will never go away. For Americans, it's of course news that the Germans or Europeans ever had any good years, much less "good years" that were wildly good, almost beyond imagining.

"People my age," she said, "we got used to the standard of living going up and up. Now the young Germans, in their twenties, they don't expect as much. They still live at home. Many of them never leave. Why should they leave? They don't have jobs. And you know what's really sad? When they get out of school, they're too old." Yes, they were too old to work, she said. "They're twenty-eight, twenty-nine, so the companies don't want them."

Then whom do the German companies hire?

"I mean the global companies. They hire the British kids."

That's what galled her, and all the Germans: the British were passing them over. It was the British moment now. Germany's was over.

Anyway, she had given up on Germany: she was waiting for a plane that would leave at midnight to take her back to South America, where she taught philosophy. How sick she must be of Germany, to flee so far away. . . . It was not a happy life. One of her German colleagues had been kidnapped. Yet she seemed to prefer it to living here with everything collapsing.

Well, I wasn't going to defend Germany to Germans. I gathered up my books on labor, European politics, etc. She took one of the books and looked at it. "Don't you think," she said, brushing back her hair like Veronica Lake, "one of these should be a German dictionary?"

No.

No, I had figured anyone I really needed to talk to would speak English. But that was not true, as I found out during a day or so of walking around alone in Frankfurt. Since I knew no one here, I decided to try my luck in Bonn. In Bonn, there were three people I had contacted through friends back in America. One of them, Tomas, was a journalist and didn't really count because I don't count journalists as people. But I had two other names.

On the train on the way there, I was shocked at how bad the news was: it was not just German unemployment. The *FT* had a story about how all the employers—three out of four—had stated in a survey they were planning to relocate some jobs to Poland or some equally low-wage Eastern European country. *Three out of four!* "Germany has a new export—jobs." At least three hundred thousand jobs would be lost. When I had left, a friend in D.C.— a well-traveled, astute friend—had told me I had better go now because there would not be a Germany much longer.

I put down the *FT*, in horror.

So I began to talk or try to talk to two little old ladies seated nearby, who spoke only German, it seemed. But they were sweet, and they began giving me cookies. And just as I began to think that at least some people in Germany could smile . . . WHAM! My suitcase hit the ground. An old man, maybe eighty-something, had pulled it from the rack, and now he was screaming at me in German in a purple rage, and now he was reaching overhead to grab my overcoat, and now he was rolling it in a ball, and WHAM, he threw my overcoat to the ground.

And snarling up behind him came an old woman, who had to be his wife, and she too was screaming in a purple rage. I didn't need a dictionary to know that they were saying: YOU'RE SITTING IN OUR SEAT!

The old guy was huge, but he had no bone mass and had big hollows in his shoulders. Yet I knew without knowing that once upon those shoulders there must have rested a Nazi greatcoat, and he had probably pulled a trigger while serving in the SS. What an ass, I know: but just as I was feeling sorry for the Germans, I had come across this Nazi, and Germany really did seem dark.

The unemployment number of 4.5 million was worse than Weimar's, and here on this train, in the dark, I was being screamed at by a Nazi. No wonder the woman who was Veronica Lake had left for South America.

Anyway, I moved, and then the strangest thing happened, as

the two old ladies, now blushing, began unwrapping and passing me little sandwiches. The old man who had rolled up my raincoat and flung it on the floor started smiling at the three of us. Now he wanted to be in our little group. Heh, heh, ho, ho. Big smile: the storm was over. Some say this is a German trait. Or at least a British historian, Gordon Craig, made this point in his 1982 book, *The Germans*. Oh yes, Craig wrote, they can be the nicest people, and then suddenly they are in a purple rage and pulling down your suitcase. Then, all at once, the storm is over. "Heh, heh, I'm sorry." Maybe World War II fits what Craig wrote: they went into a purple rage, and now it's over. "We're sorry." Meanwhile, 20 to 30 million people are now dead.

I ate my sandwiches, but I was weirded out. Who'd want to live in Europe? It's too dark. And perhaps Mark Mazower is right. He is another brilliant British historian who wrote the 1998 book *Dark Continent: Europe's Twentieth Century*—maybe the best book about Europe I have ever read. Mazower argues that fascism, and not liberal democracy, is really the natural form of government for Europe, or it was after the fall of the monarchies and empires in World War I. In other words, fascism should have won out, and today Germany should be running Europe—except, as Mazower argues, it was just too evil: if it had been a little less dark, like Italian fascism, then German fascism would have won.

It all would have been different, yin and yang: we would have remained on the left, and they would have remained on the right. We would have been more like America under FDR—i.e., a social democracy—and they would have been like Chile under Pinochet—i.e., the University of Chicago would have held sway.

But Hitler had been just too evil, and somehow they're now on the left and we're now on the right. Over and over I thought: thank God I don't live here and have to think about all of this. Every time some eighty-year-old went into a screaming fit, I thought, "Oh, that's their problem." But why isn't this my heritage as well? Why is Hitler only their responsibility and not ours, in at least a small part, as well? I'm sure that's a shocking idea to my friends: we Americans are so superior. But Emerson, our greatest philosopher, wrote: "The history of every country is my own." Besides, the summer before I left, I had been in a local Chicago bar, Laschet's, and on the wall there are pictures of big fat men in lederhosen pouring beer down the blouses of German women with helmets on, all of whom must be named Brunhilde, and a woman my age, a journalist, said to me: "You're German, aren't you?" I looked blank. She leaned closer. "It's okay, we all are." It's the great secret of America: the largest of all our ethnic groups is German. "No one will talk about it." But it's partly a German country. In the 1960s, when flower power was all the rage, this journalist had had enough of the hypocrisy as she saw it, and she signed up to go to school in Germany. I mean, she went "all the way," not only going to Germany, but majoring in philosophy, and getting into trouble, and hanging out with radicals like Rudi Dutschke and the like. I gasped: though she had started life as an American, she had really gone native.

"Yes," she said, darkly: "We all are German."

Oh no we aren't.

But in another way, we all are, and not just because the-history-of-every-country-is-my-own. We Americans are Europeans: we all are from the Dark Continent. And I say that well aware, very well aware, that the majority of this country will soon be non-European or descendants of non-Europeans. But this country is a European settlement, a European outpost, a European project: we can go into a purple rage and throw a tantrum about it, but in the end, America is perhaps *the* European project. It's a point made in *After Tamerlane* by the historian John Darwin. Just as Europe made America, so America made Europe. It was the bonanza of

America that made Europe into an economic superpower that left rival blocs like China and the Ottoman Empire behind. We turned them into a superpower, and they made a superpower of us.

As surrogate Europeans, we carry the Dark Continent within us: look at the way we imprison people at rates we would expect in Europe if fascism had carried the day. Sure, in this particular sense, we're all European.

Still, I'm relieved that, being American, I don't have Hitler on my head. Anyway, in Bonn, I met Tomas and his girlfriend, B., at their car. The two of them, being journalists, did not count as Europeans, as I explained, but at least they were going to take me to dinner with another couple, two real Europeans and not journalists.

"By the way," Tomas said, "you do speak German, don't you?"

I said nothing.

Tomas turned to B. "Oh shit." Their friends did not speak English. What a mess.

I scrunched up, miserable, in the backseat. Tomas, being a journalist, turned on the news, and this was the second time, with a shiver, I heard The Bells. But this time The Bells were not from the Dom but from the car radio: they were really little bongs. So there'd be a "bong" when the story was from Prague, and a "bong" when it was from Vienna, and so on through the summary at the top of every hour.

Bong. Berlin. Blah, blah.

Bong. Wien. Blah, blah.

One could hear the little bongs bonging from every big city of the world, as one never heard them in America, even on NPR. But not once did I hear:

Bong. Washington.

But I did hear:

Bong. New York.

In fact, I heard Bong New York a lot because the UN is in New York. The Security Council was up to something. Or there was a report on world hunger. Bong New York began to get on my nerves, because it seemed to be a way of ignoring America.

What were they leaving out?

Bong. Chicago. The Brewers beat the Cubs.

Our hosts V. and his wife L. lived in a log cabin out in the woods, and I saw an ax glint in the moonlight as we walked in. They kissed and hugged Tomas and B., as I stood unembraced. The hugging unnerved me more than the German. I thought Germans were supposed to be cold. The Christmas tree was still up, but I did not hear the kids. I wish I had put that in chapter 2, since this is one of the big differences between "Barbara" and "Isabel." When Isabel hosts a dinner, you don't hear the kids.

Anyway, for ninety minutes Tomas and B. and V. and L. talked in German and smoked and laughed, and were all very loving, and I sat there alone and ate their red roast and drank red wine and said nothing and looked at all their books. V. was a businessman who ran a construction company, but he had books by Habermas, Marcuse, and the like—or maybe L. did, or they both did. Who knew? I couldn't talk to them. What a mistake it was to come to Europe! I was embarrassed, I was ashamed. And then V., who spoke no English, leaned over and pointed to the Christmas tree that was still up and said:

"You see, it's a real German Christmas tree."

What?

Yes, he spoke English, though I now realize his wife didn't. And not only did he speak English but he had lived in America—in the 1960s, the time of *Easy Rider*. And he and a fellow biker had roared on motorbikes through the South. "We rode through many small towns, and we must get out fast—before they find out we are foreigners. In America, you are not so fond of foreigners, yes?"

I was shocked. No, we're very fond of foreigners. We're not like Europeans: we welcome foreigners. He was trying to lump all Americans in with Southerners and people in small towns, which is kind of a stretch.

Best of all, this wonderful night, which I had almost ruined (well, I did ruin it for V.'s wife), I got to hear about labor law, just as the German Marshall Fund would have wanted. In fact, I saw a debate break out between V., the contractor, and B., who was a left-wing labor journalist. She said the big contractors like V. were not paying "twenty marks an hour" (oh, there was no euro yet).

"Of course we are," said V. "But the subcontractors we hire don't pay the twenty marks." Then he turned to me. "Do you understand how it works? Here in Germany we hire the Czechs. The Czechs as subcontractors hire the Ukrainians. The Ukrainians then hire the Russians."

"Who do the Russians hire?"

Everyone laughed. I was serious. But on the way back, B. was still furious. "They're not paying twenty marks." And tonight, out here in the woods, I wished I were a European. Only in a country like Germany would someone like B. attack her host for not paying the right wage and even know exactly what the right wage is.

The next day in Bonn, I found out why the German model is great, and then later, at dinner, why it wouldn't survive. I had lunch with C., who didn't count as a real German because I knew him from Chicago, where he had worked at the consulate.

"Are you happy to be back here?" I asked.

"Of course!" His three German daughters had begun talking about going to college in America. C. and his wife were aghast. The tuitions were $30,000 a year! (Again, this was 1997.) It seems in Chicago he got "hardship" pay, so he could put the kids in private schools. But hardship pay for German diplomats living in the U.S. didn't cover college.

"So we had to come back, even though I took a pay cut. Besides, I'm a Rheinländer."

But Wilmette, Illinois, is very nice.

"Oh, Wilmette is very wealthy. Too wealthy for us. Besides, even in Wilmette, I had to worry about the girls. I had to take them everywhere. Here in Bonn, I don't care where they go at night."

Germany was great.

"Well, I'm glad you're in a good mood. Everyone else is full of gloom. Haven't you seen all the stories in the paper?" I asked.

"Bah, since I've been back, people say, 'Oh, times are really tough.' Then they show you the new car they just bought for fifty thousand marks, and they tell you how they just came back from a holiday in Majorca."

"But aren't you worried about all the jobs moving to Eastern Europe?"

"No. Why should I be? There's nothing over there." (As one German said, with some exaggeration, "They don't have any roads.")

"Besides," C. went on, "our whole trade with Poland, Hungary, all of Eastern Europe, is less than our total trade with Switzerland alone."

"But won't it go up because of rising labor costs?"

And here C. got me thinking about the weakness of the whole flat world idea. "Labor costs aren't rising," he said. "Besides, it's much worse when the mark goes up. Let me give you an example. Last year the mark rose 10 percent against the dollar. Let's assume that labor costs here in Germany went up 3 percent— which would be a huge rise. In fact, they didn't go up at all, but let's say they did. Even so, labor makes up less than a third of the price of a finished good. So what's one third of 3 percent?"

"Uh, 1 percent."

"So that's 10 percent due to the mark, and 1 percent due to higher labor cost." His point was: it's ridiculous.

I quote this and step out of the time signature here to be anachronistic and say how right C. was. Ten years later, the *FT* and *The Economist* began talking about how the German unions exercised wage restraint and controlled labor costs, but this was almost meaningless in terms of competition. Sure, with Agenda 2010, the German government brought down the "social payment," but that's a more significant cost for the service sector than the global exports. Indeed, that's why a social democracy concentrates on what it can sell abroad.

But I'll get to that later.

What C. did worry about was unification, East German unemployment, etc.

"Why don't you lower the wages of Germans in the east?" That's what the Ayn Rand–types argued.

"If you lower the wage in the east, then the higher-skilled ones move to the west. We want them to stay in the east."

"Oh, I see the problem. You must be a pessimist."

"No, actually, I'm an optimist. You see, the manufacturing sector will save us. Yes, we'll restructure, but we won't do it the way you did. The middle-class way of life here depends upon it."

C. turned out to be right. Still, Germany had a lucky break because, as it restructured, most of Europe was switching to the euro. That meant the German manufacturers did not have to struggle as in the past when the mark rose against the lira or franc or the currencies of its other rivals.

Whether C. was counting on a switch to the euro, I don't know. But he also didn't believe that Germans could disinvest from manufacturing the way we in the U.S. did. For one thing, it's what people *did* here. The best and brightest did not go into banking and finance, because London and New York had all that action. Sure, there was a certain culture here, too. But the laws created that culture. Labor law made it harder. Every time there was a lay-off, there had to be agreements with works councils. There had to be closing plans. There had to be severance pay. There were "conditions, conditions, conditions" on getting out the way we did. Tougher bankruptcy laws made it hard for big business to walk away. They could not go into Chapter 11 and dump their pension and health obligations. It was the power of labor not just "against" or "outside" the firm but deep "inside" the very structure of the big German firm that made it harder to deindustrialize the way we did.

And maybe in a social democracy, there are just fewer investment alternatives. There is the fact that, because people have public goods, there are fewer alternative ways to profiteer. Businesses can't make the same profits on health or education the way they can here, since in Europe, unlike in the U.S., the state will not pay for these goods at whatever price the market will bear.

And to the extent they stay in manufacturing, they cannot use day laborers and temporaries the way we do to staff our factories, poor and powerless people who have no say in anything. Yes, in Chicago, some of our factories use day laborers and temps. I suppose it's partly so that businesses don't even hire or fire anymore— they have no connection with the workforce but deal only with their straw bosses. The Germans have to employ people who sit on their corporate boards.

In the U.S., our elite, scoffing, might say that there is just not enough labor-market flexibility to allow Germany to adapt to globalization as we do. But it's precisely because of our flexibility that we can't compete. What the laws manage to do in Germany is to keep people together and to hold onto their skills in groups. Co-determination, works councils—in other words, worker control—keep people in groups, rubbing elbows with each other, and all this rubbing of elbows helps build up human capital. Indeed, for some economists, while not applying it to Germany, this is now a fashionable idea. Think of all the buzz about the "knowledge" economy, which, in the world of academic economists, is an inquiry as to how knowledge drives economic growth. For finding out about this new economics, I refer the reader to David Warsh's 2006 book, *Knowledge and the Wealth of Nations*, which introduces us to economists trying to untangle the connections between the kind of knowledge that comes from groups and economic growth. German worker control contributes to a group interaction that over time not only builds up but protects a certain amount of human capital, especially in engineering and quality control. This kind of knowledge is not just individual but group knowledge. It's the kind of group knowledge that our efficient "flexible" labor markets so readily break up and disperse. It's our flexible labor markets that make it so hard for the U.S. and the UK to compete. We spend vastly more on basic research than the Germans do: U.S. companies are unrivaled. We spend far more on higher education. But with our flexible labor markets, we're unable to capitalize on this research and education. Sometimes we try the Japanese model of work, but we never try the German, because we don't want to cede any real control to workers. Supposedly it's a great mystery why Germans keep investing in manufacturing and even prospering, despite the claims that the German education system is broken (okay, it needs help) and they aren't spending enough on research (okay, they aren't). But they're doing something right. What is distinctive about Germany is the privileged position the worker has within the firm. And it's that privileged position that explains how our own middle-class way of life can survive. Putting more money into education is a waste of effort. Putting more money into basic research is a waste of effort. We already spend enough. In fact, we have every factor of production going for us: we have much more land, more labor, more capital, much higher levels of formal education. But with our flexible labor markets we cannot develop the human capital or knowledge needed to wean ourselves away from turning out crap. In global competition, the U.S. has almost every comparative advantage over Germany, but the one great comparative advantage Germany still has over us is that it is a social democracy. Yes, I admit Germany has its problems. "You have to take them seriously!" Okay, as an American, I can crow about not having the problems of Germany. But *we're* losing our middle class, and *our* problems are even worse.

So why didn't I go back and tell people that? Because I still didn't believe it: look at their unemployment. Many expected and still expect the Germans one day to vote out the German model.

And while Germany was not disinvesting from itself, all the global capital was going to the U.S. All the hot money went to New York. And the fear was that, as capital became more global, German companies would not get any money precisely because they had ordinary workers sitting on the corporate boards. Would Bear Stearns or Merrill Lynch want to put money into a company where a guy whose job was watering the office plants was a director?

Bear and Merrill and Bank of America expect a director to be— well, someone who's not going to wreck the company.

So Germany was dark, and in the years to come, Germans I met would often say, "How do you find us?" "We're all depressed, don't you think?" "Is anyone saying anything good about us?"

It's odd now to think of them so depressed while we Americans were so merrily going deeper into debt.

On this trip I wanted to meet depressed Germans. So, I ended lunch by telling C., "You know, I tried writing to a lot of Germans, but no one wrote back."

C. was puzzled: "Can I see a copy of these letters?"

I handed him two or three, and he started laughing. "They are dated December 27," he said.

"So? It's now January 9."

He stopped laughing and gave back the letters. "They're still on vacation!"

No wonder Germany was dark! The Germans were in Majorca.

Fortunately, one German, whom I'll call M., was not away in Majorca. And that night at dinner, it was he who convinced me the German model would not survive. We had met after I had walked all afternoon looking for the parliament building of this tiny political capital. "Oh, it's over that way." "Where?" "That way." Some citizen of Bonn would point vaguely to India. I'd walk and find nothing. Where did they put parliament? By the way, the good people of Bonn were delighted that the capital was moving to Berlin. Bonn was an old university town, the home of Beethoven and Robert Schumann, and most people living there had no interest in being the capital of Germany. When I asked people in English or in my rocky German where to find the parliament building, most of them were clueless.

M., though, hated the idea of moving to Berlin. I met him for dinner at a place as tiny as anything in this tiny toy town of a capital. M. liked the chef here: "Extraordinary man! He is a German trying to make haute cuisine out of German food. Do you know it, in America?"

"Sure, we have German restaurants."

"Bah, these are dreadful, I think. They are an embarrassment."

The restaurant was tiny; everything in Bonn seemed tiny, and they say one reason the politicians wanted to go to Berlin is that in tiny Bonn everyone could hear what the politicians were saying. M. continued to talk about the importance of cuisine: "You see, people are writing in our magazine about the connection between eating and eros."

"Eating and eros?"

He smiled. "I mean eros as a form of knowledge."

We started on the soup. "It's in Genesis," he said. "The apple: yes? One takes. One eats. There is knowledge."

"What should I know about Bonn?"

"About Bonn: yes, people say, 'Bonn is so provincial.' Provincial? It's not provincial. There is chamber music, there is new, experimental theater. . . ." To M., it was just a plot of the right, after unification, to move the capital to Berlin. "Because now 'they' are back . . . all of them, the Prussians. . . . Adenauer never wanted to have Prussia back."

Konrad Adenauer was the chancellor from 1949 to 1963.

"I thought Adenauer wanted unification."

"Bah! Of course not." And now that the Prussians and the right wing are back, they want the capital back in Berlin. "And what do they say about Bonn? 'Oh Bonn, it's so Left Bank, it's so Rhinish.'" He explained that Rhinish, for Rhineland, was a code word for pacifism.

I told him my maternal grandfather's father had come from the Rhine. His name was David, and he had been sent to the U.S. as a young man because the family did not want him to be drafted into the army—Bismarck's army.

"Good!" M. said. "Then you know what I am saying. Resist! Unification with Prussia was a disaster."

In fact, years before, I had once asked a German woman at Harvard Business School what she thought about unification. To my surprise, she said, "It means Germany will be more Protestant and less Catholic."

That was an odd thing to say. So I followed up: "And what does that mean?"

She paused. "It means we'll have one week less vacation."

Actually this turned out not to be true, but Germany is not really a country but a series of princedoms, and it's East v. West (that's the real division), and North v. South (no, that's the real division), or Catholic v. Protestant, or BMW v. Daimler-Benz, but tonight it was Left v. Right. And as I ate, I began to see it as M. did, and became more and more upset myself. M. appealed to me as a Rheinländer, to go back to America and tell people how unification imperiled everything.

Why didn't someone try to stop it?

"Some of us did try. Ah, we could have stopped it." He meant the SPD could have stopped it. "It took a two-thirds vote. I wrote a long minute and laid out the problem. Some of us said, 'Stop. Let's keep it, East Germany, a separate country, at least for five or six years,' because we couldn't afford it. It would ruin the whole country."

Specifically, he meant that, with the higher taxes that West Germans would have to pay to bail out East Germans, it would be impossible to keep the welfare state. It would be impossible to keep the system of collective bargaining. M. laid out the trap into which the left had fallen: to bail out the East Germans, the new Germany would have to run a deficit or cut benefits. Well, as they were about to introduce the euro under the Treaty of Maastricht, they were forbidden to run a deficit that might have weakened the new currency throughout Europe as a whole. So they would have to cut back the welfare state.

It was the revenge of the Right. It was the revenge of the old

USSR, which hated Germany: East Germany was like a car bomb that the USSR, as its dying act, had rolled into this paradise of social democracy, now so much better off than the Russia that had won the war.

The West Germans opened the gates, the Russians rolled it in, and kaboom.

I could see it from the point of view of the West: good, Catholic, decent, even pacifist maybe (though I had my doubts), the land of Heinrich Böll, Konrad Adenauer, and all the small merry people who put on funny hats. Now, once again, they would be under the thumb of Prussia, which was not so much a territorial state as a state of mind, a militaristic place, a Germany of tall German women, unsmiling, who rode on horseback cracking whips.

Ugh: it was horrifying. And now the capital would be in Berlin: I now hated Berlin. I had no desire to go there.

But I admit, I later came to think maybe M. had exaggerated. And I'd like to say here that what I "later" thought was wrong. Whether it was the Grandmother's Soup we ordered or something else, M. was right that unification did imperil everything. It's not that Germany moved to the "Right" or Germany moved to the "Left." Rather, what was unique about unification was that Germany had two of everything.

It had a Right: but it was a nasty Prussian Right and, at the fringe, even a neo-Nazi right. And it had a Left: but it was a nasty Communist Party Left, even a screaming left. The new Right would undermine the old Right, just as the new Left would undermine the old Left. It was bringing in a whole new set of swing voters, a different kind of Right and a different kind of Left, which were small in number but just arguably big enough to decide, yea or nay, the future of the German model.

And then, to my horror, I began to realize M. thought I could help him. "You're a labor lawyer, yes? You are with the unions in America."

"Well . . . yes."

"You must go back to the unions in America and tell them what is happening."

"Wait . . . unions in America . . . these are not like unions in Germany . . . they . . . well, there's no one to tell."

"But then you must tell your friends in the unions. . . ."

"Look, there's no one to tell! There's no labor left, it's shrunk to nothing in the U.S., and there's no one to . . . I mean, there's just no one to. . . ."

"Okay, okay," he said. "I see the problem!"

It was too dark in Bonn, and I wanted out, in part to escape the Prussians. On the train to Hamburg, I calmed down and took a look at all the soldiers. On trains, I'd often see these German soldiers, sitting alone, late at night, kids, little kids, all dressed up like soldiers, but really like children. I'd think: Do their parents know they're on this train? There is a draft in Germany, but they seem to make a point of picking out the most waiflike little boys and dressing them up and putting them on trains to go around Germany, kind of like scarecrows, because the adults on the trains cringe and look away—Oh my God, we can't send that little boy into battle.

You can see why it's so hard politically to round up a contingent of these children to go off to fight for NATO. Seriously: *do you want a child to die?*

Meanwhile, sitting with these little boys, I was going north to Hamburg, which was even deeper in the dark. Hamburg was eerily empty, and I guess here, too, people were on vacation.

They were certainly not in the stores.

I have struggled with all the reasons why Germans do not spend. And it's the rich especially who sit on their money. The savings rates of Germans are high but very uneven: the poor save nothing, the middle class save 5 or 6 percent of their earnings, but the rich are hyper-savers, certainly compared to Americans at the top. Hamburg in particular is fabulously rich: I often heard that it was the richest place in Germany, maybe in all of Europe. What's a puzzle is: what exactly it is that people up here do with their riches?

That's the question I put to S., a lawyer who was a friend of a friend. She and her husband had invited me to dinner. She lived in a big, glorious, white building, and we talked in her office, a big, white room. As we talked, she was e-mailing a letter, making our dinner, feeding the kids, phoning a client, pouring herself a drink, and chatting with me.

The one question I was dying to ask was: where is the maid?

But instead I said, "So what is the economy here—what is it people do?"

"Media, public relations," she said.

"Public relations: that's what makes the town go?"

"There's a lot of old money in Hamburg," she said.

"They hire people to get their names in the paper?"

"They hire people to keep their names *out* of the paper."

Later I read a paper for this book: "Marketization of Production and the US-Europe Employment Gap." The authors, the great labor economists Richard Freeman and Ronald Schettkat, partly explain the gap as follows: Germans spend more time preparing meals while Americans eat fast food and takeout. In that sense, we "marketize" much of what Europeans regard as family life.

So why don't the rich spend?

My friend L., an American priest who now lives in Germany, is puzzled too. He says, "I see people in the stores." And now that I have been several times to Germany, I would also say, "I see people in the stores." But now I think that the rich travel so much outside Germany—Italy is down the street—that maybe the reason they are not in the stores every day of the year is that they are out of town instead.

Still, it's true, the savings rate of the better-off people is very high: so why is that? I can think of many reasons. They need not pay big tuitions—like $50,000 per year now at NYU—to send their kids to first-rate schools. That's the first thing that could explain it: the rich can't blow the same amount of money as our rich do on what they get back as public goods. That's the whole point of the chapter about Barbara and Isabel.

The second big reason is the chilling effect that even an unequal social democracy has on "flaunting it," because at least people pay lip service to equality. After all, Thorstein Veblen wrote *The Theory of the Leisure Class* in what was the Gilded Age, not in the more egalitarian post–New Deal 1950s, when our savings rate was high. (While Galbraith may have scoffed at our private consumption, people were not drowning in private consumer debt.) It's not just equality but the spirit of equality that has held down Veblen-like conspicuous consumption: perhaps an uneasiness around working people who have real political power at the firms where they work. Now many people say, "Well, that can't apply to Germany, because it is becoming more like the U.S, rich v. poor, etc." Some would say, "All over Europe, the middle class is stagnating, and the inequality is growing."

Yes, I know, I might be wrong; and yes, I saw the front-page story in the May 1, 2008, *New York Times*: "For Europe's Middle-Class, Stagnant Wages Stunt Life Style." According to the story, the percentage of Germans in the middle class is declining, because—here a consultant at McKinsey is quoted— "Germany is tied to old industries." To the contrary, the old industries have made it the leading exporter in the world, and while fewer people work with their hands in these industries, they still spin off what are really the most desirable types of service jobs. No, the middle class is in decline primarily because we're counting Berlin, the old GDR, where the old industries that propped up the Soviet Union have disappeared. Even so, the decline is small; and for a long-term comparison, the best evidence I can find is from a 2007 study by Thomas Harjes, an economist at the International Monetary Fund. One can look it up online: "Globalization and Income Inequality: A European Perspective." Generally, from the late 1970s to the early 2000s, Harjes found that on the Continent—in contrast to the U.S. and the UK—"inequality rose modestly or even declined." The Gini coefficient, which measures inequality, has actually *dropped* in many advanced European countries as globalization of production has increased. For example, in France, even in the past few years, inequality has not gone up; over the last twenty years, it's even dropped—yes, dropped through the storm of globalization. Meanwhile, in the same twenty years, in the U.S. and the UK inequality has soared. In the UK, for example, which has almost as much "labor flexibility" as the U.S., the Gini coefficient has shot up 30 percent. And even in these countries, modestly well-to-do people like Barbara do not have high savings rates: when there is huge inequality, such people have to maintain their relative position by spending, not saving.

But is it true that in Germany the percentage of the population that is middle class is dropping?

Yes, I admit, it seems so. But even the alarmists (and I'm thinking of European economists like Stefan Bach, Giacomo Corneo, and Viktor Steiner) end up describing what is only a modest decline, at least in the old West Germany. In their much-cited 2006 study, they stress the big rise in inequality is in East Germany, where an economy that serviced the old USSR more or less had to be scrapped. Still, the three economists are measuring inequality based on market incomes, not the government transfer payments people end up receiving. What's more interesting is what Bach, Corneo, and Steiner concede: unlike in the U.S., there is not much increase in inequality in people with jobs. In other words, inside the framework of worker control, there is no increase in inequality. It's unemployment that is the problem; and since 2006, German unemployment has sharply dropped. "But don't I read that the elite in Germany are making more money?" Yes, there's a catch, which the three economists admit: they're not making it from super salaries in co-determined firms. Rather, unlike Americans, they are making it as entrepreneurs, i.e., from their own start-ups and ventures. After all, remember, as John Schmitt has pointed out, Europeans, including Germans, are more entrepreneurial than we are.

Still, I admit it feels like inequality is going up. How could I not think so? I did not hang out in Munich or Stuttgart, which has the kind of affluence that in the U.S. I have seen only in Chevy Chase or Bethesda, Maryland. No, I spent too much time in Berlin, which is not at the "edge" but right in the center of hammered East Germany. Worse, in Berlin, I hung out with arty freelancers who feel cut out of Germany, Inc. But in the old West Germany, which makes up the bulk of the nation's GDP, Thomas Fitch and other economists say it's as egalitarian as ever. And that's pretty extraordinary when one thinks about how, in Germany, the world really has changed.

In a way, there *should* be more inequality than there now is, especially in terms of salaries within the big firms. Yes, while wages may have "stagnated" for the middle class, it's also true that over time the middle class has worked less. No, I'm not talking about unemployment, even though that's a part of it. Over in Europe,

Jared Bernstein has pointed out, the Europeans often take their productivity gains not in the cold-cash terms of higher wages but in the softer form of leisure. In Europe, in Hamburg, in Munich, there is a global elite that is working longer and longer hours, while the middle class is cashing in with more leisure instead. If the elite choose to take their gains in the form of income and not leisure, then that seems to me fair, so long as the middle class have the same choice. Perhaps the choice is not all that free, but at least the middle class get something out of rising productivity and economic growth. In the U.S. or the UK, our median-income families get less per hour and have to work longer, too.

What is burned in my brain about Hamburg is the loneliness of the "Swimbody" in the arcades over the water, the Alster and the canals. Since I knew no one, and it was cold and dark, I spent a lot of time in the mall-like arcades, which have the elegance of the shops on New York's Madison Avenue or even those of Bethesda, Maryland.

In window after window on this arcade, there was etched, in an elegant way, a word I had never seen in English or in German:

Swimbody.

From what I could tell, if you were rich and a woman, you wanted to be a Swimbody, and there was a whole column of mannequins who were these Swimbodies begging women to come into the stores. But it was all empty. London tweed coats were "stark reduziert," but no one was buying.

Every Swimbody, shivering: how cold it must be up against those plate-glass windows.

Everything: *stark reduziert.*

Only a consumer with a heart of stone could stay out of these stores. But I can't even say why the people of Hamburg did stay out of these stores because I didn't see anybody in Hamburg at all. Occasionally as I walked along an arcade, I would run into a cluster of people. But usually as I stepped along the glass arcades, it was just me and the Swimbodies and stacks of *Hitler's Willing Executioners*, which was not just the best-selling book in Germany at the time but seemed to account for 10 percent of total GDP. I asked a tiny shopgirl where I could go for lunch. "It's so expensive around here," she sighed. "I always bring my lunch. But maybe you could try the Mövenpick."

Isn't that like a HoJo's?

But I went to the Mövenpick. I sat at a counter, and I was shocked by how many elegant business-types, probably in PR, were sitting at the counter, too. Desperate for any human contact, I tried to make small talk with the businesswoman about two inches away from me. "I'm from America," I said.

"Oh really," she said. "We were just there—in New Orleans. In America, for us, my husband and me, that's our favorite city."

Before Katrina, I disliked people who said, "Oh, New Orleans, that's our favorite city," partly because I'd never been there. But it was better to talk to a human being than to a Swimbody.

"Yes, New Orleans . . ." I said, trailing off. "But I find whenever I'm in the mood to go to New Orleans, I end up going to New York." I thought that might one-up her, but she topped it.

"Oh, New York! My husband and I go there all the time."

"Oh?" I said. "How much vacation do you Germans get?"

She frowned. "Very little! None, in fact. It's rare now you can even get half a day off."

"I'm surprised."

"And when we do . . . oh, New Orleans is where we'd *like* to go . . . but we're too exhausted."

It turned out that she worked in—well, public relations. It seemed S. was right; maybe everyone in here *was* in PR. Well, I said, maybe New Orleans was too exhausting a trip, but what about New York?

"New York," she said, "this really is our favorite city." In fact, she and her husband had talked about leaving Hamburg, which was so exhausting, and moving to New York.

"Can I ask why?"

I could hear her stockings rustle, unpleasantly. "Why? With the taxes I have to pay here, I have to work half a year just to make money for *myself!*"

I tried to give her the chapter 2 "Barbara v. Isabel" argument and say that, because of her high taxes, she doesn't have to pay for anything, and that's why she has all this money to go off to New Orleans and New York, though it's hard to squeeze in when she gets only six weeks off and twenty-seven other paid holidays. "In America," I said, my voice rising, "we spend almost as much in taxes and we don't get free school or the big pensions . . . we don't even get police and fire, really, in some cases. . . ."

"I don't think so," she said, scoffing.

"Oh? You've been to New York? Hamburg is clean, it's rich, it's . . . fabulous. . . ." Of course, the people are aloof and impossible to meet, but I left that out.

"Fabulous?" she said. "It's falling apart. There are drugs, prostitution."

"Oh, come on," I said. They've got five drug dealers, all of them in front of the Hauptbahnhof, where the cops can watch them, and of those five, at least three of them are undercover cops themselves.

But she would have none of it. "And the immigrants! They go around and rob, but 'they,' they don't dare to send them back." She did not say who "they" were.

"Well," I said, thinking of home, "at least there aren't any *armed* robberies."

"There are!" she said. "Some are—some of them. Don't you think we should send them back? But our politicians, they say nothing. We can't because of . . . oh, 'what happened.' Because of . . . 'that,' no one here can say anything."

Now, I don't like to play the Nazi card with a younger German, but this woman really irked me. "Well," I said, "let's face it, maybe because of 'what happened,' you guys really shouldn't be saying anything." But baiting her only made it worse.

"Fine, but with all this crime, people are moving out."

"Where?" I said. "New York?" I started laughing.

"We go there!" she said. "It's not that bad."

Now both of us were shouting. Later I thought: Good riddance—send her to America.

But wait: I *am* an American! And when I read in the *FT* how the up-and-coming business-types are leaving Germany for the U.S., I have conflicted feelings: (1) It's good for European social democracy, because it's a safety valve, letting out the alpha male or free-market Republican-types who'd try to undermine it. But (2) it also means there are more predators in the U.S. I just bet that when she and her husband got here, they began making sub-prime loans.

Still, I had met a European.

After this, I met no one in Hamburg. Or I met no one until I went out on the ice my last night in town. It was the week of the "Glühwein Festival," when the Alster has frozen over and the ice is thick and solid (one hopes), and people go way out to little tents in which teenage kids serve up this heavily spiced wine called "glühwein," and as everyone gets shit-faced, they look back at the white city and blast out "Funky Town." And out here it's easy to meet Europeans, but after a glass or two of glühwein, you can't even remember your own name, much less theirs. They must call it glühwein because it has the effect of drinking wine and sniffing glue together, and I knew after a glass or two that when I woke up tomorrow, I would not know any Europeans. Hamburg was not my town, and I was now frightened of going to Berlin.

But still: look at Hamburg! There it was, far away, ringing the shore, and every building was as white as a block of ice and as white as a burning candle, and it was both the summer white of Monte Carlo and the winter white of poor Shackleton stranded on the shore, and way out here on the ice, drinking glühwein, I could look back and know I would never break into this city, and the white wall of it would keep me back. I was so discouraged and tired, and Germany was so dark. It was tempting to lie down and curl up on the ice, and though I'm not really sure, maybe that night the Swimbodies came out to pull me to land.

Now I went north up to the Baltic port of Kiel, where on January 12, it was dark by 2 P.M. on a Saturday afternoon. I was to meet friends of Ed and Kathy, a German couple whom I will call Gerhard and Renate. Once they had lived in Washington, D.C., where, in my opinion, they had seen America at its best— neighborhoods like Cleveland Park and, even better, Bethesda and Chevy Chase, Maryland. Ah! Now they were up here in the dark in Kiel. Did they miss the *New York Times* and Dupont Circle and the Starbucks where people squeeze in with their laptops to apply for their grants? I know it's uncool to say, but I *love* Washington, D.C.

I'm sorry: but that's what I think.

And at that moment, with Cleveland Park on my brain, it was a shock to walk around Kiel: the houses are small!

Of course the Germans don't subsidize the supersizing of houses as we Americans do with our tax code. "Ah, so you admit Barbara is better off than Isabel because she will end up in a bigger D.C.-type house?" Sure, Barbara really is better off than Isabel. Except that, when the housing bubble finally bursts, Isabel's savings aren't wiped out.

As I said, Kiel is a Baltic port, where boats like big white birds fly north to Scandinavia. The kaiser used to come up here to see his navy; and there is a monument for the sailors who died gasping for air in the U-boats. (It honors their victims, too.) In my whole time in Kiel, I felt claustrophobic, too. The tiny homes seemed as cramped as U-boats. "Still," I thought, "at least they aren't money pits." I could see why Germans can stash so much money away. But I could also see why, gasping for air, vacationing Germans love to head to Death Valley, where at least they are alone.

A German once said to me: "I was in the bookstore the other day and I reached to get a paperback and a woman walked right between me and the book. She didn't say a word!" Yes, people are packed in.

It's not just the houses: they must feel trapped inside their towns. It could be Kiel or Stuttgart, or ten or twenty other cities: they are precisely 2.5 or 3.2 miles, or whatever, across and will never be another inch wider. In Chicago, I have a sense of . . . a vast "Chicagoland," where at this moment at the far edge, someone is building a new mall.

Still, that night at dinner it amazed me what Gerhard and Renate had done with the much smaller space they had here. They had hollowed out the house, so there was one giant room, which had the feel of a ski lodge in Aspen. And we had red wine and a red roast, and a fire burned in the fireplace. If we'd just had a few more lawyers, I'd have felt I was back in Washington, D.C. They told me about Germany. I gave them the news from America: how there were still fifty stars on the flag. No new states had been admitted.

Then I told them about my project and how I wanted to show how Germany, with its high wages, was struggling with globalization.

Gerhard paused. "That's your thesis?"

"Yes."

"You think globalization is the problem?"

"Uh, well, yes . . ."

"What about unification?" He was incredulous that I was missing the real problem. "Right now," he said, "I'm paying the equivalent of a hundred dollars a month, or more, for a 'unification tax.' It's right out of my paycheck, and that's on top of my normal taxes, which are really high." He noted that others (who aren't academics) are paying an *extra* $200 or $400 a month in taxes just to help the East Germans, who don't really like the West Germans anyway, and vice versa.

And I want to write about globalization?

I pleaded with him: Look, I can't go back and tell Americans that the problem with the German model is unification. In my country, people know what globalization is. But most of them—there are exceptions, sure—know there used to be a "West" and "East" Germany and that's about it; they don't want to hear about it. (And forget about the people who have no idea.) They want to hear about globalization.

That night, I despaired of my whole project. I was also tired of it. What was I doing up here in Kiel? I was tired of the dark; I was tired of living out of my suitcase. Now the next morning I was to leave for Berlin. The last thing I wanted to do was to go to Berlin: "the capital of the forces of darkness," as a friend said.

Berlin. Ugh.

Only a few days ago I had told M. that, like him, I was Rheinländer, and not a Prussian. He had said, "Resist," and I had every intention of "resisting." I didn't want to go to Berlin, which is, aside from being steeped in monarchy and militarism from which my grandfather's father had fled, foul and dirty, as I had seen when I'd visited briefly a few years before. Besides, a spring had sprung out of my suitcase.

It was sticking me, and I had no way to fix it.

Fortunately, I was among Germans. Early the next morning Gerhard fixed the spring and took me to the train and we shook hands and that night I was in Berlin.

For two days in 1993 I had seen Berlin, and at the time there was no "Berlin" in Berlin. The U.S. Army had left. No one spoke English. Now that the Wall was down, Berlin as a "cause" was history, and the Kohl government had cut off all the subsidies to keep the hipsters and gallery owners. Yes, as unlikely as it sounds, in 1993 it seemed that even the hipsters had no future in Berlin. For now, "Berlin" had no way to sustain itself. It had long ago lost its real economy: cut off from the West except by air, the old big firms had moved to Stuttgart or Frankfurt or someplace else. Now that the Wall was down and Communism had collapsed, Berlin actually seemed more Communist, bleak, and gray, and just as there was no West Germany to keep propping up West Berlin, there was no Moscow to keep propping up East Berlin.

So when I showed up briefly in 1993, there was no there "there," no Berlin in Berlin, and in the middle of it, in the old center, was a big empty nothing, a few big black buildings and what seemed like a lonely Mister Softee truck, without any Mister Softee.

That was the middle of Berlin: this one little truck where you could get a little hamburger and a Coke.

It shocked me at the time: I was there on a junket for a labor-law project, and I had even specifically asked my hosts to send me to Berlin for a day and a half. I wanted to see it because Jim Yuenger, who was the foreign editor at the *Chicago Tribune*, had

said to me one night at a dinner party in Chicago, "Berlin's my favorite city in Europe."

It seemed a cool thing to say, and none of us could top it.

I was dying to say, "It's my favorite city in Europe too." But I
didn't because it seemed to me that first I ought to go there.

Of course he meant the old Cold War Berlin, and by the time I
got there Jim Yuenger was dead and that old Berlin was gone. A
student I met said, "This is just a big dumb city in the middle of
nowhere." I cringed because that's also how people talk about
Chicago.

Of course West Berlin *was* a bit like a Chicago-with-no-economy,
with a few Michigan Avenue things on the Ku'damm, like Louis
Vuitton. But for most of us, who came in by the main train sta
tion, named the "Zoo" because it's next to the Zoologischer Garten,
it just seemed like the setting for a movie starring Burger King.
That was the choice in the Free World: stay in West Berlin, which
had now emptied out, except for girls in black stockings with black
balloons eating French fries with their boyfriends at Burger King,
or push on to East Berlin and try to hunt down that one Mister
Softee truck going around. Of course, that could have been a cool
thing: for I had read books like *The Spy Who Came in from the
Cold*, and it was a kick to find out that Berlin, which had already
seemed like the end of the world, had broken through this shallow existential darkness into a deeper darkness, a nothingness beyond the imagining of John le Carré. My British guidebook at the
time had warned me not to expect anything more than a Lionel
Richie concert. But still I kept looking for the real Berlin that
would deliver more than an ice cup from a wannabe Mister Softee truck, because in college I'd read about the Berlin of—

Hannah Arendt,

Max Beckmann,

Walter Benjamin,

Bertolt Brecht,

Albert Einstein,

Lotte Lenya,

Paul Tillich,

and Sally Bowles, though not necessarily in that order. Even though I knew the Nazis and the Red Army had pounded all of that Berlin to bits, I knew that something, even in tiny pieces, must still be around. And I dragged my suitcase around the city for those two days trying to find even a halfway decent "Berlin café," and with two hours left before I had to leave, I went into Tourist Information at the Zoo and said, "Please, before I leave, I want to see . . . something, or anything, that would be . . . you know, the real Berlin." The young guide nodded. "Look, I'm not some American looking for *Cabaret* or anything, but you know . . . coffee, or. . . ." He knew just what I meant and told me to drag my suitcase up to platform 3 and take the next S-Bahn to Charlottenberg, where he said there was a gallery with a little art-book section, and that would be the "real" Berlin, in this tiny store, where I could spend about five minutes. And so I ran and made the train in a second flat and went down the staircase banging my suitcase and . . . it was closed! It closed at 4:30! I got back on the train and wept. Ah, how I hated Berlin.

But now I was back.

The station, the Berlin Zoo, was more strung out than ever, in an evil-clown sort of way. Still, being German, it was immaculate. I went to the Hotel B., which was under a dripping highway, and when I got there, I couldn't find the lights. The staff was gone. Since I knew a lawyer, V., whom I'd met at the consulate in Chicago, I called, desperate: "I can't find the light, and no one speaks English."

"Wait," V. said. "I'll come by and pick you up."

When he said, "I'll come by and pick you up," I assumed he'd swing by in a car. Instead he came by on the U-Bahn, which is slower than the S-Bahn and travels underground. Well, he found the lights, and he assured me the Hotel B. was nice. We could go out to eat here, in Friedenau, famous for its war widows, etc.

"Okay," I said, "but let's go somewhere else."

"East or west?"

"East!" I said. I knew it had advanced beyond a wannabe Mister Softee truck, and I felt the thrill of going into the "Communist" darkness, but we still ended up at a yuppie-type trattoria.

The East was under construction. When Reagan said, "Mr. Gorbachev, tear down this Wall," he spoke on behalf of real-estate developers from all over Europe. I never saw so many construction sites: big cranes bobbing like Big Bird even at midnight in Berlin. They had overbuilt. Whereas once the East-was-Red, now the East was in the red, in a way unimaginable for Germans, and in the years to come, many people like my friend Father L. would say:

"Berlin is broke."

"Berlin has no money."

"Berlin has no economy."

And it's true: there's nothing for people to do. But there is one big thing Berlin has, and it has it in a bigger way than any other place I know.

Berlin has kids.

It has kids the way Berkeley has kids, and while I saw the kids all over the place on this first night in 1997, I would say there are far more of them all over the place right now. That's what I tried to say to Father L. and others, and still do: it's got kids. And all over Germany, sober, prudent Germans with high savings rates are giving their kids money to blow on cafés in Berlin.

Even on my last trip in 2009, I was in shock: each trip, even more kids are in town, and while the café-per-kid ratio was maybe 1 to 6 in 1997, I have seen it trip by trip increase to 1 to 5, then 1 to 3, and, though I'm just eyeballing and don't have the numbers, I'd say that as of April 2009, it's 1 to 1.5.

Readers are rolling their eyes and thinking: "Next you're going to say it's 1 to 1."

Reader: I've just been in Kreuzberg, on Saturday night, April 2010, and I think it is indeed 1 to 1.

"Yes, but that's no kind of economy."

Why not? Everybody's mad that Germany isn't spending enough, but then, when they do spend, everyone says, "Well, this isn't right, they shouldn't be spending all that money in Berlin, and tsk-tsk, that's no kind of an economy."

I say: Lighten up, bankers of the West! If Germans want to blow their money in Berlin, let them blow it in Berlin. Maybe the whole problem of the German economy is that the parents of the "university" kids are not spending as much as U.S. parents are because kids in Berlin are going to universities like Freie for free. It's perfectly logical that the kids at Freie or Humboldt would be hanging out in cafés while kids at DePaul or Northwestern, deep in debt, are working late into the night at second- or third-shift jobs.

Berlin *does* have an economy, and it's the kind of café-life-on-steroids economy that a lot of U.S. cities would have if we had social democracy and universities were free. Wait: don't I believe in manufacturing jobs? Sure I do; and that's all great for Düsseldorf. But there should still be a Berlin. And I could smell the coffee that first night in 1997. V. and I got on the S-Bahn, which whooshed like a futuristic monorail straight across the sky, though it's a 1940s type of missile, like the one that whooshes at the start of *Gravity's Rainbow*, and while if Berlin were a true U.S. city, it should take us fifty minutes of fighting traffic to get to the East, the S-Bahn flew us in ten minutes to this city-of-the-future, the developers' Berlin. They had started with a big complex of court-yards called "Hackescher Höfe," and I'd die of embarrassment in 2010 to go someplace that is so touristy, but in 1997 it was right up on the edge: the young Hannah Arendt might have been in here buying clothes. There were shops, galleries, and a big walnut-brown central European–type café-diner on the ground. It felt like Soho under Communism. I asked V. about all the kids. "There are now thirty thousand at Humboldt," he said. "And there are about another fifty thousand at Freie University." (That is the "Free" University the U.S. Army had started in West Berlin when the Communists cracked down on Humboldt.) "And there is the Technical University in the center, and that has forty thousand maybe." And V. himself was helping start a new kind of school, a "Hochschule." This "Hochschule" would go in the space between a university like Freie and a German vocational school.

I knew I had to ask about education in Germany. An American will ask: "What's the education system like? That's what I want to know!" For us, if Germany is outcompeting us, it must be "the schools."

Then here's the biggest shock I can give: yes, Germany is out-competing us by far, but the schools are a mess. They don't send enough people to college. The vocational schools are falling apart. Because of all the money used to bail out the East Germans, the schools are broke.

What's that mean?

It means schools don't matter as much as we think. When our politicians—and I single out the liberals here—say we have to send everyone to college to be competitive in the world economy, they're ducking the real problem. First, we're never going to send everyone to college. Roughly three-quarters of our adult citizens (twenty-five and over) have no BA and never will. Our country is a high school nation. Germany, too, is a high school nation. Every developed country is a high school nation. Second, even if we did send everyone to college, we wouldn't be better off. We spend far more on college education and we can't keep up with a Europe, whereas, in Germany, the education system is often a shambles and yet the country prospers.

So what *does* matter?

Economists put a premium on education, but what some put an even bigger premium on is the development of skills and problem solving in groups. That's just a fancy way of saying that the right kind of corporate governance and the right system of labor laws count for more than which country has the highest percentage of people going to college.

So I kept telling myself: it's all about the labor laws. Education doesn't matter, it doesn't, it doesn't.

Still, I had to ask about it. But first we had to eat. We went to the ground floor and I kept looking up from the menu to stare at the kids. From what I'd read, I wouldn't have thought that so many kids in Germany were even in college. Of course, who knew if they really were in college? Lots of kids circling around big college towns aren't in college at all.

I turned to V. "Can you tell just from looking at them which are from the East and which are from the West?"

"No, you have to talk to them," he said. A kid in a T-shirt is a kid in a T-shirt.

"But in the U.S. I read you can tell a *Wessi* from an *Ossi* by how fast they walk."

V. winced.

He also winced when I said "Herr Ober" to the waiter, the way Michael York did in *Cabaret*.

"That's so old-fashioned," he said.

It's what my guidebook said. "How do you get them?"

"You make eye contact."

I thought: Great. We'll be here for hours.

Here's another thing about social democracy: you don't have to leave a tip. That's right, V. said. "You don't have to leave even 5 percent. Sometimes I leave nothing."

At this point, a German man, poor, shabby, or maybe he was a Russian, said, "Pardon me, sir . . . pardon me, for interrupting, but did I hear you say that sometimes you can leave no tip, nothing?"

V. looked annoyed. "It is proper, sometimes, at a hotel."

"Where is such a place?" he said, as if he hadn't heard. His voice trembled, and then he was shouting. Up to then I'd thought: "This-could-be-a-restaurant-in-Chicago," but . . . well, we don't have characters from Dostoyevsky screaming at the diners.

Meanwhile, a newsboy had come right up to us to sell a paper! Yes, I mean a newspaper! I gasped. A little boy stood there like Jackie Coogan in *The Kid*. In half an hour, three different newsboys came up to our table. Okay, the education system is less than perfect. What matters is that Berliners around me were buying papers. They were continuing their education as adults!

To me, this is vastly more important than "how-many-go-to-college," for the test of education is how many continue reading as adults. It's especially important in a social democracy that high school grads, as opposed to college grads, keep reading. For in this new global economy, high school grads, in Germany and elsewhere, still have one big competitive advantage over college grads: *there are more of them.*

If they can just read the papers and go out and vote, they can vote themselves a better deal—even if their skills are worth less.

I turned to V., and tried to gurgle: "They're . . . they're selling newspapers in this restaurant." V. may not have understood because he said, "Yes, but you can get the papers over there." He pointed to a rack of dailies where I could have gotten them all for free—big national papers like the *New York Times* or the *Wall Street Journal*. And I admit, later even a journalist scoffed about the kid—or three different kids—trying to sell me papers at my table. "At our paper," he said, "we sell only . . . maybe two thousand papers doing that." I admit, they don't use children anymore. "Germany has changed." Yes, the newspapers are smaller.

But come on: there's still a newspaper war in Berlin. People still continue a reading life after college—or heck, even if they didn't go to college. It's stunning to me that people from the U.S. come over to look at German "education" and they never see all this adult education—unknown in the U.S.—going on all around them. And why is there even still a newspaper war in 2010?

Well, of course it helps that German papers get nice tax breaks. But I'd say there's a business logic to staying with the printed word, even if the big German dailies have been bleeding money. In a social democracy, collective decisions still matter to people. And if people need half an hour a day to stay up on what's happening and not just three or four minutes to skim the news online, then it's just more user-friendly to do it the old Gutenberg way.

And if one day it's not, the big German firms may still spin off these thick papers as not-for-profits, just as in some European countries they already do.

But how would this explain the continued reading of books? As I said in chapter 3, I get on a tram or subway in Frankfurt, Hamburg, Berlin, or Bonn, and it would be normal that, out of twenty people, five or six are reading the paper. At least five are reading books. Half the time in Chicago, in an entire El car, I see no one reading anything, not a paper, not a book, not even the *Red Eye* forced on us for free. And I take the DePaul, Northwestern BA–besotted Brown Line.

Yes, I can see Americans reading in Washington, D.C., in the Metro, at rush hours, and in Manhattan, of course, I can go and gape at all the readers on the 1 train. But Chicago is a hip, global city; it's not like the rest of the Midwest, where even if they've got a Starbucks, they don't have a single copy of the *New York Times*. "Do you mean that in thirty or more years in Chicago, you have never seen someone read *The Economist* on the El?" Sure I have. I've been to the state fair. And on State Street, I've seen a man dance with his wife. But outside of Barack Obama's neighborhood in Hyde Park, do even well-educated people in Chicago read? No. Recently, my friends Jim and Cornelia went house hunting in the most opulent part of the North Side, and Jim said to her: "Notice anything weird about all these homes? You don't see any books."

That's my point: if you own thirty or more books, or you are reading any book at this moment, you may protest all you want, but you were born on the wrong continent. Paradoxically, if you own more than 130 books, you were born on the right continent. Because if you own more than 130, you must be a professor at a U.S. university, and you make more than you would as a European professor.

That's because, in the U.S., we believe in higher education, and the drug companies give universities a lot of money to do corporate-type research.

So that night I was pumping V. about education partly to find out why people read. The problem was we were in a bar, with a young kid at the mic croaking like Joe Cocker and blowing out his vocal cords.

Over the croaking, I had to shout: "Can you explain to me about tracking?"

"Yes, let me explain." In the dark he took out an envelope. On the back of it he drew three columns.

"Let's start with the first column: this is what we call 'The Royal Road.'" He said that's for the kids who go to the "gymnasium" and then go on to the universities, which are of course free. "Now, in the second column, we will put the 'Dual Track.'" This is not high school, and it's not junior college either, which might be our closest equivalent. Instead, it's a kind of high school with pay, an apprenticeship in a "craft," like the craft of being a stonecutter in a Gothic cathedral, and it's so medieval that it's hard to find an equivalent.

By the way, did I say that the high school kids are being paid? Germany's greatest single education idea: pay the student to learn a trade. Of course, in the U.S. we have a similar idea: that's how my niece got a degree in engineering. But she went to Marquette. These are kids who in effect just get "high school" degrees. And as the kids learn a skill, they work and get *paid* in an employer-union setting; they receive not just a skill but a political education, too. That is, as they receive a skill that they can later use to get a higher wage, they are "taught," or at least "made aware" of, how not to use it, i.e., to collectively withhold it to get a better deal. Otherwise, they are merely generic "knowledge workers" who can use a computer but have no real specialized skills to withhold.

That's why, to our astonishment, the German unionization rate is higher in the manufacturing or "export" sector (80 percent) than it is in the public or civil-servant sector (40 percent). In the U.S. or the UK, it's quite the reverse. While I don't want to overstate it, that's the special edge that German education has over U.S. education—it can turn out some high school grads who know how to take collective action to protect their skills.

To us that's shocking: "How un-American." But this is the education that our great American philosopher John Dewey recommended for us. It's education in collective action as well as practical skills. With Dewey, that's the part our educators miss. As he would tell us, the "Dual Track" is a track that gives us not just a "skill" but a political identity. That's what is "dual": as kids invest in a skill, they are taught how, politically, they can protect their investment.

But then we get to the hard one: the *third* column. The kids who come out of this column are the high school grads without the skills—and, perhaps worse, without a political identity. Why would they read the papers? In the new global division of labor, there are only so many "Dual Track" skills the export sector can take in. That's the problem that Germans brought up to me over and over, saying in effect: "The ones who come out of the first column are okay, and so are the ones in the second, but for the ones in the third column, there's nothing to do."

And—yes—as labor loses its clout, column two shrinks while one and three get bigger. "Yes, you're overlooking the problems."

No, I'm not, but a shrunken column two beats *no* column two.

Columns one, two, three—the whole thing's paradoxical: the tracking system has helped keep the social democracy stable by allocating skills to high school grads and pushing them into unions. Yet it's also unjust: it's an affront to the tenets of social democracy.

I went back to V.'s drawing, the three columns: "Don't you have to open up this Royal Road?"

That's the U.S. way: to send everyone to college. It turns out, though, as we push more onto the Royal Road as the only way out, it's still only a few who get the BA. Why do we keep trying to do this? On the other hand, morally, it's hard to turn a kid away from college. A German woman, a teacher's daughter, told me how—to her father's horror—they put her brother on the Dual Track.

Think of her dad, an intellectual—and his only son, pushed onto the Dual Track.

But V. told me there's another side: switching from the Royal Road over to the Dual Track. His own sister did it. She had to scheme to get *off* the Royal Road and start over on the Dual Track. Why did she do it?

"She wanted to make jewelry."

And the Germans don't let just anyone make jewelry. She couldn't say, as in the U.S., "I'm a summa from Yale and I want to make jewelry." Sorry, girl, you have to go get a degree. Actually, I shiver, thinking of anyone, on purpose, stepping off the Royal Road. It has the darkness of a Grimm fairy tale.

What happened to her? I was afraid to ask V.

Yes, what if *my* sister went on the Dual Track? Even I might push her to get a degree. But wait: on the Dual Track, she's got a degree. Indeed, though it may not be a college BA, the Germans are even more fixated on their little certificates and degrees. It's not just the Dual Track: the German way of life is about quality control. Every piece of paper has to be the same size, the same quality. Everyone has to have a certificate. Back in the U.S., we bust unions and offshore everything, and we don't even care if the workers made it out of grade school. I think of my firm's suit against George Soros and his Wall Street colleagues. They took over Outboard Marine and shut down the union plants and outsourced the work to here, there, everywhere. And when the engines start blowing up, they just pull out of the businesses. The Germans—rigid, inflexible—may subcontract out, but at least co-determination puts some quality control over how recklessly they do it. And it's no accident that we have a German pope, Benedict XVI, who even has an encyclical that carps at subcontracting. Sure, it's a matter of social justice. But I'd bet Benedict as a German would be concerned about quality control.

Still, V. said, German educators want to change the system.

Why? "They want more flexibility. We want students to be generalists, more like Americans."

"Generalists?" I said. "V.! They don't know anything, they don't
read the paper, they, they, they . . . they don't even vote!"

I had to shout over the kid singing like Joe Cocker and blowing
out his vocal cords.

"Can you hear? I said they don't even vote!"

V. nodded. "I see." He paused. "I must find out how many of
our students vote."

They don't need generalists: they need more people with skills.

In the old days, the real spending on education was done by the
German employers: it was the employers who paid for all those
skills on the Dual Track. Well, in a global competition, the employers have cut back on this kind of education. Now it's up to the
government, which has failed to deliver. According to the UK's
Guardian (May 8, 2008), the German economy had a shortage of
almost a hundred thousand engineers, not to mention other labor
shortages. Meanwhile, if anything, the U.S. had a glut, which is
why so many of our engineers end up in sales.

Locked into an engineering-type economy, the Germans are
lucky to have such a skilled-labor shortage. It's a problem I wish
our own country still had.

On the way back, we took the S-Bahn, and as we shot across the
sky, I became a little starstruck with Berlin. Okay, it's cold, it's
soulless. Maybe it's depraved. It's also Protestant, Prussian. But it
was so raw, so unfinished: even the Reichstag, which I could see
lit up under construction from the window of the car. I turned to
V.: "Why do they still call it the Reichstag when they've got the
Bundestag inside it?"

"That's a good point," V. said. "I'm glad you noticed that."

I paused. Wait: there's no answer?

No. But there it was. And I thought of it: in 1933, the Reichstag fire and all of that. I looked at the cranes on stork legs bobbing up and down in those dark Reichstag pits.

The Reichstag: sure, I felt a shiver. But it's hard to take a building seriously that had just been wrapped by Christo.

Yes, Germany is dark, and Berlin is darker. But it is not so clear in Berlin what part of the dark is now faux dark and what part of the dark is real. After all, I had just come here from Chicago, where, in public schools all over the city, children are being murdered. Poor Brecht spent much of his life comparing Chicago and Berlin: and it was pretty fair to compare them once upon a time. But in terms of evil, and not just Brechtian color, Chicago has pulled away.

For example: I'd like to see just one monument in Chicago, somewhere, to all the children who have been murdered within a few miles of me just as I've been sitting here writing this book.

Yes, that night, I was sure Berlin would be Brechtian in a fun way: where it's safe and no one gets hurt. I'd get here what I can no longer get out of Chicago at all. But I now know, years later, that it's not very Brechtian here at all. On my last trip, in April 2009, the only little buzz I could get was to pick up my *Financial Times* and head down to the "Kantine," which is a lunchroom in Brecht's old Berliner Ensemble Theater.

The food is practically free, and I line up for the kind of goulash that has been sitting in some tureen since the collapse of the GDR. And it's eerie to watch the kitchen crew slop it on the plate. The cook, the staff—they look like they've been pulling the wagon of Mother Courage. And in the next scene, the two who seem to be deaf-mute are about to be shot.

So you tell me: is this Brechtian Berlin, or is it all just an act?

Still, in 1997, it seemed eerie. Once at a party in Chicago, I met a British bon vivant. He touted to us a new, magic elixir. It was a juice that was an extract of what's left of the Berlin Wall. "It's an extract of all that evil," he said. "You drink it, and it's supposed to flush all the evil out of you."

Yes, people come to Berlin because they want to drink the Kool-Aid.

And it does have a noir side, even in the way it hands out public goods. On the U-Bahn or the S-Bahn, while one is supposed to buy a ticket at the machine, there is nothing to stop you or me or anyone who does not know the system from just walking on. On my third day in Berlin, before I had taken the trouble to find out how to get a pass, I just walked on, and an undercover cop came up. In English: "Where's your pass?" Uh-oh. I smiled, touched my jacket, and being, uh, an American, I pretended I couldn't even quite speak English. "Uh . . . officer, I'm just an American, and . . . and I've just . . . come . . . and. . . ."

And what?

"Get off." He pointed.

Ah! I was going to jail! Of course, being a lawyer, I knew how to beg, but at that moment, I knew what the old Berlin was like. This guy was a serious cop. I should have said, "Why don't you have turnstiles instead of the honor system?"

It's so GDR, isn't it? The whole thing is some kind of Hitchcockian trap. Sure, you can get on the S-Bahn, no ticket, just walk on, do it every day for weeks, but one day, someone will come up and arrest you.

He let me go: I was a minnow. I should have thanked him. It's for this kind of faux terror one comes to Berlin.

At least in 1997, the city still seemed a little frightening. Certainly the joblessness was real. "Soon, in Berlin," a German professor later told me, "there will be no-go areas." V., though, seemed skeptical of all this. He even told me about a TV show called *Ten Years Ago Tonight*. For example, if "tonight" is January 16, 1997, I could see clips from the news on January 16, 1987. V. said it was the same news, albeit limited to West Germany: "Unemployment is at 2.3 million!" "Immigration is changing everything." So V.'s point was that if someone told me about the crisis of the German model and how unemployment was worse than ever, I should say, politely: "Pardon me, this is very interesting—but wasn't this just on *Ten Years Ago Tonight?*"

And I must say, almost every day up through 2007, the stories about Germany could have appeared on *Ten Years Ago Tonight*. But then unemployment did begin to drop.

Ah, Berlin, once it was so poor—now it's like Berkeley, all students and cafés. Ah, what made me think it could just go on as it was—changeless, outside of History?

I wish it were just the way I saw it on the S-Bahn in 1997: I liked it when it was raw and unfinished. But at the same time it was so orderly and European.

If I really ever did get Berlin, I remember the exact day, the exact moment, when I got it: Saturday night, January 16, 1997. By myself, I had gone to a performance of Beethoven's *Missa Solemnis*. It was not the Philharmonic but the Berliner Orchestra, the East Berlin symphony, for at this time, Berlin awkwardly still had two of everything: two city centers, two symphony orchestras, two left wings, two right wings, and not just two but three opera companies. And now I was stepping out into the square called the Gendarmenmarkt, which has at each end two identical churches, like two queen-size chess pieces that can check each other and still be mates. And all of this made the scene so eerily "Europe," even if a Planet Hollywood was just a block away, and it seemed to me that not one of us at the concert dared to speak as we came out on the square and saw an old man with a violin playing in the moonlight next to a little red-haired girl, holding out her beret, where we could toss in our little coppers. In the stillness of central Europe, as if I were the elector of Brandenberg, I dropped in my little coin.

Click.

And with that "click" of that one coin, I knew I'd crossed some kind of line: *Ich bin ein Berliner*. I'd paid the entrance fee.

From that moment on, though I never forgot I was an American, I forgot I had a job. Part of the appeal of Berlin was that it was poor, and broke, and nobody worked. How long could that last? Now the other day, here in Chicago, a lawyer my age—my age!—came up to me and said, "Hey, my wife and I were just in Berlin—that's really a happening town!" I think of that girl with the red hair, and I feel sick.

Why was it so great?

It was the only city that for a moment, dialectically, tried to hold the best of East and West in a single body politic. It was unstable: it could not last. In a sense, East Berlin was "the East," the world of *Animal Farm*. But in one odd way, it had also become the opposite of *Animal Farm*: one of the great fears that Orwell and Josef Pieper and others had about Communism is that, like Boxer the horse, we'd have to work and work until they sent us to the glue factory. But by the time Communism collapsed, it was the opposite of *Animal Farm*: no one really worked. "We pretend to work, and they pretend to pay us."

They also pretended to consume.

West Berlin was the opposite of *Animal Farm*. It was free, like the West, politically and culturally. But in one tiny respect, at the time the Wall fell, the West, compared to the East, was becoming like *Animal Farm*. We in the West were working the longer hours—we were becoming the old Boxers.

What was new about Berlin after 1989 was the way it brought together the West's old freedom from the politics of *Animal Farm* with the East's old freedom from the workday of *Animal Farm.* While it's a pretty unstable compound, for a while it seemed to hold.

It was certainly holding in 1997.

Now I was a Berliner. I know: a few days ago, I was going to be a Rheinländer. But here I would say it's the Rhine, or Rhineland capitalism, Catholic Germany, that created the labor law. It's Rhineland capitalism, or Catholic Germany, that put in the safety net. But I have to admit in fairness that it was in godless Berlin I saw this Rhineland capitalism in effect. I was part of a short EU program for outside-the-box Americans like labor lawyers who might like to meet their European counterparts. Part of this tour took me for a day or so to Berlin. While I have already complained how I saw nothing of Berlin, here I have to confess: I did get into a labor court. As part of this whirlwind EU program, I was set up to meet a union-side lawyer named Eckhardt, and I had expected that I'd get a few moments to chat about globalization and all of that. I took out my notebook and got ready to write. "That does not really interest me," he said. "And since you are a labor lawyer, I thought you might like to come with me to court."

Like most older lawyers, I detest going into court. Besides, I was on a vacation. But what could I say?

So Eckhardt and I didn't try to bridge any U.S.-Europe gap. We just went to court. As we walked along and he pointed out all the undocumented Poles working in construction with no unions, I saw he was wearing jeans. "Wait," I said, in front of a construction site, "you're going to court in jeans?"

"Why not?" he said. "The judge will be in jeans."

Well, I still thought he'd take off his windbreaker, but we were almost late to court (just like in America), and he was still wearing it when he went up to the judge. We were here on a status, not a trial. He told me about his client, a bank teller, a forty-something woman who, a year or so ago, began to have aural hallucinations. She "heard" voices, and she began yelling back, even as she was dealing with customers. "So," Eckhardt said, "the bank has put her in the back room, where she can't shout at the customers." She could just go on yelling by herself.

As a result, she had sued the bank for the transfer to the back room.

"And you're representing her?"

"Yes," Eckhardt said.

"Well, she's crazy."

"Of course she's crazy."

"Why are you representing her?"

"It's her right."

I was astonished. In the U.S. a month or so before, I had represented an electrical worker, a skilled craftsman, black, who had been fired by ComEd for eating a pizza during an emergency. Because it was an emergency, he was working overtime, and all the others on the crew were breaking for a pizza, and he ate a slice. He was fired. It was all right for the others, but as ComEd explained, he was in a classification that didn't allow him to eat a piece of pizza.

And of course, because the arbitrators are terrified of management now, the firing was upheld.

And now I'm seeing this!

But it was even worse: this woman that the union was representing, for free, with this very bright lawyer, was not even a union member. Or she had not been, until she was transferred to the back room. Then she joined, for no other reason than to get a free lawyer.

"Wait," I said. "Don't you think she's using you?"

"Why?" he said.

"She blows you guys off, and then she gets in trouble and cynically signs up and gets you to represent her for free."

"It is her right," he said.

The judge came out, and he had a beard and looked like he was a rocker. Eckhardt knew him and whispered to me: "I have to be careful not to call him *du*," which is the second-person singular that, in Germany, you use only on a golf course with your foursome. But while I was shocked by Eckhardt's jeans and by the judge, I was shocked most of all by the lawyer for the bank. Yes, he had on a coat and tie, but with the bottom of his shirt unbuttoned, and I could see a bit of his belly sticking out.

Nothing happened in the status: the judge wanted a report on how the bank lady was getting along. Everyone was smiling and nodding.

On the way out, I said to Eckhardt: "What's going to happen?"

"Nothing. We're just watching things."

I hesitated. "You know, it seems to me the bank is being very nice to her."

He looked at me in surprise: "Of course the bank is being very nice to her." And that's why people can hang out in Berlin.

But of course this can go too far. After all, I'm not just a labor lawyer: I'm an employer, too. I'm not just on the left: I'm also a small businessman, running a small for-profit company.

I mean: what do you have to do here to be fired?

And I hear Berlin is a bit more laid-back than the old West Germany, but still it's a problem that worried people even in the SPD, even the ones who came out of the labor unions. A few years later, I would meet one, working for then-Chancellor Schroeder. In the labor courts, he said, the unions win 95 percent of the cases. At that time, the right was demanding "reform" and "deregulation."

In Agenda 2010, part of the SPD's response was to let management win a few more cases.

Why?

"There are two reasons," he said. "First, it's for fairness." And what's the other reason? "The second reason," he said, "is that we have to look like we're doing something."

But that was still in the future, and at this point no one was doing anything. And just as people wanted to loosen up the system a little, I met other bright, intelligent Germans who defended all of it. I think of Martin, SPD legislators like Anke F., and others who are exactly the kind of Europeans who, being on the left, never get quoted in the *New York Times*.

Every American I met at this time kept urging me to talk to people on the right. "You have to hear the other side." But the fact is, we hear from these people all the time: they write the op-eds in the *New York Times*, etc., and are quoted in the news stories. The ones we don't hear from are the people on the left.

And a great example is Martin, whom I met for breakfast in Berlin. Ah, breakfast in Berlin. Ah, that first cup of coffee, in an art gallery, next to a bus, spray-painted and upended like a turtle. Martin was a journalist, a Nieman fellow at Harvard—but, as I later found out, he was a worker too.

When I knocked Germany, he would defend it. If I said such-and-such was a problem, he would say it's-not-a-problem. An example:

"Why is Germany so bad at services?"

"What do you mean?"

"I mean, the American economy, it's service oriented."

"I don't agree. There are no services. You go into a store in America and no one can fix anything."

"You throw it away," I started to say.

"By services," he said, "you mean that in our supermarkets we have half as many employed as you do in the U.S."

Fine by him: let people bag their own groceries. "We can't have two labor markets, the way you do."

Yes, two labor markets: the one for the baggers and the other for those who drive off with the bags in their SUVs. In America, fewer people can jump the Wall that divides one market from the other.

In America, that's okay. But in Germany, it's on the scale of a constitutional crisis.

But I pointed out that they were now keeping the stores open until eight, so they would have to be hiring more people into service jobs.

"I don't agree. They already talk now of scaling back to seven." The whole thing irritated him because he was on the works council at his Berlin newspaper. "On the works council, we have to approve new work schedules. Who wants to work from eleven to eight at night?"

"People want to work," I said.

Didn't I get it? If the stores stayed open till eight, then management would want the works council to let people work till six. Then people would start eating out at McDonald's, and. . . .

Soon, we'd all be fat, with hypertension, and never see our kids.

At the time, I was astonished a guy like this would waste time on a works council. Here was an important journalist, a Harvard fellow and all of that, yet he was deep in meetings over what time the cleaning crew went home at night. How many people did he represent?

"We have 450 employees," he said. "They elect us for nine years. And during that time, we can't be fired."

So he told me much of what Wigand later said about the firing process, etc. He began to open up when he realized I was not an

American coming to bash the German model. Remember, at this time Clinton had just signed a bill ending "welfare as we know it," even when the only welfare we "knew" was welfare for nursing mothers, or with small little kids, and the idea of kicking these women into the workforce . . . well, it repelled a lot of people in Europe. Of course, one could think up a "politically correct" case for it, namely, that the mothers themselves were so sick, impoverished, drugged-up, physically and sexually abused, that it was better to separate them from the kids. But of course that wasn't the reason we were doing it. And it was shocking to Europeans, who had welfare—yes, a lot of welfare, even for the men, and my God, certainly for children. That was the biggest problem I had in getting Europeans on the left to open up with me: yes, I was for Clinton even though I'm for labor and he isn't, not especially, and I'm aghast at what he did on welfare, and I have nightmares about Larry Summers.

How can you be for Clinton? It baffled them.

Well, Bush came in, and now they know.

"Anyway, up to the last moment, I thought Clinton wouldn't sign the thing."

Martin said, "That's what I thought, too."

I paused. "Do you think our liberals who call for flexible markets—do you think they know what they're saying?"

He became grave. "No, I don't think they do know." He thought a big difference was that the middle class in Germany had once been—well, poor. "You must remember," he said, "the Germans on welfare now, they are living the way we in the middle class did in the 1960s. In our family, we were middle class and we thought we were 'well-off.' But in the 1960s, we only had a used car. To have *one* used car was a very good thing. And food—we had cheese, but only two kinds. . . ." His point: when we say Schroeder and the yuppies came from the middle class, we mean they had nothing or very little. So German yuppies, unlike U.S. yuppies, hesitate to cut welfare.

To the contrary, the odd thing about Agenda 2010, which was supposed to cut welfare, was that it actually raised it, a lot. Under Schroeder, the SPD-Green coalition cut back the long-term unemployment benefit but increased welfare. The shock was that many who had scoffed at welfare now saw it as a good deal. Suddenly, all sorts of Germans without jobs—some who had never had jobs, ever—now applied to get on this new higher "basic grant." So in trying to cut back on the welfare state, Germany ended up enlarging it.

You'd think at the moment, during the election, this would be a raging issue: but it wasn't.

Well, isn't there cheating?

"Yes, of course," he said. "The single men, that's where the cheating is."

I was speechless: *single* men, not even dads or anything.

But welfare for single mothers: that was great. "Because many Germans feel guilty about this: if our child credits were more generous, there would not be single mothers. The families would be together."

Besides, welfare was a good thing if it kept the "two labor markets" from developing. At this time, many on the left, like Martin, had that hope. He and others were against some of the very things that people on the left in America were trying to promote. For example, he was against the Earned Income Tax Credit (EITC). To him, that was awful. "You have taxpayers paying for jobs."

He was against the minimum wage. "Yes, we don't want the taxpayer stepping in."

I think he meant the government: what he wanted was the unions, the whole labor system, pushing up wages. To him (and other Germans), the minimum wage is a way of lowering, not raising, wages. To Germans on the left, welfare is a way of protecting the middle class. And Martin's unspoken point is simply this: our middle class isn't going down because of globalization. Our middle class is going down because of welfare reform.

We're collapsing because we are so damned mean to the poor.

But couldn't that happen here?

Look at the unemployment: isn't welfare to blame for that?

No, Martin would have none of that, of course. It's all East Germany: that's why Germany could not run a deficit, could not have a Keynesian-type shock, as some on the left urged. That kind of "stimulus" had already gone to propping up the East Germans, who had no industry, no jobs, nothing after the collapse of the USSR.

But there was another threat to all this welfare, it seemed to me. "I'd like to ask you something that would seem strange. Didn't this develop because Germany was a 'Christian' democracy? There's a religious basis to it. But from what I read, no one is a 'Christian' anymore. So how can you keep a 'Christian' democracy going if no one goes to church?"

I expected a denial. Instead, there was a long pause.

"This is a good question."

I waited.

"Yes," he said, "the unique thing about Christianity is the idea of grace, or the idea of a gift, a free gift, something which comes to us and cannot be earned. Without some idea of grace, unearned grace. . . ."

Well, this was the Lutheran spin. And I realized at this moment: he was not named Martin for nothing.

But would it continue?

I tried desperately to get an interview at IG Metall; when the big day came, I was already too sick to make it. After visiting

Berlin, I got the flu, the shakes, which lasted for weeks. But even if I missed IG Metall, at least I got to see Heinz.

He was a retired labor leader—actually, a senior statesman—but mostly he was just a huge bear of a man always on the move. And everywhere I went with him, union members, SPD pols, circled him, protected him; everyone adored him. A few years ago he had passed through Chicago, and I'd shown him around. (Who asked me? I can't remember.) Now he didn't just return the favor and welcome me. He took over my life.

In Chicago, at a wild talkfest that went on for hours, we had talked the world. As for the future of social democracy, Heinz was clear. "Things are worse than Weimar."

Or rather:

"THINGS ARE WORSE THAN WEIMAR."

He didn't shout. That was his normal voice: even when his voice dropped to a whisper, it could fill a city block.

He had phoned me when I had gone back to Frankfurt to meet with people at IG Metall, but I was too sick. The whole trip was now a bust. . . . I was too sick to meet anyone. At the Hotel Ibis, a kind of Howard Johnson, I was in bed, lying there, waiting to die, when the phone rang:

"GUTEN MORGEN! HALLO, HALLO!"

"Heinz," I said. I tried to sit up. "I was going to call you. . . ."

"CALL ME? I HAVE BEEN CALLING YOUR OFFICE IN CHICAGO. YOU DID NOT GET MY MESSAGES?"

"No." (How had he tracked me to the Ibis? Even the office didn't know.)

"SO NOW WE WILL COME BY AND PICK YOU UP. WE ARE GOING TO A UNION CONFERENCE."

I said I was supposed to go to Mainz.

"WHEN YOU ARE SICK OF OUR UNION PROPAGANDA, THEN YOU CAN GO TO MAINZ."

The next morning he came to get me in a big car with his lady friend, three or four aides, a court chaplain, and a whole retinue of people, and anyone could see I was too sick to go anywhere.

"WHAT? YOU ARE SICK?"

"I'm really sick."

"THEN DON'T STAND HERE IN THE RAIN. GET IN THE CAR." And so we were off to Heidelberg.

Thank God I did because I saw a whole world: Heinz's. And because, in Heinz's world, things were always worse than Weimar, it meant paradoxically things were better. Or at least it meant that Heinz and those like him were on a hair-trigger alert. What could get past them? I began to underestimate how much things really were at risk.

In Heidelberg, we picked up more union officials and went to a big lunch with SPD politicians who fawned over him and bowed and scraped. I was startled at the way SPD politicians groveled so in front of Heinz and others. In Washington, D.C., one would never see the Democrats grovel like this. Yes: they grovel a little, but here it's quite shocking. Yet German labor people go around slamming the SPD.

I asked Heinz, "What exactly is wrong with the SPD?"

He said in a low voice: "I WILL TELL YOU LATER."

But he forgot.

After that, we left Heidelberg and went up to a retreat. It was up here on this mountaintop that I got to see one reason German unions thrive and American ones don't. On the mountaintop there had once been a big resort or spa. I understood that there were four of these union resorts or ex-spas: there was one in the Alps; one in the Harz mountains; one at Bad Orb; and a fourth in Sprockhövel, near Berlin. They were supposed to be education centers, but they seemed to function like sanatoriums—like the TB sanatorium where Hans Castorp arrives at the beginning of

The Magic Mountain. A union steward came down to the train station to fetch me and the other patients—union members, of course—and take us all up to the top. My fellow patients seemed to come here consciously to escape from capitalism, or "mobbing." Later, at another one of these centers, I met a doctor, whom I will call Dr. O. Though not an MD—she was an economist—she did wear white, and she took part in what I'd call the "cures." During our walk around the place, which had seventy-eight rooms, she told me some people up here suffered from "mobbing."

"Do you know what mobbing is?"

"No."

"It means people have to work against each other."

Oh. As she explained, it's people trying hard not to be the one who will be laid off. Explained that way, "mobbing" is something that has been going on in America for years. "Look, I'm working here on Saturday night, and no one else is!"

But she smiled when I said this was a sanatorium. "No, no, this is for education mostly." She explained that people came up here to be on works councils, to handle layoffs, or changes in working hours. Up here they had to train people to fight American-type downsizing: or what she called "slim enterprises," which require fewer people to work longer hours. Now she frowned. "These works councils, they are still approving too much overtime! Often, they come up here and they have heard, 'Oh, "slim" enterprises are good,' so we have to work with them to correct this. Our economics department—it has shown . . . the number of jobs saved by the reduction of overtime . . . this is now acknowledged to be quite substantial." As she spoke, I found it hard to believe that the employers and the Kohl government were paying for all this.

But to "help the works council" was considered a service *for the employer*. And what I saw up here—the training, the classes, even the rest cures—made me catch my breath. "This is pure genius," I thought. Right before my eyes, I could see the unions unloading onto the works councils all the negative things that dragged us down in America. Over here, the unions let the works councils handle firings: so it's not the union that is spending dues to help (sometimes) a real jagoff keep his job. "Hey, let the works council do that." Over here, the unions let the works councils fight the work-rule changes, all the legalistic stuff that bogs unions down in America.

Of course, in Germany as anywhere else, unions always have a somewhat bad image, because employers and journalists and various servile types love to trash them—and besides, even when unions are strong, they're weak. So the good part is that unions can concentrate on the big things, like wage bargaining and national politics, but the bad part is that they have a weaker presence in the shops and plants. Still, as a labor lawyer—and I came here as a labor lawyer—I found the message I needed to bring back to our dying unions in America: Hey, let's stop burning up all our dues on people who may not even be capable of holding a job at all. Let the works councils defend them. Don't sweat the small stuff, the grievances. Do the big-time national politics instead.

We were up here to do politics. Professors who teach Marcuse and Adorno roared up in their BMWs to tutor us on what Kohl was doing. I'd said to Heinz: "But they'll be talking in German!"

"DON'T WORRY, I WILL TRANSLATE."

So I sat with him, waited. Not a word. "Heinz, what are they saying?"

"IT'S NOTHING INTERESTING." Here I should say that Heinz once had been the head of the public employees' union—

a very big deal. But he'd had a heart condition. In 1982, his doctor had told him if you don't quit now, you'll be dead within a week. Still, even in retirement, he was a rock star.

But here's the paradox: because Heinz was a kind of rock star, he seemed to be in the wrong country. Here was a guy born to lead a strike. (Heinz felt the same way.) To an American—yes, to me, whose first job as a lawyer was with the United Mine Workers—the Germans don't seem to strike enough. It's strange: it's this very thing, co-determination, the worker control, that makes it harder for the workers to go on strike. It's too consensual. Heinz must have found it galling to be German. When I praised the works councils, the consensus, etc., he would frown: "BUT THE GERMAN WORKER WILL NOT STRIKE."

"Why not?"

"OH, THEY WANT PAY FROM THE STRIKE FUND." (Being German, they want a paycheck, even on strike.)

I wondered if the French workers had strike funds.

"NO, IN FRANCE THEY DON'T GET PAID! BUT IN GERMANY, IT'S 'OH, WILL THE BOSS FROWN ON THIS?'"

But the flip side is that when German workers *do* go on strike— which is rare—the "bosses" sometimes join the strikes! I didn't believe it when I first heard this from Professor Kathleen Thelen, now at MIT and a great expert on the German labor movement. What? They walk the picket line with the workers?

Yes. Just before I came, in a big strike over sick pay, that's what some of the smaller employers did. I saw the photos. But remember: these employers don't bargain over wages, over health care, over all the things that lead to shoot-outs with small employers in the U.S. The big employers at the top meet with the unions to set the "economic" issues.

So the big global companies tend to be nasty to labor, and the little guys seem nice. In the U.S., if anything, it often seems the opposite. Sure Walmart is awful, but in my experience, the smaller employers in the Chamber of Commerce seem to me the worst. By contrast, in Germany, it's bizarre that I can have a friendly chat with a lobbyist at the BDI (Bundesverband der Deutschen Industrie), which is the "nice" employer federation, as distinct from the BDA (Bundesvereinigung der Deutschen Arbeitgeberverbände), which is the "mean" one. Now, at the nice one, they weren't necessarily that nice, but at least they said things like: "We're concerned that we're laying off too many workers," etc.

Heinz told me the whole history. At night, down in the Bauern-Stube restaurant, we sat and drank beer and forgot about the lectures. After World War II, Heinz had come back from America, where he had been a POW. He was thrilled to have been captured: he was a child soldier, from an anti-Nazi family. He became a waiter at the officers' club and rode around in roadsters, and he loved the U.S., and even the U.S. Army, even though he was a POW and also way on the socialist left. But the U.S. Army was full of New Deal left-wing types, and Heinz thought that the army had helped create the German labor movement. Even Eisenhower was a kind of "labor hero." We sat in the Bauern-Stube and drank beer, and it was a lot better than the lectures. "EISENHOWER GAVE THE ORDER—TO WORK WITH THE UNIONS." Heinz made a big point of this: even before the 1949 Constitution, the Eisenhower "administration," if one may call it that, came up with and pushed the idea of works councils, shop-floor representation. "EISENHOWER WANTED CONSENSUS." I make this point because many scholars both in Germany and in the U.S. try to downplay the New Deal's role, but to Heinz, who was a first-person witness, the New Deal was huge for Germany.

But it was because of Eisenhower that Heinz rarely got into battle. I asked: when he was president of the public employee union, did he ever have strikes? "NO." He paused. "IF THERE

WERE, I MADE THEM OFFICIAL." He did get to go on strike, of course. Maybe his favorite was his strike against the U.S. Army officers' club. It was a kind of revenge on the army for pushing works councils, co-determination, and consensus.

Because the old left was dead, Heinz shot to the top. In 1964, he met George Meany, the old cigar-chomping plumber who was head of the AFL-CIO. Meany said, "So when did they make babies the heads of unions?"

"I SAID TO HIM, IN MY COUNTRY THEY ARE SO YOUNG BECAUSE THE OLD ONES HAVE MADE SUCH A MESS OF THINGS. PERHAPS IT IS DIFFERENT IN AMERICA." And Heinz said that Meany laughed. "AND SO WE BECAME FRIENDS." And he knew them all—Brandt and Helmut Schmidt, a more conservative SPD chancellor, but Heinz seemed to love the guy. Brandt also had his faults. "BUT IF I WERE IN A PRISON CELL AND COULD PICK ONE PERSON TO STAND UP FOR ME, IT WOULD BE WILLY BRANDT." But Heinz was *really* on the left. "OH, I'M A REALIST. WE LIVE IN A MARKET ECONOMY. THERE HAS NEVER BEEN REAL SOCIALISM, NOT EVEN WHAT WAS IN RUSSIA." But he was scornful.

One night, I confessed to him that maybe I was hanging around with too many people on the left. "If I go back to America," I said, "people will be upset that I talked only to labor people and not to employers. You, Heinz, must know some employers. Can you set up some meetings?"

"YOU WANT TO SPEAK TO AN EMPLOYER?"

"Yes," I said.

"WELL, YOU MUST TELL ME RIGHT AWAY SINCE THEY ALWAYS SAY THEY ARE SO BUSY." He didn't think they had much to say. "THEY ARE ALWAYS SO SAD. OH, PLEASE,

THEY SAY—WE MUST HAVE MORE PROFIT—THEY NEED MORE PROFIT TO HELP THE STARVING FAMILIES THAT MAKE THEIR SAILBOATS."

In the end, we all got sick of our own propaganda, and Heinz and I and others went down to the city of Heibrunn for lunch. There I met one of his former union officers, a young woman even further to the left than Heinz. She was now on the city council, and her special job was to help tenants who could not pay the rent. "I'm now a city official, and once a year there is a custom among the politicians—the custom is, you must sit and have lunch with your political enemy."

"That's very nice," I said.

She gave me a scornful look. "This is the *first* time I have had to do it." So far as I could tell, the Christian Democrats were sitting far away from her, and she was here with Heinz and me.

She had fought with Heinz, of course, for not being far enough on the left. But that was different. And when he introduced me to her he said, "WE FIGHT AND WE KNOW HOW TO MAKE UP."

Of course Heinz never set me up with an employer. Nor did I care. I can read what they have to say in the U.S. press or the *FT* or *The Economist*. To get the other side from a "socialist" like Heinz, alas, one has to buy a ticket and go there. But in Berlin— during a cocktail hour at the local U.S. Chamber of Commerce— a consultant named "Melanie" was upset I was not hearing the other side. Fortunately, she knew the vice president at a bank here. "I'll set up a meeting," she said. So the next night, at 5:30 P.M., I hurried in the dark to the "Mendelsohn Bank." I'd written down the number as 49251 Französische Str., but I seemed to be miles away from it.

Ah! I was now late, and lost: Melanie would be furious.

I stopped a man who looked like Joel Grey in *Cabaret*. "Where is the Mendelsohn Bank?"

He grinned a skull-like grin. "The Jewish Bank!"

"What?"

"The Jewish Bank! It's over there."

To spite him, I went in the opposite direction. Why take directions from an anti-Semite? I stopped a ragged man selling pretzels.

"I don't know," he said. "Why don't you phone them?"

"I don't have a phone."

"Here, use mine." He flipped out a cell phone.

Since he seemed to be a beggar, I thought I should give him a coin or something. Anyway, when I phoned the bank, I found out the address was not 49251 but . . . 49 *to* 51.

Damn. Why do Europeans do that?

It was dark, but in the bank the chandeliers were blazing, imperially. It was the kind of bank where Bismarck came for loans. As I sat in a golden antechamber, out came a secretary with a cup of tea: "Mr. A., our vice president, has been called away. Can you talk with Mr. Z. instead?"

It's a relief for me to talk to less important people. The younger man looked about thirty. But in America that's old enough to run a presidential campaign.

"Is this on the record or not?" he said.

I gaped. Did he think I was a journalist?

"Oh, never mind," he said, in English. "But I'm not a political person, I'm a practical person."

He looked tanned, rested: I bet he spent his twenties on the beaches of Sri Lanka.

At this time, there was a common view in Germany that the world would no longer need its high-quality goods. Somehow the fact that they kept selling them was just a fluke. Thanks to Americans, many Germans—intellectuals, businessmen—had talked themselves into thinking German-type capitalism wouldn't work anymore. On the left, Wolfgang Streeck had presented this case in a much-buzzed-about paper: "German Capitalism: Does It Exist? Can It Survive?" He said there were vanishing investment opportunities because the Germans were running out of new things to make. It was *The Decline of the West* all over again. It was inevitable.

Mr. Z. seemed to take this view.

"We don't have any ideas! That's the problem in Germany. We need more ideas, more new enterprises."

I expected Mr. Z. to go on about Bill Gates, Microsoft, or some kind of technology. But to my surprise what he had in mind was—

Limousine service.

"Let me give you an example," he said. "To get to the airport, what must I do?"

"Take the train?"

"Take a taxi. I have to take a cab. But why not take a private limousine? Maybe not in Berlin, but in Frankfurt there would be a great demand for this service."

"Why aren't there limousines?" I asked.

"It's the people," he said. "The people themselves have to change . . . we must be more free, more open-minded. We're still too old-fashioned. You know, there is one strict way of hiring people. . . ."

I guessed what he meant: people had to stop thinking of themselves as stonecutters on Gothic cathedrals and learn to be valets. But I decided to press: "Do you think maybe there is too much job training in Germany? I mean, the dual system, and all of that. . . ."

If Mr. Z. saw my trap, he didn't care: "Yes, perhaps—it could be. They think, 'Why should I go off and be a street cleaner?'"

And I thought of the Berlin cab drivers and the London ones.

The Berlin cab drivers could be grad students in physics or just free spirits. I'd just taken a cab here, and the driver said, "You're an American? I have been to America . . . to see . . . *your King!*"

Heh, heh.

"You saw Mr. Presley," I said.

"Ah!" he said. "You know!"

In London, they were "modern." In London, they say, "Yes, guv'nor," and they looked as nervous as I did in the Mendelsohn Bank.

But I worry that I am being hard on Mr. Z., because he was de-lightful company. For example, I asked him: "Last night I was over in Savignyplatz, and you know what it's like there even on a Tues-day night? Every place is packed! So if things are so bad here, why are these restaurants all jammed?"

Mr. Z. laughed. "That's a good question! Do you know our economist Norbert Walter? He was telling a group of us, 'We Ger-mans are worse and worse off . . . but at higher and higher lev-els.'" And there was something delightfully young about him in his pride in the fact that Germany was unified. "I *like* Unifica-tion." (He was the first German who said this!) "Economically? Oh, yes, there are many problems, but . . . I *like* it!"

And I was excited for him to be, well, young and a banker in Berlin. When I said so, he shook his head. "No, no."

"But isn't this the city to be in?" I was thinking of all the cranes outside, bobbing for apples.

"No, no, the city to be in is Frankfurt!"

"But isn't it in Berlin where people are having the great conversations?"

"No, no, it's in Frankfurt where they are having the conversa-tions! Oh, late at night, we go out, to the restaurants, and we talk . . . that is where you have the conversations!"

And at that moment I could see that he could glimpse Frankfurt as being on the scale of London or New York, the center of all the financial speculation (well, gambling) that brought the melt-down we're now in. And as much as I like Mr. Z., it was Germany's salvation in the end that Frankfurt lost out, and that it was in the U.S. and in the UK where the financial sectors became bloated and the limousines took people to the airports.

After two months, I came back to America. Well, I had to go back to work. And while I was going to write up my notes—I promised the Marshall Fund—I just was too busy at work. But perhaps I lost heart.

Yes, when I had gone there, I already knew what I was going to think. But now that I was back, I wasn't sure what I could write. I had dragged my suitcase from hotel to hotel. I'd gone from Frankfurt, to Bonn, to Hamburg, to Kiel, to Berlin, back to Frankfurt, to Bad Orb, to Munich, and even to Amsterdam and London, and halfway through it all I got sick, really sick, a wild fever, lying on my bed in hotel rooms in the dark. Feverish, I'd wake up, read about the unemployed, and then go back to bed and sleep for twelve more hours.

And although I got better before I left, I was thrilled to come back to Chicago and go to the office. "Forgive me," I said to everyone. And for the next four years I took no vacation.

Yes, I had to admit: Germany was dark. But with no social democracy, it would have been a lot darker.

5

Clash of Civilizations

Meanwhile, America had become dark. There was the nightmare of *Bush v. Gore*. We did not seem like a democracy. We had big tax cuts for the rich, and payday loans for the poor. Every day I went to Caffè Baci and read the *Financial Times* and would root for Germany and hope that, in terms of GDP, it would do a little better. Many a time, in the half hour for lunch, I would think: shouldn't I be back over there pushing up GDP? I kept thinking, as I said, that in the 1930s people on the left went to die in Madrid. In the same way, it's our duty to spend in Berlin. Yes, that's how people like me could help European social democracy, by giving the GDP a little push, like the young woman on the swing in the painting by Fragonard. So I began to dream of going back to Berlin. Yes, it had to be Berlin. It's not just because it's the German town for Germans who can't cut it in the rest of Germany. No, it had to be Berlin because it was the only place I'd ever been really idle, as idle as the man in the movie *Claire's Knee*.

But it's a lot of work to be completely idle; and when I say I wanted to be idle, I also wanted to have a job, something to do as a break. And it was in 2001 that a German friend said maybe I could come to Berlin to teach—for a month or two at least.

"What would I teach?" I said. "I don't know anything."

"You could teach American labor law."

"Are you serious? I mean, I'd have to do it in English. I can't imagine why a kid would want to take a course in American labor law—in *English*."

"To the contrary," he said, "the only reason for the kids to take it is that it would be in English." They wanted to hear it in the mother tongue of Pearl Jam.

Ah, but I would have to prepare lectures, and it turned out that in some of these law classes, the professors lecture for three hours straight! I wanted a job: how else could I get any sense of routine life? But this would be a lot of work.

And who would take my class?

But it turns out that, in Europe, they also have courses like "Moby Dick, Lincoln, and the Beginning of Queer Fiction," just as we do, so maybe I could get away with "American Labor Law: What a European Should Know." No, it did not seem so odd. In the *FT*, the big German global companies, which hated "consensus," were sending their young middle managers over to the U.S. so that, at a tender age, they would learn how to fire people. I could imagine myself telling the European left the way we do it in America, where we have a much meaner, Puritan view of human nature and think the poor will not work unless they are paying interest rates of up to 400 percent and live in constant terror. Of course I wanted to be balanced.

Somehow I got a two-month grant from Fulbright and a chance to teach at Humboldt. So in April 2001, I was headed to Berlin.

At O'Hare, I was still trying to settle the Dickieson case and set up a deposition when I got on Lufthansa and had to turn off my cell phone.

And we were up in the air—and soon they were bringing brötchen and I was already in Europe.

I pulled out some of my notes from 1997, and I had packed my trusty copy of Wolfgang Streeck's "German Capitalism: Does It Exist? Can It Survive?" I expected in Berlin people would argue about the German model as they had before.

But what I read on the plane was Jared Diamond's *Guns, Germs, and Steel: The Fates of Human Societies.* Yes, I know, it was a bestseller, so I broke my rule in buying it. But in a way it gets at part of the difference between the European and American models. For long ago, Diamond writes, we humans faced the choice between the "hunter/nomad" and "farmer" ways of life. Now, the surprising thing is that the hunter/nomad societies had a better diet, a higher quality of life, and the farmer societies had it worse. So why did people move from the hunter/nomad model to the farmer?

Simple: the farmer model could sustain a larger population, though at a lower standard of living.

Unlike the hunter/nomad model, which produced high-skilled "hunter" jobs but not enough of them, the agrarian model produced a lot of low-skilled jobs, jobs, jobs, or what some would now call "McJobs." In a sense, while the higher-skilled hunter model led to a better way of life, the farmer model was better at— well, giving people work to do but not with very high rewards.

That seemed to echo the U.S./Europe debate. The European model, like the hunter model, may produce *better* types of jobs, but the U.S. model, like the farmer model, could produce far *more* jobs. As a result, it could support more people, though some would have a lower standard of living.

As I slept on and off, I thought: maybe we had a choice like the one people had in 10,000 B.C.

Then I was on the train to Berlin and I was floating. Just as on Lufthansa, I could see the kilometers per hour:

180

190.

I'm in the air. I saw the little white windmills, beating their wings. Green, green: I want you green. Then, bang, we were in Berlin.

When I hit Berlin, I phoned the caretaker of the IBZ Guest House, where I could stay for two months without moving my bags. The IBZ Guest House is part of Freie, even though I was teaching at Humboldt. "Where are you?" said the IBZ Guest House lady. "You're at the Zoo? Then you must take a cab." For at 1 P.M. on a Friday afternoon everyone goes home, and this seems to be true all over Berlin, though people are counted as working until 5 P.M. The super told me that one key, yes, just one, would open up three doors: to the outside gate, to the suite I shared with two men, and to my tiny little bedroom.

How German!

Groggy, I called up the Fulbright contact and told him I was here and that I had been trying to call up experts to talk about the German model. After all, I still had to finish up my report to the Marshall Fund, from four years before. Anyway, I complained to him that at 2 P.M. on a Friday, no one was at work.

"Of course not," he said. "You're in a socialist country. You won't find anyone at work."

"But if I can't talk to anyone today, then I won't have anything to write up on Saturday and Sunday. What am I going to do with this whole weekend?"

He paused. "Why don't you try relaxing for a few days?"

Relax? Of course, he is right. In terms of relaxing, I wish I could have hit the ground running. I wanted to meet people— now. Back in the U.S., my German tutor, who was German but of Korean descent, complained to me about this kind of thing. She was critical of the way Americans wanted to have instant friendships.

"Here," she said, "in America, you meet people and you hit a certain level very fast. In America, at first there aren't any boundaries. But then later you have to go back to the start and try to set up boundaries."

"And it's different with your German friends?" I said.

"Oh, yes. Over there you start out with the boundaries. They're all set up. And then, because they're there, you can really go deeper."

She said it was true as well in the way Germans took up topics, say, in economics or in history. It wasn't how we do it. "In an American university, people want to cover a subject, but do it only once. You talk to someone about a period of history. 'Oh,' they say, 'I covered that when I was nineteen.' But in the German system, the idea is you keep coming back to the same topic, through your life, only at different levels of maturity. You keep going deeper."

Sure, I wanted to go deeper, but we Americans don't have a lot of time. I'd hoped that, if I could find six typical Europeans, I could follow them around and write up what they're like. That weekend, I looked up V. and his wife and told them I needed to find six typical Europeans. A., who was V.'s wife, frowned. "What six Europeans would you think are typical? I don't think there are six typical Europeans." She was right. Joschka Fischer? Pope Benedict XVI? It was ridiculous. There are books where the writer (usually a journalist) has followed a subject around for three or four years. Even if I could, I wouldn't have the nerve to write up someone's life like that.

But—I could tell you how *I* lived.

After all, I was kind of a European. For two months, I even had a European job. I even lived with two Europeans, both scientists who would leave in the morning two or more hours before I woke. Each of us had our own bar of soap; otherwise I'd have had no clue they were around. The IBZ Guest House was a big complex, with married grads and their kids. But it was so tomblike I never heard a single child. Around eight o'clock in the morning, I went out and bought a banana. By ten or ten thirty, I was in my office at the law school. Until two or so, it was like being on a ghost ship: except for my secretary, Mrs. Kley. But right at two there suddenly would be students everywhere, and until eight at night, the place would rock, kids filling up classes, etc.

I had to learn my new routines, like buying the banana at the Turkish fruit and vegetable stand. It was fun, in my old age, to tell myself:

Be flexible

Be flexible.

But I also had to tell myself:

Don't move

Don't move.

This time I'd stay put, and let Europe come to me.

The name of my neighborhood was Wilmersdorf, a kind of middle-class neighborhood in the old West Berlin. At night, I often went to L., a neighborhood place: but what a place! At ten at night—even on a Tuesday or Wednesday night—just as I was leaving, I'd see middle-aged windbreaker-type couples coming in for dinner! Who knows? Maybe, thanks to someone's negotiations on the works council, these two working people had just come from the opera. Sure, I might expect this at the law school. A faculty member told me she had gone to a faculty reception that started at 10 P.M. But out here in Wilmersdorf, these were plainer folk strolling in to have dinner as late as ten.

But the big shock in this two-month stay was how many four-day weekends I had. I don't mean three days: I mean four four-day weekends in just two months, April and May, which are not even the summer vacation months. At lunch back in America, I used to rattle on about my weekends.

"Four four-day weekends," I said.

"No!"

"First, there was Easter: that was Friday, Saturday, Sunday, and Monday."

"Then?"

"Then there was May Day, which was on a Tuesday, so Monday was off."

"Then?"

"Well, Ascension Thursday: did you ever hear of that as a holiday? And of course people took off Friday too."

"And what's the other?"

"Well, Pentecost, though Berlin doesn't make a big deal of it. But I vaguely recall there being four days off."

And here's the real clash of civilizations: "Christian America," where churchgoers work and shop on Sunday, and "post-Christian Europe," where Ascension Thursday is off. How big a clash? One night, I'd gone out to visit V. in Potsdam. Before driving back to Berlin, we decided to wait for rush hour to die down, so we went for tea and cake. Then, at 7 P.M. on a Tuesday night, we got on the autobahn. V. was surprised: "I can't believe there's so much traffic, I don't know why, I don't know why. . . ." Then it hit him. "Of course!" he said. "It's Ascension Thursday!"

"What? But it's only Tuesday!"

"Yes, but people want to get a jump on the weekend."

You laugh? These four-day weekends were like crypts for Americans. Just as centuries ago, people used to fear being buried alive, I used to fear being trapped inside Humboldt with no food or water for an entire four-day weekend. At night, the lady janitors sometimes locked me in, as my sentence for staying late. So the women became my jailers.

They also locked me out when I went jogging in the Tiergarten. On Saturday around five, I'd slip out of work to go run. I'd run down Unter den Linden. I'd run past the Reichstag, where, on the roof, the backpackers would cuddle and look up at the stars. I'd run on through the Brandenburg Gate, where the kids in black bang bang banged the drums slowly to remember Chernobyl and all of its dead, and then I'd burst free, into the woods, running where the king of Prussia used to hunt foxes and where Joschka Fischer and his two bodyguards now came to jog.

Why oh why did I ever stop jogging in Berlin?

When I came back, the building would be locked. I'd bang on the door: "My clothes are in there!"

Once, I was in a panic because I had to get in and get my clothes and meet B. for dinner. When I arrived, late, I told her how I had had to hunt down four janitors, none of whom spoke English, and all of them staring at me with folded arms near a bust of Karl Marx, and beg them, though I had no ID, and stood there in my little running shorts, please to unlock the building so I could get back to my desk.

I was an American: let me in the office!

After I told the story, she shook her head. "I do not understand."

"What don't you understand?"

"You worked . . . today? But it is a holiday."

I could have said, "Every day here is a holiday." Really, I had to do a little work here, and besides, I had to keep up with my practice in Chicago. But instead of snapping at her, I blushed.

It's all the innocence of Europe: "But it is a holiday."

How could I tell her the way of our world?

But this was not the only clash of civilizations. As a "European,"

I needed all this time off since I had to get everything for myself. It was not just that I had to do my own laundry: the laundry room was always closed. At the IBZ Guest House, it was open for two hours, ten to noon: you had to stay home from work to wash your clothes. When I brought my shirts to the dry cleaner, the German woman who ran it looked at me with contempt: didn't I have an iron? Each time I expected her to throw it back at me to do myself. And her place was in the Friedrichstrasse, where the American tourists would go. I wouldn't have tried to get my shirts done in a less neoliberal part of town.

I once confided this to an economist at DIW, a think tank in Berlin. "Yes," she said. "It's hard to find someone. But there is a feeling in Germany you should do these things by yourself."

I found a place, I told her, that would do all my laundry, wash-and-fold. But they told me to come back in three days. Meanwhile, they would keep my underwear.

It turned out she had a friend, also an economist, who had written a paper about her attempt to set up a business doing wash-and-fold laundry. "She charged thirty marks to take clothes to the laundry. Thirty marks—that's not really a lot of money." But the business fizzled. "It's just that, as she wrote, there isn't any demand."

What about a maid? I have a cleaning service in America, once every two weeks.

The DIW economist shook her head. "To bring in a maid—most Germans would regard this as an invasion of privacy."

"It's just the maid coming in," I said.

She frowned: "Why would you want a stranger coming into your house?"

Look at poor Walmart: it went bust in Germany, lost out to Aldi, and one reason supposedly was that Walmart had baggers, people who put the merchandise in the bag for you. German shoppers were shocked. Why would anyone "wait" on you like that? So they all went to Aldi, where they could dispense with these servants and put their own things in bags.

Well, in America, we don't need the time off because we have so many helpers; all this extra European time off might only make us miserable. It's not enough to have "time off" in itself; we need to have it off with safety nets. That's what occurred to me as I talked with the DIW economist. After all, this woman—whom I'll call L.—had lived in America. She had friends in America. She liked America. I think most economists do. So, since she knew America and she knew Europe and she was an economist, where did she think she was better off?

At first she seemed about to say something careful, like, "Oh they each have their own advantages." But she stopped herself.

"Maybe," she said, "maybe I'm just being a German, but for me . . . it's better to be over here."

"Why?"

"It's to know you're *secure*," she said. "I have friends in Britain, and when I go there, all they talk about is mortgages, their houses, the value, all of that. Yes, in Britain you can do very well, even better than here. But even if you get savings, something might happen, inflation might eat it up, and, in a country like that, you can never be secure. There's all the energy in worrying about money! Here in Germany, I'm free to take all that energy . . ."

She seemed here to inhale, as if she were trying to find her atman, or breath.

". . . and I'm free to use all of it, all that energy, for something else!"

She seemed to exhale.

She didn't say so, but the implication is that Americans and the British might as well keep working. Why give them free time?

They'd just worry about their money and their free-market inse-
curity and tie themselves in knots. When we work, we don't have
to think.

I wanted to challenge her: how can you Germans be so secure?
You have a great safety net: the pension at that time was 67 percent of working income. By age fifty-five, they'd be out in their
golf cleats finishing the front nine every weekday at noon. Yet if
the number of active workers "paying in" kept dropping, the system would collapse.

Or at least the younger workers would pay staggering sums.

She scoffed. Yes, there was a problem. "But this thing about the
whole pension system collapsing . . . it's a technical problem, it's
not 'fundamental.' For thirty years, while this generation ages,
there will be a problem. Then there will be no problem."

Thirty years?

Yes, well, Germany had a Thirty Years' War (1618–48). I
wanted to say, "Thirty years? You'll never survive that."

Instead I asked her: "Do you think people read more over
here?"

"Yes."

"How can you know?"

"With my American friends, I do not see how they would have
the time."

Sure: who needs data? It's logic. If I could work the hours of a
European, think of all the energy I could free up just to read.

Or even to pray: I don't see how Americans have the time even
for that. I know, Europeans don't go to church, and given the horror of the last two world wars, I can see why they may want to give
organized religion a rest. But in the next millennium or so they
may change their minds about all this, and at least they have time
every week to give it some thought.

———————————

My own private clash-of-civilization came only when I had to teach my class. Except in class, I had no sense of any "clash." Sure, Humboldt was a big barn of a place, formerly a palace, with a bust of Karl Marx scowling down at the kids who'd be outside getting tans where once, long ago, Nazis burned books. Otherwise, it seemed American. Or at least it did in the PC pool, which is where Ms. Kley sent me when my PC was on the blink. ("See? You have to hit 'Save.'" "Oh.") If this was the PC pool, these four kids were like the lifeguards. With these four, living, breathing Bill Gateses, I had no clash of civilization: these Germans had morphed into Americans.

If I felt homesick, I'd go down and banter with them in "American." For example:

"Come on, you guys are from Seattle. Don't give me this stuff about being German."

"Come on, get off, yeah, we're Germans."

"No way."

"Way."

"What did the Cubs do yesterday? Don't pretend you don't know."

"Come on, I don't know about the Cubs. . . ."

Of course, they had cultural clashes with other Germans.

Once, as a joke, I said, "How do you explain the difference between Microsoft 'Word' and Microsoft 'Vord' to the kids here?"

It's a lame joke: how the "W" is pronounced as "V." In college, we freshmen got confused between Max Weber (as in "Weber" grill), whom they made us read, and Max Weber (as in "Veber"), whom we talked about in class.

They became very serious: "You think that's funny, but that is one of the biggest problems we have."

But that was 2001, a long time ago, and I can't believe "Word" and "Vord" can be so big a problem now. Now with each trip to

Berlin, more Germans even sound like us. When I came here in 1993 and there was only a single wannabe Mister Softee truck, I was dividing Germans who could speak English and those who couldn't. Now I divide them into those who speak English just the way I do and those who aren't there yet. That line is getting fainter, just for actuarial reasons, all over the world. I'd say it's the biggest single planetary change in my lifetime—bigger than global warming and bigger than the rise of Asia. And in some way I can't articulate, I think it's connected to those two. When I could see this in Berlin in 2001, I mentioned my astonishment to an older woman, a longtime Berliner I'll call W. It's more astonishing than I know, she said. "When I came to Berlin in the 1980s, it seemed no one spoke English except at the U.S. base, and there was only one place, the Odeon, where I could go to see movies that weren't dubbed but still in English." When the Cold War ended in 1989, she kept going to the Odeon, but the U.S. Army was gone, and no one was in the seats. Then, somehow, the Odeon started filling up, and then it became packed. Really, what happened?

Instead of an accent, the kids now have a "look"—that's how I would put it. It's the look of the face, or the look *on* the face, of someone who can speak at least one or two other languages. So even if they can fake "American," it's not an "American look." At Humboldt, I could see posters for parties and pictures of kids partying and even ones where the kids seem to be wasted, but there's still this look, and I can tell just from the face, wasted look or not, whether or not this reveler can speak two or more languages. So when I strolled around Humboldt, I felt I was home, in America— in particular, Planet Hollywood, a place I've never been.

Then I walked into my class.

I was in a foreign country when I walked into my class.

First, they could barely speak English. That's why they signed up: they were trying to learn. That's what Professor A. had predicted: "The only reason to take your course is that it's being given in English." In the U-Bahn I used to see the ads with a big guy, arms folded, over block letters:

Yes, I speak English: WALL STREET English.

That was before the crash. Anyway, I think some of the kids were hoping to learn Wall Street English.

Second, to my surprise, not a single kid was German. In fact, the students were foreign grads dropping in from abroad.

Why no German law students in my class? In a German law school, every student has to concentrate fanatically hard on passing the German bar. The bar exam lasts not three days, as in the U.S., but several grueling months. No serious German law student in his or her right mind would waste a credit on a course like mine—on U.S. labor law—which never in a million years would be on a six-month German bar exam. So how many students even take these offbeat boutique-type courses, which are packed in the U.S.?

Two, three students. Maybe five.

Professor B., who came to audit, was shocked I had ten students.

"Congratulations," he said.

"What do you mean? I've got ten."

"There are professors here who would love to have ten students," he said.

That included me, since I soon had only six.

Instead of Dortmund or Düsseldorf, my students came from France, Belgium, the UK. I had twins from Samarqand. With the kids in my class, I was in a real clash of civilizations. Though I tried later to talk about Taft-Hartley, the Civil Rights Act, and

ERISA, we never really got beyond our first disastrous class on "Employment at Will." I'd thought that, in the first class, I'd explain how, in the U.S., people could be fired for any-reason-at-any-time, or for *no* reason at all. "Here's an example. I work for you for twenty-nine years, one year from retiring. One day I wear a yellow tie to work. You say, 'I don't like your tie. You're fired.' In the U.S., you can do that."

A kid who looked like the kid in *The 400 Blows* said, "*Mais non, c'est impossible.* This is not possible!"

"Yeah, well, I can tell you it is possible."

"No."

"Yes."

And in the next class, I'd have to go into it all again. "How is this possible?" etc. Since no one ever took notes, maybe they forgot what I'd said. But it bothered me that I seemed to make Americans out to be monsters.

I decided to soften up Employment at Will. "Sure, we fire people for no reason, or for the color of their ties—yes, we do. *But we don't do it every day.*"

It's just not that bad.

"Look, you have to remember, in America, we're basically nice people. I mean, we really are. It's a nice country, it's a first-class civilization, so . . . I mean, there are things like laws, but there's also custom. And we don't literally fire people all the time. . . ."

Of course, I didn't tell them how often we *do*: that Americans have, on average, six jobs by age thirty. After that, it gets worse. But why go into that?

Later, Professor B. came up: "That was very good." (There had been a little applause.)

"Thank you for coming," I said.

"This is what we are supposed to do!"

Maybe so, but it was agony. The class started at five. It was May. The sky was blue. Outside, in the beer gardens all over Berlin, they were clinking their glasses. Meanwhile, in our unpainted classroom, I could see the chalk dust in the air.

I'd cough. I knew the kids were also dying for a beer, but, waterless, I had to gasp on through the damn course. And why inflict American labor law on these kids?

Ugh. But it had gotten me into Europe.

Every Wednesday night I would start at 5 P.M. and have to "teach" for three hours. Even by 6 P.M., I'd be out of gas, but somehow it would get over, and still in the sunshine at 8 P.M., I'd go running in Berlin.

Ah, Berlin, in the woods!

London and Paris have their precious gardens. But Berlin is wilder and full of woods. What capital has woods, living, breathing? I'd run through them out of breath. In Mitte, I could see Joschka Fischer jogging between his bodyguards—or, much farther out, I could see the hunting lodge, full of antlers, where once I sang a song to B.—or even, rarely, I might run by a couple who did not want to be discovered (so unlike Paris, where so many couples do).

Alas, I'm not cut out to be a teacher, which is as close as I can get in America to a European-type job. If I had been a European, I wouldn't have dreamed of being a teacher, since I can get some of the lifestyle in a nonteaching job. By the way, I am baffled why Americans teach part-time as adjuncts at "night," in "night classes," when half the class is in a coma.

It's as if by working two jobs, we could somehow work our way into a European type of life.

But if I could have a real European life, I'd surely do something different, like operate a windmill. I would get a lot of Victorian novels and lock myself in, the way lonely old guys live in a light-house on the Isle of Man.

Still, while I wouldn't want to be a teacher, the life of a European student has a certain appeal. I had asked Professor B.: "Do I give them a reading list?"

"No," he said, "this is a lecture course; there is no reading."

"Well, what about exams?"

"No, no exam."

"Is there a paper?

"No, there is no paper."

"Well, do they get credit?"

"Yes," he said. "Of course!"

Damn it! I really had been born on the wrong continent. I should have been born here, sitting in classes without doing any of the reading and raising my hand occasionally to say, "But this is impossible!" In my self-righteous anger, I forgot that, in my youth in the 1960s, because of student riots and Vietnam, they had canceled my college exams sophomore and junior year.

And in some ways it can be a horror to slog one's way into a professional career.

Indeed, late one night, with a raven sitting on my desk, I heard a knock, and a student poked her head in. "Hi. Looking for someone?" I said.

She blushed. "I am here to see Professor C. I work for him. I am his assistant."

"You are? Well, he's been on sabbatical for three months. He'll be back next September."

"Oh." She seemed upset.

"Look, I don't want to seem critical. But you can't have been working for him that hard, if—"

"I know," she said. "I have not been around." She groaned. "It is a bad time. You know about exams here? They will go into January."

(This was April.)

"Right now," she said, "I am in the middle of them."

Then she told me the awful truth. The bar exam, which is a three-day blur in the U.S., goes on for months. The pass rate is 60 percent. She gets only two tries. And then, if she doesn't pass, she's out, forever, even though she has been studying law, just law, only law, for her entire student career. It's frightening to think: if they fail, what do they do for the rest of their lives? In the U.S., it's not the bar but the first year of law school that's tough; but, compared to the bar in Germany, our One L is a lark.

Imagine, not one year in the U.S., but two, three, four, five years waiting for this big six-month exam, which almost half of them will fail! "It's ridiculous," said Nina, my *New York Times* friend. "Even to be a waiter over here, they have to apprentice two years." On a later trip, I met an American expat who told me: "I wanted to open just a little computer shop here, and before I could do it, I had to show the authorities not just my degree or ré-sumé, but my transcript—they wanted to see my grades!"

I was about to tell Professor C.'s assistant: it's so much easier in America.

But something about her seemed American. "You speak En-glish so well," I said. (In 2001, I was still noticing that kind of thing.)

"I *used* to speak it," she said. "But now I'm so full of . . . *Gerecht*," the word for "law," and when she said it, she seemed to be about to spit. "After all, I grew up in Laguna Beach."

"Laguna Beach, California?"

Yes, she was from Laguna Beach, where her father, a German, had taught American cultural studies, which out there is probably *Baywatch*, and she had grown up on the beach. If she had stayed in America, right now she'd be in marketing or something, and maybe reading things like *RedEye*, if she read anything at all.

"So," I said, "where would you be better off, in the U.S. or Europe?" I knew, for the purpose of my book, I'd get a bitter answer.

"Oh," she said, "my family, it's here, and that's so important to me, but . . . but . . . oh, America!" She sighed. "I think, in America, it's better for a woman. In America, I could work part-time as a lawyer, but here, to be a lawyer, everything is ten hours a day, and if it's part-time . . . you're off the career ladder. . . ."

She seemed to think this didn't happen in America.

But look at the time she put in: years. I can see why they want to reform the schools. But still, do they want to be like us?

Of course, I know, it's changing over there. Yes, apprenticeships are going, etc. One hears this all the time. "Yes, we're becoming like Americans." But any American can see how shallow a claim this is. In terms of teaching soft skills, breaking down the idea of a career, we're far ahead of them. How to be more pliable, to adapt, to work as a team: or at least that's the claim about the way we live in the "new" capitalism, the U.S. and UK kind, in a haunting book by the sociologist Richard Sennett, *The Corrosion of Character: The Personal Consequences of Work in the New Capitalism* (1998), which I read on later trips. And it's true, even in the law, as I can testify. Even in Harvard or Yale Law Schools, or especially there, they don't expect you to practice law, i.e., to come out with a real skill. After all, we're expected to hold six or seven jobs. Only a minority of us went on to practice law, or do it now. To Sennett, it's moving from job to job that destroys the old-fashioned sense of character, i.e., mastery over one's life. To look at the blurbs on the cover, Sennett's book has had more acclaim in Germany than over here, since Germans are actually worried that they are losing this sense of character. And it's true, by German standards, it's all collapsing. But by our standards—and I'm writing this book for you and me, in America—it's fascinating that so many people still do get some weird little skill that they can control how they use.

It's not just this young woman from Laguna Beach: it's the apprentice for IG Metall. Mastery depends on willing one thing: one *Beruf*, one career. "Oh, Germans have always been that way." Well, it's easy to write it off that way, but each generation has to choose, really choose, to keep this kind of thing going. Anyway, it's all relative. Sennett's point is: we used to have a bit of it, too. Look at Willy Loman, the hero of Arthur Miller's *Death of a Salesman*. Even in "sales," which is Sennett's bugaboo, Willy Loman has a "career," a sense of craft that is practically medieval, literally doing the same job, learning the product, going deeper into it every year.

And to a labor lawyer like me, the paradox about the American emphasis on "team" is that, in the U.S., there is no real sense of "team." Take a look at their depositions: there are so many hostile, sullen people. Based on what I've seen, I'm inclined to believe Wolfgang Streeck when he makes a standard point about the U.S. and German models. While Streeck was pessimistic about the German model, he still notes its advantages. In the U.S., for example, where the corporation is authoritarian and undemocratic, it's easy to make decisions. The hard thing is to implement them. The people at the bottom aren't involved. That's partly why, to compensate, we put so much effort in telling business majors: "Be a team player." And we hope they buy tapes that say, over and over: "Hey, we're empowering you." "You are the boss." In other words: do what we tell you. But in Germany—with co-determination, works councils—it may be more difficult to make decisions initially. But Streeck claims that, once decisions are made, they're easier to implement. And I heard almost the same Streeck-type claim from two or three different Europeans: "It's amazing, when you go to the U.S., and you suggest something, the Americans say, 'Let's do it.' But then it turns out later, it never happens. But here in Europe when you suggest something, everyone says, 'Oh, we can never do that,' but then later it turns out it actually gets done."

Sure, I felt guilty—I still do—when I think how I'm preaching mastery and not drift, when what this poor girl wants is just to go back to Laguna Beach, i.e., to be one of us.

Well, I did feel sorry for her.

But I couldn't let myself feel sorry. No, put away the surfboard. Stop reading *RedEye*. Pick up a skill other than learning how to submit.

I know the German education system is broken. The universities are running out of money. Humboldt needs a paint job. They score low on the PISA tests. A professor blew up at me: "Do you know the minister of our federal state has to approve the questions on my exam?"

Sure, but, bad as it is, they're going to outcompete us because they aren't going to turn into a nation of "temps."

And I believe the Germans and the French and the Scandinavians and all the rest of them are learning one thing, one "skill," that makes Europe a bigger threat to us than China. One day, at the current rate, it is English that will be the second "mother" tongue.

Do people in our country grasp how threatening that is?

I know the threat is supposed to be in manufacturing. And I may just be trying to justify my hanging out at Humboldt, which seems an unlikely place to get any insight into the battle between the U.S. and European model. Okay, I should have gone out to Wolfsburg and toured the big VW plant. I kept meaning to do so. But didn't Hitler plan the city of Wolfsburg in the 1930s as a showpiece of the Reich? No, I don't want to go out there.

So instead, during the week, I'd just go to lunch at Dussmann and eat cucumber sandwiches under a waterfall (yes, there was a true indoor waterfall in 2001), and then I'd go up and browse the kind of English-language books that one usually could find only in London.

Under the waterfall, I'd often think how much higher the German GDP would be if it were truly a "flat" world, in a linguistic sense. What would it be like if Germany wrote in English, spoke in English, sang in English, just as we do?

It used to be, in the time of Weimar Germany, that the U.S. stood for mass production while Europe stood for quality or craft. It is said that, in Weimar, the bestseller was *My Life and Work*, the autobiography of Henry Ford. That was the avatar of the U.S. model: Ford Motor Company. But that's certainly not true today. Nor is it true that mass production is the especially distinctive thing about the U.S. model. Today the U.S. economy, which is so much bigger, has not just one company like Ford but three of them—three companies that are our colossi that straddle the world:

Disney (or maybe it's Viacom)
Microsoft (or maybe it's Google)
Goldman Sachs (or maybe it's . . . Goldman Sachs).

And what allows them to straddle the world is the comparative advantage in having English as our native language. The Germans can't do Disney: Mickey would be too strange in German. The Germans can't even do Microsoft if German kids have to think twice if they're using Microsoft Word or *Vord*. And while Germans can be global players in banking, I have to think not speaking English can hold them a fatal nanosecond behind their own subordinates in London and New York.

What we have instead of mass production is the lock on the global language, which helps explain why Europe doesn't do, or can't do, Disney, or Microsoft, or Goldman Sachs the way we do.

But that's changing.

English is the official language of the EU: that's what the French have to use to speak to the Germans and vice versa. And all around me at Humboldt, I could see how the kids, knowing no Americans, were sounding as American as you and me. When these "European socialists" have English as the mother tongue by 2025 A.D., they may globally outcompete us not just in widgets but in things wrought with words.

Then what will we do? Let's hope for global warming. At least we can sell bananas.

One shock about Germany to me is that so many people are not engineers but "cultural" types, in opera, music, and theater. Look at publishing. And they also still have newspapers, of course. They seem to have a better gift for selling culture on a mass basis than we do.

And they're doing better now that more of them have started to lighten up. I remember that, on an early trip to Dussmann's, I decided to buy Kafka in German, his *Der Prozess*, or *The Trial*. I took the book up to the cashier, flipped out my credit card. Frowning like a border guard, she turned it over, and squinted at the signature. "Do you have any other identification . . . ?"

"What? I'm an American."

"Then I would like to see a passport."

"I need a passport?"

Maybe for *The Castle*, but not for *The Trial*.

Come on: I tried to josh her out of it.

No, she was serious, as if about to call a cop. I could see myself sitting that night in a Berlin jail with someone from the consulate saying, "I'm sure we can clear this up. . . ."

But that was long ago; in Berlin, they've all lightened up, hey, they're American, there are no more GDR types, and they're way too hip now to ask for your passport when you want to buy *The Trial*.

But that's what makes them dangerous: the more they lighten up, the more likely it is they will outcompete us globally one day. It's also intriguing to see a European model that is peopled more and more by people like us. That's why I hated to see any back-sliding, or cutbacks in the welfare state, before they get to a flat world, where the U.S. and Europe get to compete on an even plane linguistically.

Yes, the center-left soul in me understood why there had to be cutbacks, why the SPD had to make it easier to fire people and make the other changes known as "Agenda 2010."

As a Green Party staffer later said, quoting the line in di Lampedusa's novel *The Leopard*: "We have to change, so everything can stay the same."

But I hated to see it change. It was as if it would mess up the experiment. And that's what led me to do the strangest thing in my "life-as-a-European." It's when I stood up and told them to hold the line at the Party of European Socialists Congress in Berlin.

Well, here's how it happened. There was such a congress in May 2001. And it was not so "Socialist." Tony Blair almost came. And there were a handful of ex–prime ministers.

I went to hear one of the ex–prime ministers, António Gutteres of Portugal, give a talk. To a lot of elderly academics, he was saying that, while the EU may exist formally, there is still no European "idea."

It was all very European: he even quoted Jürgen Habermas. But I kept thinking of my old college teacher Sam Beer. "The problem with the European Union," Sam had said, "is that you

can't have federalism for its own sake. There has to be an *idea*."
The ex–prime minister said the same thing: "We have a formal
European Union, but we do not have, as yet, a corresponding European civil society, a European public opinion." There was as yet
no European "idea."

These elderly Socialists clapped. Were there questions? When
no one else went up to the mic, I decided to go up.

"Yes?"

"Mr. Prime Minister, you say there is no 'European public opinion.' But isn't antagonism to the U.S. . . . . isn't that creating a European public opinion?"

Around me the Socialists started clapping. Some even began to
tap their canes. Trying to talk over the cheers, the ex–prime minister acted as if he did not understand: "Oh no, my American
friend, you must not worry! While we have our disagreements, the
bonds between Europe and the U.S. are now stronger than, blah,
blah, blah. . . . So, no, no, my friend, you should not worry. . . ."

Worried? I wasn't worried. But I had gone back to my seat.
Later, I decided that he knew perfectly well I wasn't worried. The
people around me now tottered back to their professorships. That
night, alone at Dussmann, when the waterfall was turned off, I
was aghast at what I'd said: had I really been touting a civil society based on antagonism to the U.S.?

Ah, it's my country! I love it. I even live in the Midwest. What
can be greater proof that I'm a patriot? I noticed that Barack
Obama put on his flag lapel pin only when he went east to the
White House; so long as he was in the Midwest, that very fact
was patriotism enough.

Still, didn't George Bush, Fox News, and the GOP in general
help create the new Europe? In 2001, the war in Iraq was yet to
come, but there had been *Bush v. Gore*. In May 2001, *Der Spiegel*
had a cover mocking Bush as "the little sheriff." In 2003, I saw

concrete barriers all around the U.S. Embassy in Berlin, so no one could get near. It was galling; in front of the Russian (former Soviet) Embassy, there were no barriers, no walls. It was as if, trading places in Berlin, we were now the USSR. On a later trip, over New Year's Day in 2005, the one where I caught up with Wigand, I stayed for free at the American Academy in Berlin, thanks to Marie U. The resident fellows were gone for the holidays; I knocked around the enormous place alone. Yet every night lying in bed, I knew out there, in a police car, two cops were awake, guarding me: if only I could have had the money that the Germans spent guarding me! Okay, it was not me but the building, which carried the dangerous name "American." Of course, it was the Middle Eastern terrorists they feared. Still, so long as Bush and Cheney were around, European socialism was safe.

No, the European idea has to be a lot more than that.

I lunched with another professor, C.O., who seemed to be a classmate of Joschka Fischer. He not only looked but smoked cigarillos like Marcello Mastroianni, and maybe could have been him, if Mastroianni had studied not under Sophia Loren but Max Weber. How I wanted to smoke a cigarillo as he spoke.

"European social policy, this is a whole new field of study." Pause. Inhale. "But you say, 'What is it?' I think there are four main areas. First, there is a set of issues as to . . . we would say exclusion, or 'who-will-have-access-to-our-labor-markets.' And here there is no 'harmonization,' but great differences between the countries. Then there is a second set of issues, pension issues. I am very pessimistic about harmonization here. The third set of issues, these relate to family policies."

He paused. "Do you know what tax splitting is?"

"No. What's the fourth?"

"The fourth set is that of labor-law policies. And here I think there is a real potential to harmonize our labor markets."

The point was that in Brussels the Germans and the French were pushing rules on works councils that would make all European companies more like German-type than U.S.-type companies. The big issue was whether the "Social Partners," namely, Management and Labor, could impose these rules by majority vote.

I had asked another professor: "Do these rules come from the Commission or the EU Parliament?"

Neither: they come from the Social Partners themselves. The Germans seemed to believe that the German system could spread.

I sighed: "It's so civilized," I said to C.O.

"But America, too, is such a civilized country," he said.

"Oh well, yes," I said. "Sure, I mean if you're talking about New York and New Haven and all that." That's where he goes. "And it works incredibly well, given that no one is really skilled at anything. . . ."

"I know," said C.O. "In America, when I am in the travel bureaus, I have to help them."

"Sure, of course, go into any place, people are nice. But they can't really do anything for you. . . ." I should have added: of course we're civilized. Look at our universities, full of professors who commute over here from Europe to get the higher pay. But as C.O. pointed out, not all of them do. "My daughter should, for career reasons, go to the U.S., but she won't. . . . She says, 'I won't step foot in the U.S. until they stop giving guns to children and do something about the death penalty.'"

I gaped at C.O. "That's what she says? That's what I think!"

I decided to tell him about my thesis: that even people who are at the top or are in the top 20 percent by income are better off in a European social democracy than in a country like the U.S. I started listing all the material reasons why they might be better off—free college, vacations.

It seemed to me I forgot one. "I can't think of it," I said.

C.O. leaned over. "They would get to live in a just society."

Yes, that's what I had in mind.

I thought about it when I marched on May Day, when the Socialist Party Congress was in town. Peter S., a labor lawyer, had called me up: "You must come and march with us." He'd be marching with his union, IG Metall. We were to step off at 10 A.M., yes, in the morning—unthinkably early in Berlin, even on a weekday. Every kebab stand was closed. I had a headache from lack of coffee. When I met up with Peter and saw the men and women with whom I would be marching, I could have burst out laughing. I was back with the Steelworkers I'd represented in South Chicago! *I was home.* These were my clients. Even racially there was some similarity. There were no blacks, but it was much the same mix of white and brown. In America, one hears so much about the difficulty of Europe integrating Muslims, but all those people should go to a May Day parade in Berlin, where one would marvel how easily it happens. I asked my friend Peter: "What percentage of the members of this IG Metall group are foreign-born?" He said that, in Berlin, the foreign-born member-ship of IG Metall is 42 percent! In Germany overall, he said, it's 8 or 9 percent, which, on a national basis, also seems high. To my surprise, he said that the percentages had dropped thanks to unification. In other words, the percentages were higher before 1989.

Now I blushed: "Peter, I know the answer to this, but I have to hear you say it, because in the U.S. people won't believe this. But do the foreign-born get exactly the same wages, the same deal as the native-born?"

"Yes." He was kind enough not to look at me as if I were crazy. He knows the way Americans who come back from Europe get all these idiot questions: "Well, do they let Turks into unions? I'm sure they don't," etc.

Two memories of the march under the blazing sun still stay with me. First, I was amazed that so many of the marchers seemed like such suburbanite AFL-CIO types, whether white or brown. They had the same slight bellies hanging out of the same slightly untucked T-shirts, just as I remembered in the union halls of South Chicago. Whether white American, or Turk, or Latino, it seems that T-shirts are untucked in this way all over the world.

The only thing missing were the SUVs.

Second, there was not just rock-and-roll, but, unlike the canned stuff on the radio, it was German rock-and-roll, with the lyrics not in English but in German, blaring from the backs of trucks. Somewhere ahead of us, there were real German kids, rocking in real rock bands. I started out with Peter and his intern, a young law student from London.

I said to her: "I think this is the first time I've heard rock music in German."

She said she was surprised to hear them rock in German, too.

"It's also so multiethnic," I said. I added that, compared to Berlin, London must be more so.

"Oh," she said, "it seems more so here than in London."

"I can't believe it's more multiethnic than London."

"The Turks and the Kurds, the way they have taken over Kreuzberg—it's so interesting. You go on the U-Bahn, and you see whole families, mothers, everyone traveling together."

I wanted to turn off, but Peter said that if we kept going, there would be beer and brats. Great: now I was even more eager to turn off. But I decided to keep marching. This march was both more cheerful and angrier and edgier, classwise, than an AFL-

CIO Labor Day march in South Chicago. I counted seventy cops, but I might have passed a hundred more. A lot of them were cheerful. I even decided to stop and look in the side mirror of a police car to comb my hair. A woman cop laughed and in a low voice said something to me in German. Who knows? If had a better grip on German, I might be married to her today.

We finally got up to the big park, where a Milwaukee-style tailgate party was going on in the old East German Communist part of town. It was eerie. We had passed through the "new" Disneyland Berlin, with big blue-and-green glass boxes for big global firms like Daimler that pretend to have their "world" headquarters here when the real principal offices were back in Stuttgart. Somehow, this new Berlin seemed to be menacing that morning, and, looking up at the Disney-type hot air balloon that often hung over this part of town, I wondered if cops up there were tracking us.

We passed out of Mouseketeer Berlin and now gathered in front of the old Communist GDR "Palace of the Republic," a building that was even uglier than McCormick Place, which is Chicago's own homage to Stalin. The Palace of the Republic had been the parliament of the old GDR, but, as Peter said, it's also where GDR kids had come to party. "I know what you're thinking," he said. "It's awful."

"It's evil."

"It's evil to you," he said. "But the Palace of the Republic not only held the parliament—it had the world's biggest dance floor. They could make it very intimate, like a club. And for many young East Germans, this is where they danced and first fell in love."

How chilling to have one's first kiss captured in a photo by the Stasi.

"And here are the statues of Marx and Engels. See, their backs are to the Palace of the Republic. People in the GDR used to say:

no wonder we can't do anything: Marx and Engels have turned their backs on us."

I turned away to a much happier scene. The Kurds kept kick-dancing in a chorus line. The Fritz Weinecke Orchestra was serving as the oompah band, and someone handed me a beer, a flat urine-like thing that, behind a Port-O-Let, I had to spit out on the ground. But while it was a happy scene, it was angry too. For at that moment, the Schroeder government was already planning its little nip-and-tuck of the welfare state. While they were right, I didn't want them to do anything that gave comfort to the *Wall Street Journal*.

In 2001, the SPD-Green government had not yet come up with the changes known as "Agenda 2010." But Schroeder was hinting that he might cut back the benefits for long-term unemployed. The idea was to force them to take jobs that they currently disdained. Recently, in *Bild*, the chancellor had even said, "There is no right to be lazy." "You see," said a Humboldt professor, "Schroeder is a genius at what I call 'preemptive phraseology.' He can come up with the slogans of the CDU before the CDU can." But this infuriated the left. One sign said:

WER —WAS IST FAUL, HERR KANZLER?

Peter said the word "faul" could mean "lazy" or "rotten," depending on whether the antecedent is "wer" (who) or "was" (what). This picketer had crossed out the "wer" to put in "was," so with the "wer" crossed out, the sign read not "WHO IS LAZY, HERR CHANCELLOR?" but "*WHAT* IS *ROTTEN*, HERR CHANCELLOR?"

Get it? Well, I shouldn't try German. But I also saw a sign that's easier to translate:

DU BIST CHIC . . . ICH MUSS SCHUFTEN.

That's plain enough: "YOU ARE CHIC . . . I MUST SLAVE AWAY."

Many of these marchers may have been allied with Oskar Lafontaine, who had broken away from the SPD to form a new
party, now called Die Linkspartei, "the Links" or "The Left." The
left was already fighting with the left. It was true in France as
well. That was a bad omen for European social democracy.

But still there is a far left that is furious: that night, radicals
would set fire in empty buildings.

This May Day got out of control. And I was shocked at the anger
in unions like IG Metall. But maybe they were especially angry at
the SPD-Green government, because the unions had quietly decided to hold down wages too. They were afraid in 2001: even the
export sector seemed in peril unless there were cutbacks.

An SPD staffer complained to me: "We took criticism for doing
the same thing that the unions had decided to do." For the unions
had signed on to what some call the "dirty deal," to hold the line
against wage increases relative to those in other European countries. Maybe, as they marched in protest, some of them felt guilty.

But at least they march.

At least there still is an IG Metall: with its 2.3 million members, it's still about as big as it was in 1973. Even if that now
counts East Germans, it's still astonishing, when in the U.S.
we've seen our own United Auto Workers and Steelworkers practically disappear.

At least there is still a membership that can march.

While the Germans may have held back on wage increases at
various times, look at the steady decline of real wages in the U.S.
From 1973 to 2005, productivity in America went up approximately 55 percent. Put another way, output per hour went up 55
percent. Meanwhile, the average hourly wage dropped 8 percent!
Harvard's Richard Freeman, perhaps our leading labor economist,
once wrote: "If in 1973 any economist had predicted such a pat-

tern, the American Economic Association would have carted him or her off as mad."

In *America Works* (2007), Freeman also wrote that if real wages had risen with productivity in roughly the same way it did in Germany and other countries, then the American worker would have been making $25 an hour on average in 2005 instead of just $16. Since Freeman wrote, it's gotten even worse, especially with the financial meltdown of 2008.

Is anyone marching? No.

And how can I explain this to the kids in my class? I can't. And when I look back on that year, I now regret that I pulled my punches. Oh, I told the class, we're nice people. We don't really fire people for the color of their ties. But more and more, in effect that's what employers do. They use big temp agencies to staff even the running of the plants that make things like Weber grills, which we supposedly could sell abroad. With temps, if they don't like the look of a particular worker, poof, he or she is gone: not even fired, just not called back the next day. Steve Franklin, who was the longtime and superb labor reporter at the *Chicago Tribune*, estimates there are a hundred thousand or so of these temps working in Chicago-area plants.

Is anyone marching? No.

At least in Europe they march. Still, in a certain mood, I can agree with *BusinessWeek* or *Forbes* that the left is naive, etc. They can't go back to the 1970s and keep adding new benefits. It's true that, in our flat world, the German industrial sector is doing great; and so is France's, and so are other high-wage social democracies. But they still have to make room for China, India, and the rest.

I knew, or half knew, they would have to cut back. Didn't I know that, without the cutbacks of Agenda 2010, young workers would be paying 30 percent of their wages to keep up the pensions of retired Germans?

No, I didn't.

Because of the U.S. problems, which obsessed me, I suppose I didn't take their problems seriously. (I know! I know!) Yes, it's true. At least on the pension issue, I could not see the beam in Europe's eye because I was so conscious of the blindness of its American observers.

I admit, too: I hated to see it change. It was probably the invasion of Iraq that kept the changes from being worse. Thanks to our Bush and Cheney, who may be the saviors of the German model, the left stayed in power and kept out the right at a time when the right would have made much bigger changes than Agenda 2010. It was fortunate that "our" side, not the right, did the cutting back.

But there's another reason I gave less attention to what was going on—I was having too good a time. Even on a weekday night I was going out to dinner at ten and staying up to 1 A.M. I did try to get in breakfast by noon.

For once, instead of my just waiting for my life to begin, maybe it *had* begun.

Near the end of my stay, I met up with S., an American friend who had helped me get the Humboldt gig. "How's it going?" he asked.

"Steve, I've never been so happy in my whole life. And there's just one thing making me miserable."

"What?"

"It's going to end! I'm dreading it. I have to go back." I'd have to go back to a U.S.-type life of work, work, work.

"You'll poison the whole experience if you worry about that," he said. "Just enjoy it now. And when it's over, it's over."

That's what I came to think about the European model. Maybe one day, Europeans will have to work till they drop as we do in

America. So? Then the Europeans should just enjoy it now. When it's over, it's over.

But because the Europeans really do enjoy it now, they keep coming up with tweaks in the model to make sure it goes on and on.

6

After the *Krise* (2009)

April 2009. Just back from Berlin—in this year of what Germans call the "Krise." We use the clunkier "global financial meltdown." But let's use the brutal German word:

The *Krise*.

While the U.S. may have set it off, it could hit Germany even worse—6 percent drop in GDP in 2009. Why? With no credit, there's no world trade, and, unlike Americans, the Germans feast off their exported goods. So the "Krise" ought to be a disaster for Germany. Yet for the first time, I worry about the U.S. model even more. Now, with both a huge trade deficit and a huge fiscal deficit, the U.S., more than ever, is in the clutches of foreign creditors. Think of our net external debt, how much more we in the U.S. owe people outside the country compared to what they owe us. Our net external debt may be as much as $3 trillion (that's $3,000,000,000). Driven by our trade deficit, this figure is projected to grow this decade at the rate of $1 trillion a year. So predicts Yale's Jeffrey Garten in the December 14, 2009, *Financial Times*. On the other hand, though Germany has a large external debt, it is a net creditor as a country. In that sense, unlike America, Germany is debt free. It has a freedom of action that our country no longer has.

I know on the right and even the center I am dismissed as a European-style liberal. But my question for those on the right is as follows: do they care about the sovereignty of our country? Then they better start taking seriously what the Europeans do.

During the trip I kept seeing the face of Larry Summers (still in charge, oddly enough, twelve years later), so worried, begging me: "Can you get Germany to stop being so competitive?" He and his team plead with the Germans: "Stop running up the score! Give us debtor countries a chance."

Isn't it embarrassing to be on our knees, asking our creditors to stop playing against us so hard? Maybe, as a debtor country, we should "restructure," with "European-type" socialism as a model. At least we could run a surplus.

In 1945, Keynes said the U.S., as a creditor country, had a duty to stop running up its exports at the expense of the debtor countries, like his own UK. But why should the creditor countries do a debtor country like the U.S. any favors? I wonder if they grasp that on Fox News. Americans still seem unaware that it's not just East Asia but the socialist Europeans who have outcompeted us in global markets as we sink deeper into debt. Thank goodness the debts we've run up are "denominated," or payable in our own dollars, and not in the rising currency of a creditor country, as is normally the case with a debtor country. Otherwise, we would be like Argentina, and there would be riots in our streets. But while it seems unlikely at the moment, that day may come upon us, suddenly, like a trap.

And aside from my embarrassment that my country now asks Germany to stop being so successful, I was also for the first time worried about our unemployment. No matter who did the measuring, our unemployment rate in 2009 ended up beating Germany's. Here is the count given by the International Labor Organization (ILO):

UNEMPLOYMENT (PERCENT)

	Germany	U.S.
2000	10.7	4.0
2005	11.7	5.1
2009	8.2	9.3

Source: International Labor Organization (ILO).

I was unnerved by this reversal of fortune. I felt happier in Germany when it was just Germany that was dark. And as things had turned upbeat there, I felt much more alone at night. It was also a mistake to come when three of my closest friends in Berlin were gone—oddly enough, for different reasons, they all happened to be in America.

But this was the only time—April 19 to 29, 2009—that I could get away from work. I had to go somewhere, right? And if I'm going to be alone, I'd rather do it in Berlin than any other place in the world. This time, I stayed at the Hotel Kastanienhof, where Mrs. M. was so kind. Thanks to her, I ended up marginally happier than Christopher Isherwood in *Goodbye to Berlin*.

I thought of my law partner emeritus Leon Despres, who would die at age 101 just as I came back from this trip. The first time I went to Berlin, I went into Len's office and asked: "Have you ever been there?"

"Sure."

"Really—when were you there?"

"Oh . . . 1926."

"Yikes: *1926*? You went, like, in Weimar!"

"Oh yes." He and his friends went. He told me how demoralized he and the other kids were when Coolidge had won in 1924.

"So, Len, what was it like, I mean, Berlin?"

He paused. "It was the first time I was in a gay nightclub."

Yes, he had truly been in Weimar.

But he said it took him a quarter of an hour before it occurred to him where he was.

But my other great mentor, Sam Beer, had died at age ninety-seven just a few weeks before Len did. He had gone to Berlin on a hiking trip a few years after Len's visit—in 1932. It was all over.

The Nazis were now goose-stepping. The Kit Kat Club had shut.

For Len, it was a lark. For Sam, it was dark.

For me, though, it's just a place that gets happier on every trip. Even in the *Krise*, it's hard to say, when I walk around here, that Germany is dark. I still remember when all I could find was a beat-up wannabe of a Mister Softee truck.

Now, twelve years later, just within a block or so of the Hotel Kastanienhof, where I'm staying, I can count at least ten cafés. But the street scene is misleading, because there are even more cafés in the courtyards hidden off the street.

Berlin's not a movable but an unmovable feast. It's got a confidence not even the Krise can crack. "But what's the basis of the economy?" There isn't any, not in the German sense. There's no industry. But the money keeps pouring in. They have political capital here, so it's like Washington. And the kids are here because it's so hip, so it's like Berkeley or Portland, too.

As a result, the basis of the entire economy is just hanging out.

Prenzlauer Berg and Kreuzberg are packed with kids, kids, kids, spending their parents' money. Can there be any world capital so completely supported by money from Mom and Dad?

I try to think of stodgy German parents, blowing all this money on parties in Berlin. As my American friend Leo says, "Germans take out insurance on everything. They take out insurance on their windows."

Yet the kids come to Berlin, where they can break all the rules. Worse, there are now Americans.

To my horror, I pick up the *New York Times* travel section and gasp to see another what-to-do-in-thirty-six-hours-in-Berlin, how cool it is, etc. Of course, I dislike this, and I much prefer the old Berlin, a city of squatters and slackers who knew that life was meaningless. Of course, some of that old Berlin is still there: I went to see the Hieronymus Bosch painting made up of panels on the Passion, with the last panel being the tomb with Jesus shut up inside and a huge vulture on top looking for carrion. This year on Good Friday, the priest had said with such distaste, "There's such a rush to Easter." Well, there is no rush in Bosch. And I can still go, as I used to, to the Pergamon Museum, so frightening, to look at all the Greek statues that have no eyes. The first time I went, in 1997, I'd just started to read Herodotus in a pretentious sort of way and had the shock of finding one story after another of messengers being blinded, and the blind statues I saw there seemed to have come out of the dark and terrible book I took around with me that winter.

All that I can still do. But I can no longer sit alone as I did late at night at the Café Oren, a once quite hip Israeli spot where the waiters inside would wear black and white like members of a string quartet and outside in the baby tanks the German cops wore green. I'd come late at night to the Oren and pull out of my book bag all the twentieth-century histories I'd bought from the floor with all the English-language books at Dussmann's and sit by the white candle, which Cecelia, my Soho-type waitress, lit, and try to pretend I was a Berliner. It's here in 1997 and in 2001 that I read all I could of Eric Hobsbawm, Fritz Stern, and so many others, and first came across Mazower's thesis that fascism should have been the natural form of government for Europe but the Nazis were just too evil. But still the more I read, the more it seems to me this "inevitable" triumph over evil was a kind of blind luck. And I'm quite persuaded by Richard Overy's *Why the Allies Won* (1996), which argues that the inept Soviet Union, improbably, and almost impossibly, defeated vastly more efficient Germany, and if that isn't providence, an inept evil empire wiping out what should have been a less inept one, I don't know what is. I say all this because so many people come to Berlin to grandstand about all their issues with theodicy: i.e., if God supposedly exists, why is there so much evil? Only there is a reciprocal side that no one ever bothers to mention, i.e., if God does not exist, why hasn't evil won?

Well, the Café Oren is gone.

Now each time I go, Berlin keeps getting nicer, more upbeat, and it's a little hard to bear. Still, this last trip in 2009, I was hoping it would have a bit of the old darkness back, with capitalism cracking up, etc.

Yet while I was there, the whole place seemed in a festive mood. Of course the far left was happy. Near my hotel there was a big sign:

COMMUNISM: YES WE CAN.

It was right near the park where, on May Day, I had spit out the beer. And of course no one wants the GDR back. It was just schadenfreude, delight in others' troubles. Oh, to be sure, a few people like Ms. G. from the Bundestag tried to sound depressed. The economy was contracting fast. "Soon," she said, "there will be riots." Yet when she said this, we were on a big party boat, rocking on the river, getting tan, drinking beer, calling back a waitress who looked like she spoke more than five languages.

Come on, six new cafés must have opened while we drank that last beer. There weren't going to be any riots!

Or at least not in Berlin.

Yes, on this trip I met a few others who told me the end had come. "Oh! I think the capitalist system is over."

But really they don't think it's over. They just think it's over for us, the Americans. And that puts them in a festive mood. In fact, it's all the better if the same U.S. model revives. It just makes them more competitive.

What if we're in a whole new era due to climate change, an era of limits? That's great too. Is the world running out of oil? Hey, bring it on. The Germans think they have an edge in green technology: after all, they're making machines. Looking ahead to a world of limits, the CEO of Siemens is quoted in the paper this week saying, "Germany will lead the next industrial revolution."

It's true the collapse of world trade hits Germany hard. But it also means, sooner or later, Germany will come back. In the U.S., we are running up an unsustainable public debt on a much bigger scale than Germany in order to reinstate a system that was running up an unsustainable private debt.

We have no serious chance of leading the next industrial revolution. As the old-timers used to say during the Great Depression, "They ain't got nothing to pump it up with."

Well, we have nothing to pump it up with, other than the big banks pulling it out of us.

So I understand why it is so hard for Germans to be glum when the U.S. is so humbled, and even our "recovery" is so ominous. As we rocked on the river, Friday night, at happy hour, Ms. G. was actually in a good mood: "You aren't a superpower anymore," she said to me. "You're not a military superpower; you can't even handle Afghanistan. You need us to help. And you aren't an economic

superpower anymore; you're in terrible debt. We all have to prop
you up."

"Uh-oh," I thought, "she's going to pick up the check." As an
American, I insisted that we split it.

This sense of national well-being in the midst of the Krise began to wear on me. As the *FT* once wrote, when things turn out
badly, the Germans cheer up. "Everything has collapsed. What a
relief!" It is a different kind of schadenfreude: a joy in one's *own*
sorrows. But there are other reasons why the Krise has put them
in such a good mood.

First, here's a world disaster one cannot blame on the Germans. It's true, we Americans have tried. "They didn't spend
enough." While it's also true that a lot of German bankers drank
our Kool-Aid, it was the U.S. that threw the party.

Second, as an SPD official said to me, "I think at this moment
people in Germany are proud of our system." With all the safety
nets, the Germans are not being laid off the way we Americans
are. At this time, this SPD official—Mr. W.—was working in the
Arbeit und Soziales, which is the German version of the U.S. Labor Department. But that's a misleading comparison because, in
a country with a real labor movement, it's a much bigger deal.
"We're actually responsible," Mr. W. said, "for half of the entire
federal budget." (He means the pension system and all of that.)

It was a Friday afternoon, before I was going to meet Ms. G. It
suddenly hit me what a major government job he had. "Look," I
said, "I don't want to take up your time . . ."

"Oh, come on," he said. "It's Friday afternoon."

Ah! Berlin's still Berlin.

Yes, I guessed he was a union member himself; and it turned
out he was. For the next half hour he explained how the government was paying employers to keep people at work: *full-time.* So,

for example, the German federal government pays for the three extra days to keep someone working on the job all week.

As I write, people in the U.S. are working an average of only thirty hours a week. But in Germany, thanks to the welfare state, they're working full-time.

"No wonder you're paying out half the budget."

"It's cheaper than paying unemployment," he said. "And the employer still has to pay the social contribution." The idea, Mr. W. said, was to have people already back at work when the "real economy" recovers.

"The idea is that, for the first time, we will try to be ahead of the real economy."

How long can they do it? Eighteen months.

The upshot is that, even in the Krise, Germany has lower unemployment than it did in 2003, when there was no Krise. Over his head, I saw a headline from the front page of *Bild* that year:

5.2 Millionen
Tut Endlich Was

Roughly translated: 5.2 Million Unemployed! So Do Something!

I asked about it. He turned around. The figure had shot up to 5.2 million because the SPD Green government had decided to count people on the basic welfare grant as unemployed. For years, the CDU, under Kohl, had not included them.

When they did so, the country went nuts. "We brought truth to the process," he said. "And that was the end of the Schroeder government."

But thanks to Agenda 2010 and the "dirty deal" on wages, and other things, the number of unemployed then came down to just

3 million. Even with the Krise, it's only gone back up to 3 million as of December 2009.

It's sad to see: for it was the SPD that brought down the unemployment rate and made all the fixes for which Angela Merkel got credit as the chancellor of the coalition government that succeeded Schroeder's. Now the election was coming up. And the SPD, which, as junior partner, had put a check on Merkel and kept her from turning into a right-wing Margaret Thatcher, would probably be voted out.

By doing everything right, the SPD had done everything wrong. In the coalition government, it couldn't criticize her. It seemed to the left the SPD had sold out. "Its image is not clear," as a lawyer delicately put it to me.

Look, SPD—which side are you on? And it was even harder to tell when it disappeared into second place in a coalition government.

Yes, in a few months the SPD would be out. I wondered if the cuts had been worth it. All they did was antagonize their base. After all, maybe it was the world economy and not Agenda 2010 that had brought Germany back.

Mr. G., who was Mr. W.'s colleague, explained the real benefit: "The great thing about Agenda 2010 is that it shut everyone up." Even the employers have shut up. "And the journalists were the real problem. They were full of alarm about gridlock." He smiled. "Now some of them have lost their jobs. So now they are full of nice words about the safety net."

In fact, he didn't think the cuts were big. "We have actually made the safety net stronger than ever." Here's how:

1. Unemployment. Yes, after eighteen months people have to go on basic welfare. But the SPD increased the basic grant. And this had the unwitting effect of making welfare "respectable." My friend Simon had said, "After the SPD raised it, everyone was

shocked that now all sorts of people began to apply for it." Indeed, Mr. G. said: "If you have two or more children you can do better on the basic grant, or the *Soziale Hilfe*, than you can probably do in the workplace." He paused, corrected himself: "No, three children."

I wanted to stop him: "You admit this?"

Of course, we're in Europe, where single men can get welfare. So why is the left mad? Mr. W. explained: "By cutting the unemployment after eighteen months and raising welfare, we took the 'good' long-term unemployed, who had 'paid in' for their benefit, and put them in the same class as the 'bad' welfare people who had never worked at all."

Example: Let's say I really am a stonecutter on a Gothic cathedral. But now I'm lumped by the government in the same bunch with Ms. Q., an "artist" who has never had a paycheck in her life. So the "serious" unemployed, who feel demeaned enough, now have to get in the same line for unemployment with the deadbeats like Ms. Q. It's all insulting, etc.

I guess it is, but as an American, I'm astonished that they get in effect a *guaranteed income for life*. I'm all for attacking the SPD for selling out, but first let me just marvel about it all for a second.

2. Pension. Yes, I hated to see the public share of the pension drop. But Mr. W. said, "We couldn't have young people in their twenties paying 30 percent of their wages to support retirees." I had been naive to think it could go on.

In Germany, unlike the U.S., there really is a technical problem, one that may last for thirty years, as B. said. So for the time being, the pensions, which used to pay 67 percent of working income, now pay just over 50 percent. Still, as Mr. G. said, "*It's not that bad.*" Why?

"The new system now has three pillars," Mr. G. said. "There is the public pension, from the government, which pays 50 percent.

Second, there is the collectively bargained pension, which pays more. Third, there is the individual account, in which you can put 4 percent of your salary." So, he said, on average, Germans are still going to get a pension of 67 to 70 percent of their income.

And of course people will work longer. But some people were still retiring at fifty-five, or they would "take unemployment" for two years and formally retire at fifty-seven. Didn't people get restless? I heard four different answers: "No." "No." "No." And "It depends," from a German friend of mine. "My father retired at fifty-five. Once he saw that the money was okay . . . he found out that he liked to volunteer." But he had an uncle who did not volunteer, and he got restless.

I thought: Because Germans work in heavy industry, maybe they are more sensitive to people being used up. I said this to another SPD staffer: "Yes, people can now work longer, but aren't you forgetting that people can get used up physically?"

He shot back: "People get used up *mentally*. Shouldn't we do something about that?" Yes, in Germany, they raised the retirement age to sixty-seven (which means it is more like sixty-five). But that doesn't mean people should work more: they should work about the same, but just pace themselves, with longer leaves, more time off.

See: in Europe, everybody keeps trumping me.

Hey, I'd like to work till eighty: but I'd like to pace myself.

Meanwhile, in the U.S., people have to keep working into their eighties. Our Social Security pays only 38 percent of working income—for many, even less. And there are very few union contracts anymore. And people have no savings. And in 2008, we lost over *one trillion dollars* in our 401(k)s. In January and February 2009, I had gone door to door in my little run for legislative office—yes, I ran for office. It was a shock. There are all sorts of little old ladies who live on $600 a month—that's all! Really, how can people in America live on $600 a month? And they're not even classified as "poor." So as I went around knocking on doors, I began to say, "We have to raise Social Security, at least up to 50 percent. Ma'am, you need more Social Security, a lot more."

One frail old woman stared at me until she got it, and then she touched my sleeve and said, "Oh! That would be *wonderful*."

I felt awful when she touched me: though we're well able to raise it, the idea that we will is a political fantasy. Meanwhile, in Germany, as one SPD staffer told me, "The retirees are still rich—a lot of them make more than they did when they were working."

So the cutbacks shut everyone up. Germany also did a better job of keeping a lid on the banks. One lesson we can learn from the Krise is to be like the Germans and set up a system of government-run banks, like the Sparkassen—I mean banks that invest in manufacturing-type jobs.

I now think: I should have written a whole book about the Sparkassen. These are the government-run banks that bail out the little companies. At least at the margin, they bail out the Mittlestand, so if nothing else, a certain skill level survives. "But aren't these banks political?"

Absolutely. As my friend V. says, "Because they're tied in with the local politicians, they know the local scene." Sure, there are scandals. But in the end, they keep some increment of money going into virtuous-type skilled industry instead of credit swaps and derivatives.

On my big trip in 1997, I went to see Herr Weltke, who at that time was the head of the Landesbank, or State Bank of Hesse, and oversaw the Sparkassen. Later, he was the head of the Bundesbank itself. Not only was he a politician, he was a Socialist, an SPD banker. I had a list of what now seem like stupid questions: "What do you think of the Dutch model?

He stared as if I had asked him about *The Flintstones*, then said in a certain withering tone: "I am not familiar with affairs in The Netherlands. . . . It is a small country."

At that moment, I felt pretty small myself.

I should have asked him: "What does a Socialist do with a bank?"

Well, it doesn't charge U.S.-type interest rates. I once asked an SPD staffer: "Do the Sparkassen hand out credit cards just like the private banks do?"

He said nothing, took out his wallet, and said, "Look at mine."

I got other people to take out their cards. The Sparkassen don't let you run up balances or let you pay for things with no down payment and then raise the rate. But a German friend told me there are terrible penalties if you go over your credit limit.

"Really? What interest rate do they charge?"

"It's very high . . . I think it is 11 percent."

Or think of this: at Harris Bank, where I keep my account, I can use the cash machine for free. If I walk a half a block to Chase Bank, I pay a fee of $3. But if I go a little farther, over the ocean to Berlin, and take out cash from an ATM there, how much do I pay?

Nothing: no fee.

The result of all this is the Germans don't have money gushing out of low-return manufacturing and into high-return finance, where we get ripped off with all sorts of usury and hidden fees. "Yes," said a German friend, "but the Sparkassen charge no less than what the private banks do."

"Sure," I said, "but then the private banks can charge no *more* than what the Sparkassen can charge."

My friend agreed. "In fact, the private banks complain, 'Oh, it is unfair that we have to compete with the Sparkassen, because they don't have to worry; the government guarantees their losses.'"

It's unfair, it's socialistic. In America, we would never tolerate such a "public option" in banking. After all, in America, who ever heard of the government bailing out a private bank the way the German government stands beside the Sparkassen?

The upshot is that the investment in the economy does not tilt away from low-return manufacturing and into high-return finance, and the machine-tool people get the loans they need before they go belly-up. Back in Chicago, I go to court to get bits and pieces of pensions when manufacturers go belly-up.

How often has this happened in the U.S. because no Sparkassen were around? It's just heartbreaking.

Wolfgang Streeck thought the German model was doomed because the big old private banks would pull out money from industry. Capital would become global. It would go to where it could get go-go–type returns. And Streeck was probably right. But the system is not perfectly "global," and just enough capital stayed in Germany—where just enough capital stayed out of financial products—for the German model to survive.

Indeed, the very fact that Germany did not get the hot money, that Frankfurt "lost out" to New York and London, to Wall Street and the City, may be the very thing that saved it. On the one hand, Streeck was right: it could have used more capital. On the other hand, it did not get too much: the financial sector did not bloat up, there were no bubbles, there was no excess liquidity, sending bankers on a mission to get people to take out bigger loans, and live richly, and plunge themselves into debt.

We mocked them for losing out, when really they were lucking out.

Also, after the Krise, the works councils are safe. Yes, Mr. W. said, "The works councils have really demonstrated their worth." Mr. G. said the same. "Yes, the HR department may be good in sunny times, but it is not so good in a crisis. Very often it is the HR department that is saying, Cut the jobs. The works council is trying to keep people on the payroll."

"They don't always succeed, though?"

"No, but at least it's not like France. We aren't holding people hostage."

Co-determination is safe, too. Mr. G. said, "I like to say co-determination is now our biggest export." He paused. "Of course we're not completely safe. Because of the European integration, we are forced to defend co-determination." For example, a new law allows "European-wide" companies to pick the corporate law of the country in which they have their headquarters. "We don't want Allianz and BASF to pick up and move to Britain to get out of co-determination. So we made a deal with the British—they can do what they want with their working hours, so long as we keep co-determination."

So that's what I carry back from Berlin. Does that mean the German model will survive? No!

I have two big worries.

First, after I came back, the CDU won! On September 27, 2009, election day, I knew by 3 P.M. that it was over. I could see online the tanned, sleek Munich yuppies all jumping up and down. I felt sick. I got in my car. I drove around: of course it wasn't even on the news until I picked up BBC. In Chicago, no one knew or cared. I went into the closest thing we have to a Berlin-type café and sat there, stricken. How could the SPD have lost? And in fact, all over Europe, at the moment the capitalist system is cracking up, the left seems to be collapsing. On my last day in Berlin, a few months before the CDU and the awful neoliberal FDP had swept back in, I had breakfast with S., who had just came back from America with the flu.

"Oh S.," I asked, "why is the SPD in such trouble?"

"So," he said, "right now, because of the crisis, we are in a period of transition. The question is: who will lead this transition, hmm? In most European countries, the people or the majority are center left. But everywhere the right is in power. How do we explain this?"

"Yes," I said, "how?" I was jittery: I had to leave in a few minutes, to go back to the U.S.

"First, for the social democratic parties, the crisis has come, let us say, at an awkward time—it came at the moment they were . . . entangled with the neoliberals."

"Yes, they were too pro-market."

"And there is a second, simpler reason—PR, proportional representation." As he pointed out, PR is the system in most European constitutions, though not in Britain. It means: multiple parties. That's better for the right than the left. Why? "If the CDU gets a third of the vote, it is easy to make an alliance with other parties with the FDP," the neoliberal Munich-yuppie party. "But," S. went on, "if the SPD gets a third of the vote, it is very hard to make an alliance with the left."

The Greens are willing enough: it's the Links, the far left, that is the problem.

Partly it's Michael Kinsley's point: the right welcomes its converts, while the left reviles its heretics. But there's more to it. The Links is not one party but three in a coalition. There is the old CP. There is the breakaway SPD, which walked out with Oskar Lafontaine. And then there are the kids, who are in the "antiglobalist" camp. It's a tribute to Lafontaine that he can keep these three factions together. The old CP, for example, is ultranationalist, while the antiglobalist kids have no use for Germany at all.

And it got worse, or the Links got bigger, because the SPD was in a coalition with the CDU and could not attack it. Imagine: if, in 2004, John Kerry and the Democrats had gone into a coalition as the junior partners of Bush and Cheney.

Ugh.

S. then gave the two conditions for the SPD and Links to—well, link. Both are hard.

"First, the old CP, they have to apologize for the murders." They have to apologize at least for the people shot going over the Wall.

"Second, Lafontaine has to go. You must understand: the SPD is an old party, it is a proud party. They will never forgive him for walking out on them in the first months of the SPD-Green coalition, when the SPD was at its most vulnerable."

Neither one happened. So there was no possibility the SPD could unite with the Links and win. Even IG Metall stayed neutral, and, worse, some within it supported the Links.

Ah: how will the SPD, *my* party, the left party, ever get back into power?

On the other hand, I tell myself not to despair: after all, the CDU was in power when I first became aware that Kohl was battling Major over worker control. It was the CDU that was in power when I showed up here in chapter 4.

Yes, as a good Catholic, I have to remember the papal encyclicals on labor. Didn't the Christian Democrats of Europe start out in Brussels as a little study group or book club to discuss *Rerum Novarum*? It was the CDU that was the first to tout the "social market" economy. It was the CDU that first came up with the idea of a "works council" at all. So why should I worry? Well, I do. Nonetheless, it was my friend K., a CDU man, who told me in 1997 that if Schroeder was elected, he would make the cuts that Kohl would not. Didn't he turn out to be right? Still, in 2005, Merkel campaigned as a Margaret Thatcher. On the other hand, the drop in her popularity is said to have been a huge shock to her. Who knows? Maybe the CDU will drop the "C." Or the maybe the Church will move to the right and drop the "D."

Or maybe it doesn't matter, for I think back to that time as to how unification would change things.

"It will be less Catholic, more Protestant, and that will mean one week's less vacation."

As it turns out, they kept the same vacation. So there is a danger in exaggerating the influence of the Church.

Perhaps in a thousand years, after the radioactivity of Hitler wears off, post-Christian Europe could be Christian again. Or perhaps with immigration, it could re-Christianize much sooner. "What? Aren't the immigrants all Muslim?" True, but I bet in the next century Africans will come here. After all, as Heinz says, "WHEN THE WIND BLOWS FROM THE SOUTH YOU CAN TASTE THE SAND." From the South, some if not most may be Christian; and they may have the same shiver as I did on my first night in Frankfurt when I heard The Bells.

In the meantime, the Catholic Church has a stake in propping up the European model. First, such a model is more likely than our U.S. model to give money to the Third and Fourth Worlds, where the Church has its base. Second, at least in the German version, it is a model that provides tax money directly to the Church.

Early on, I was shocked to find out that Germans not only pay taxes to keep the welfare state going, they also pay taxes to keep up the churches that so few attend. One checks a box on the tax return as to which church, Catholic or Lutheran, one wants to support. A banker (Protestant) who married a teacher (Catholic) told me once: "I pay taxes to support two different religions, and I don't even believe in God." I was in shock. When I connected up with my friend Leo, a Catholic priest, I asked him, "What do you think of paying taxes to support the Church?"

"Well, I'm an American," he said, "so I think it's awful."

"Yes," I said, "me too."

Well, I've reconsidered. Oh, I'm still for separating church and state, but I now see the advantages. What's the difference between the Catholic Church in the U.S. and the Church in Germany? Follow the money. In the U.S., we don't pay taxes to support the Church, so it begs for big money from the wealthy and well-to-do, i.e., right-wing Notre Dame alumni who snap even at the sainted Father Ted Hesburgh. Soon it's a mortal sin to vote for Kerry. But in Germany, the Church is at least not in financial hock to Republican right-to-lifers, because it gets money directly from the state, i.e., a left-wing welfare state. So the Church in Germany can be relatively more left-wing and even has an Archbishop Marx—Reinhard Marx, archbishop of Munich and Freising, which is the pope's old post—and this Marx, like the other Marx, has even written his own *Das Kapital* denouncing CEO pay raises, outsourcing, and the milder but still growing gap between German rich and poor. Isn't it a help that Archbishop Marx doesn't have to beg alums of Notre Dame for money? But I don't want to give a Marxist explanation of Archbishop Marx.

I'll just point out that he's free to call them as he sees them, just as the early Christians used to do.

But I have a second, bigger worry than the accession of the CDU and FDP: it's the decline of labor. Or rather, it's the decline of people covered by labor contracts. As Sam Beer used to say of such a contract, "That's half the welfare state." That's what the old New Dealers knew: taxpayers are off the hook because the employer provides the safety net.

In Germany, it's actually more than half the welfare state. But

fewer Germans now get the benefit of the old regional wage bargaining, though more of them may be in works councils. Even
with co-determination strongly in place, the decline of such bargaining has made Germany slightly more unequal. Germany does
need to pay more in taxes—to prevent child poverty, to cover the
gap between rich and poor. As late as 1991, unions in Germany
bargained directly or indirectly for over 90 percent—90 percent!—
of the private-sector workforce, while in the U.S. it was about 8
percent.

Now German unions bargain for the wages of 60 percent—
which is still huge, but which also denotes a huge drop. Think of
it too as a drop in the welfare state, or at least "free" welfare that
taxpayers don't have to cover. That drop means more and more
people are outside the "system," outside Germany, Inc. That's
what horrifies the SPD: it's not only that some people are going
over to the Links, but that many aren't voting at all, the way in the
U.S. an even greater number have dropped out of civic life and
don't bother to vote at all.

That's the crisis of the SPD, and they know it. On that Friday
afternoon, Mr. W. and Mr. G. knew it. At one point, Mr. W.
stopped his tutorial on Agenda 2010 and began griping about his
own union. It was just the same as teamsters complaining in my
office. "Every month," Mr. W. said, "I get my union magazine, and
I am tired of picking it up and reading the same attacks on politicians. All right: fine. But I want to know what my union is doing
about organizing."

Otherwise, it's his problem as an SPD official trying to keep a
social democracy.

"What are they doing?" I said.

He paused. "I come out of my office here and look at the security guards in this building—how many are in a union? It's one in
a hundred. Maybe fewer. Why aren't we organizing them?"

Well, I thought later, try to imagine going to Washington, D.C., and meeting a high-level government official complaining about his union magazine and wondering why his union isn't organizing the guards.

But why aren't they?

What amazed me about the SPD officials I met was the way they are trying to think up new ways to give people outside of Germany, Inc., some sense of power. Okay, they can't be on works councils. But one idea they tried in Berlin was to take names out of a phone book at random and let people sit on councils that would decide what neighborhood-level projects the government should fund. "It turns out," an SPD official told me, "they want to fund little projects, not the big ones that the bureaucrats like." Of course my friend L., who is a disciple of Alinsky, was aghast: for him, it was all make-believe. But at least some people in the SPD are trying out new ideas: something—anything—that, as in the case of a works council, lets people at every level exercise direct political power.

At least once in your life, even if you're picked out of the phone book, you have the political power to order something be done.

Later, I had coffee with the last of my German tutors, who left Chicago to be a producer in Berlin. Okay, the state covers her insurance. But she has now soured on the German model, which does her no good as a freelancer—and think of all the people like her, outside of it, with no union. What does worker control mean to her? Maybe she'd be better off if they fired more people. In Berlin, in the middle of the old GDR, it can seem a long, long way away to Germany, Inc.

"You stay here in Mitte, but go out on the U-Bahn, the U7, and walk around, and you'll see what it's like here. . . ." Of course, back in 1997, they were telling me to do the same thing. Yet I tell myself: this is not just a rerun of *Ten Years Ago Tonight*. Things *are* worse. Even if the Germans are always saying that.

I think the problem would be gone if only the unions could organize the janitors and maids. In the U.S., those are the only people SEIU and other unions seem able to organize. In Germany, it's seemingly the opposite, as if IG Metall and the others can reach only the highly skilled.

I should say, out at the end of the U7, there are mostly "white" Germans, not Turks. One dangerous thing about the weakness of labor out here is that it may lead to a backlash against a German model. For the problem with all this transparency in wages is that the native-born who are cut out can see how well—very precisely how well—some of the foreign-born are doing.

I know Americans think Germany is about to crack up over the Challenge-of-Islam and want to hear about the Turks pouring in. But for the SPD staffers with whom I talked, the crack-up really looms from the failure to organize the people in the services, the waiters and cleaners, both immigrant and native-born, i.e., the chauffeurs Mr. Z. wants to drive him to the airport; and the problem here is not just to get a chicken in every pot, but also to fire them up to want the right to stir the pot.

That's the crisis: it's one of desire. Without desire I don't think the German model will survive.

I know I will never get that across. It's just the way we Americans think: the big issue must be skin color, or Christianity v. Islam. And I admit other European countries have serious problems. But because of the way Turks and others are already in IG Metall, there has been far less tension over immigration in Germany than in France or even the Netherlands, where (in my opinion) labor is weaker at the bargaining table. Or put another way: immigration is not going to be a problem as long as labor remains strong. Yes, there are other accidental things that help: for one thing, the immigrants are largely Turks, and Turkey, thanks to Ataturk, is today an EU-type country. For Germany, Turkey is not an old colony but an ally: remember the two of them tracking down poor Lawrence of Arabia? It's true many Germans would prefer the Turks not become German citizens. But as even my left-wing friend Leo points out, "It works the other way too." Many Turks aren't especially eager to become German citizens. France is a different story. In Paris, without knowing anything about the Algerian War or France's colonial empire, one can look around and sense trouble. "Oh, but isn't there discrimination?" Of course, but they aren't going to send back any Turks. As many Germans would say, "Then we'd have no one to run our small businesses." I doubt anyone knows whether Germans are more racist than we are. It's a pointless kind of barroom argument, not one that flatters those Americans who like to make it. Naturally, they are more xenophobic than our immigrant nation, but not nearly as likely as we are to lock up black and brown people in a massive prison system. In another book—for this subject deserves a whole book—I could say that, for all I know, at least based on what I have seen firsthand, the Poles are treated with as much disdain as the Turks, even though the Poles are white and Catholic and from a country just a few feet away. But lest we be smug about the way some less educated Germans may like to look down on the Poles, at least the Germans let in the Poles, who come here to shop, hang out, get scholarships, and go back home, while we throw up huge barriers to keep them out of America, even for short trips, even when Poland has been one of our few allies in our feckless wars. While we're glad to let the Germans visit, and we bow and scrape to them, we still like to stiff the Poles.

No, the threat to the German model is not an anti-immigrant backlash or the general decline of the middle class as a whole (as in the U.S.) but the way more and more people at the margins, with no union representation, are cheated out of the fruits of Germany, Inc.

Now in a normal policy book, one would expect me to give up and say the Tom Friedman types are right, and it's a flat world where workers in Sri Lanka are beating out workers in Dortmund, and so on.

But there's something flat wrong about the flat-world thesis. Sure, there is a global division of labor. That's here to stay. Outside of the Links, no one seriously believes the unions can go on piling one benefit on top of the other, as they did in the golden 1970s, and still retire at fifty-five.

It's easy to see there are limits, but it's also apparent that, even with very high wages and great benefits, Germans and other Europeans can compete marvelously well. Indeed, the more globally competitive the sector, the stronger German labor is within it. Nothing could discredit Friedman's argument more persuasively than the partial and selective areas where labor has no clout. As one SPD staffer said, "In the export industries, union density is 80 percent, even 90 percent, and never lower than 60 percent; but in public administration or government, it is only 40 percent, and in the creative industries—" He stopped and laughed. "—It's zero."

"What about the maids?"

He sighed. He was a one-time union staffer. "You can't get into the tourist places and hotels."

It baffles me: why can't a strong labor movement organize in a low-wage sector?

"We have a lot of debates about this but no real answers."

That's why Berlin is so dangerous to Germany. It seems to me since I first came here there are more and more maids, freelancers, or just people sitting around dreaming of the day when people in the middle class start to be fired for the color of their ties, etc., so that they can take their jobs.

On the one hand, they want the Links; on the other hand, they might switch in a second to the FDP. Or vice versa.

If I sound frightened, it's because I am frightened. On the other hand, it's Europe, right? Where labor is not flat on its back. The strangest thing I saw this year is a video on YouTube, with a kind of hip-hop sound track, about a lot of German kids on strike. These were IG Metall–type apprentices, and they weren't like the kids in the cafés. Instead they wore black-and-white car coats and were from obscure little German towns, but all of them were marching, at night, both boys and girls, striking against the big global companies for not delivering on jobs. At about the same time as the strike, IG Metall held a rock concert with Bob Geldof, which drew fifty thousand people, mostly kids. Here's a shocking thing to a U.S. labor lawyer like me: in 2008, youth membership in IG Metall—kids *under* twenty-seven who *voluntarily* pay union dues—climbed yet again, this time by 6 percent. At last count, IG Metall had over two hundred thousand of these kids! As someone who ran for public office and found out why campaign staffs think it a waste of time even to bother with younger people, I wish I could get across how stunning a thing that is. Even the *FT*, which always writes off labor, has had to admit that, in Germany, unions are resurging among kids who are highly skilled.

Why in Germany are kids paying dues, *voluntarily?*

As I said earlier, I think it's an American who can best explain it. It's not Marx but John Dewey whose picture should be in the lobby of the Willy Brandt Haus, the headquarters of the SPD. It's Dewey who believed that schools should not just teach practical skills but explain why kids have to be political, to be citizens, yes, to get into labor movements to protect the skills they are acquiring. One can say that union membership is a "tradition" in certain industries. But that's just an opaque way of saying that the kids get politicized at home and school as they go through the Dual Track.

In a way, I think the answer to the problems of our country is education, but not the kind we're pursuing, i.e., jamming more kids into college or even teaching practical skills; instead, it's teaching them how, politically, to cut themselves a better deal. As long as that's going on, it's impossible to write off the European or, more specifically, the German model.

At the SPD headquarters, I met people on the left, the best and brightest, who can at least think in this framework. They grasp what their job is: to protect the way of life of a largely high school–educated middle class. That way of life is what constitutes the crown jewels. The protection of the crown jewels is a fiduciary responsibility. I hate to say so, but Democrats and Kennedy School–types (with honorable exceptions)—certainly Democratic politicians—really do not think seriously about how, in a practical way, to raise the standard of living of the non–college grad population, who happen to be, well, 73 percent of the adult population. Look, I like Larry Summers in some ways: at least he is willing to blush about the shameful number of people we have locked up in prison. But he would never be in the SPD. He could never relate to the striking kids under twenty-seven rapping in German on YouTube. If I ask most Democrats and their think-tank minions how to help the middle class, they have no real answer except to tell them to go to college. But for most Americans that's no answer, so essentially we Democrats are telling them to pound sand. If they didn't go to college, their lives are over.

And it is symptomatic that, when they look at Germany, everything that holds up the German middle-class way of life, the U.S. Democrats would tear down. So, barely in office, in the midst of the crack-up of Wall Street, the present administration was urging the Germans to get rid of the German model:

"You're relying too much on exports."

"Start producing less and go into services."

I felt like an idiot asking Mr. K.—an SPD staffer at the Willy Brandt Haus—whether Germans should stop exporting. He said, "Why would we try to disconnect ourselves from the most dynamic and innovative part of the economy?" Schumpeter argued that what makes capitalism so dynamic—what saves capitalism from the "vanishing investment opportunity"—is precisely this connection with technology. That's exactly why European socialists have a far better grasp of the dynamic of capitalism than the neoliberals in America. Even now, as I write, there is no serious attempt, or even consciousness of the need for an attempt, in either the Democratic or Republican party, to stop the bloating of the financial sector and try to reconnect the U.S. model to the most dynamic part of capitalism, i.e., buying new capital equipment or simply making things. It's not the lack of any serious attempt to hold down the returns to the financial sector, which, by pulling in all the money, has starved U.S. manufacturing. I do not just mean the failure of the trade deficit even to get on the radar in D.C., much less the failure to take any step to stem the harm to our shrinking middle class. I mean that we're so clueless that we're pushing forward with health insurance that will make the insurance industry even richer, and pile even more health costs onto the cost of manufactured goods. On the one hand I'm thrilled that we in the U.S. will have universal health care. On the other hand I'm against that private insurers can profiteer even more. Democrats do not even grasp, as Europeans do, that we cannot go on "feeding the beast." We cannot go on distributing public goods through the private market and pushing the costs onto our manufactured goods at a time when bringing the trade deficit down on a long-term basis is the biggest challenge we have. All of these things, which would obsess Europeans, especially on the left but not just on the left, we do not even think about.

Still, I realize I may be starstruck just because I got so much time with Mr. W. and Mr. G. I doubt that in busy Washington, I'd ever get this kind of time with, oh, the assistant secretary for policy at the Bureau of Weights and Measures. I was so taken with an offhand remark that sums up the gulf between the Democrats and the SPD people I met in the Willy Brandt Haus. I doubt any liberal Democrat or Kennedy School–type would say what Mr. K. did, unprompted, to me: "We need unions to manage the process." They grasp that if people aren't in unions, they are beyond the reach of government to help them. Not just the SPD but even some in the CDU understand that if people are in unions, it is far easier for them to keep society from unraveling—even more so, not less so, in a "flat world." At least it helps manage the process of dividing up productivity gains, if not in terms of more income, then at least in terms of leisure and less stress. Otherwise, there can be no serious strategy for bringing up the middle-class standard of living—which is what SPD types think about but, so far as I can tell, our Democrats do not. I'm not arguing against inequality altogether or even a bit of increase—maybe the rich do deserve more income, since they seem to be working longer hours than the middle class. I'm just arguing for managing the process.

Here's why we need the European model: we don't even have a way of talking about raising our standard of living except in terms of money. No one even thinks about how government can be used to reduce the real day-to-day stress. As we carry our loads longer, we should learn from the Europeans how to loosen our bonds Aren't we already bent over from the weight of our packs?

"Oh, you're just big on Europe because the Europeans talk to you." Sure, they practically fall all over people like me. They do so not because I'm some "European socialist" (which I'm not) but because, at least as a labor lawyer, I think the way they do.

"Oh, you understand us!" So, hey, I get respect.

But I realized once again why I'd be miserable in Europe: *it's too far away*! It's not just that I'd miss Chicago: I've already confessed that I love Washington, D.C.

Meanwhile, I've gotten tired of Berlin, as I found out this last trip.

I miss the old Berlin where, on the S-Bahn, a drunk would come up to start a fight.

I miss watching his girlfriend in the corner laughing as he tried.

I miss the old Berlin, the student housing where I lived in 2001. Down there they used to mock me for going up to the Mitte every day, to yuppie Berlin: why not just go live in Munich, if I want the *GQ* magazine kind of Germany? Welf, a left-wing Berliner I knew, would sneer about the Mitte, which I loved: "That's not Berlin! Berlin is poor! That's why the government in Bonn didn't want to move here." It's not just Hitler who hated Berlin: all the big shots do. "All the big men in Bonn, they didn't want to come here. Why? Because they know, here in Berlin, people don't give a shit about them. Nobody would be impressed with their Big Fancy Cars. People here are different. Here it's okay to be working class."

And as the rich move in, some of those people are still around, torching Porsches and the like. In a recent six-month period, unknown Berliners have set fire to over two hundred cars.

Yes, I miss that old Berlin—except that if I'd really wanted to, I could have taken the U7 and gone out to see it. Since I didn't bother, maybe I don't miss "that old Berlin" so much.

Really, I just miss *my* old Berlin, which for me once had the quality of Lincoln, Montana: "the last best place to hide," at least in the category of major world capitals. Even now I can still get a shiver out of the place. On this last trip, for example, I'd go jogging and run under the white flowers on all the trees in bloom and come to a park full of children and ice cream and wheel around and—

And I'd gasp to turn around and see a dark-brown Gothic steeple, sticking its bony finger skeletally out of the nave where Dietrich Bonhoeffer had been baptized.

Even when it's spring in Berlin, winter is everywhere.

Germany is dark.

But I don't belong. If I lived here, I'd always be thinking of the Wim Wenders movie *Wings of Desire*: that's the film where Bruno Ganz and others are angels, and they walk around in the streets of Berlin and simply observe. Yes, just as they, as angels, cannot intervene in human affairs, so I, as a foreigner, also observe. I have to hold someone else's coat. As to the future of the German model, they have to fight that fight. Yes, I might talk about "taking off my angel wings," but it's kind of ridiculous to get involved.

It's *Europe*. Besides, if I was stuck in a social democracy, I'd just have to play defense. In the U.S., I've the luck of getting to go on the attack.

When I come back here and see a payday loan store offering loans at 365 percent, yes, I could weep. Yet it's a thrill to know I can take off my wings.

"Oh, we can't have anything like Europe has, can we?" That's what some say. It's a fair question.

I think it's quite possible.

I now have stopped rereading and underlining Streeck's great essay, "German Capitalism: Does It Exist? Can It Survive?" Still, I recall his central, disheartening point that the German model, with its works councils and the rest, was simply too hard to copy in other countries. Global capitalism would force Germany into our simpler Anglo-American top-down corporate model, which everyone would use everywhere. In a way, he was making the same point as Jared Diamond in *Guns, Germs, and Steel*. Diamond argued that certain aspects of human cultures survive if they are "blueprintable," i.e., if they can be copied and used elsewhere. To Streeck, the democratic German model lacked just that quality. It was not blueprintable, which the Anglo-American corporate model was. It was too complicated, with its co-determination and worker control.

But now it turns out the German model *is* quite blueprintable. At least in the EU, many countries are now keen on experimenting with works councils. "Co-determination is our biggest export," as Mr. G. said. If it spreads throughout the EU, it may start to burn itself into our brains not just as a rival but a smarter form of capitalism, one that is not only more democratic but more competitive. It simply takes a change in law. We could even reshape our financial sector to support it. Even in the U.S., we at least thought about nationalizing banks or setting up a few brand-new government-run banks in early 2009. Okay, we did nothing. But with our old banking system back in place, the next crisis could push us into something like the Sparkassen.

Is it likely? No. Is it possible? Yes. For in America, we are born on both continents: Europe as well as here. Our claim to be unique, as a nation of immigrants, might be the biggest thing that stamps us as a European project. Aside from that, on both continents we speak English. Now that we all speak the same language, it is as likely that we can copy the models of central Europe as much as we have copied the models of the UK.

Yes, we are born on both continents. We explored the wilderness for Europe. They explored modernity for us. We depend on Mozart from them, while they depended on us for rock and roll. From the UK, of course, we stole the blueprint for our economic model. Even with Germany, it's hard to list the give-and-take. They gave us Billy Wilder, and we gave them General Eisenhower—and even vice versa, if one thinks about it in a certain way.

In personal style, they are becoming less formal, though they still have a lot of loosening up to do. On the other hand, they could teach us a thing or two about formal social structures. Just in terms of treating each other with charity, we have a lot of catching up to do.

Europe is not a continent but part of Eurasia, which is not just a continent but a polite term for the world. I love that I was born on an island continent, where so many of us are descended from people who woke up one day and thought, "Heck, I'm on the wrong continent," and got up and came here. Though we have messed up a bit, it may be even easier in this wired-up world to download the blueprints from all the continents and to exercise our greatest privilege as Americans—to astonish ourselves by making something new.

Acknowledgments

Thanks first and above all to Sarah Fan for editing this book: it was hard enough for me to write the book, but it must have been far more difficult to edit. Somehow she did. Thanks next to Gary Smith and the staff at the American Academy in Berlin: they gave me a wonderful Holtzbrinck Fellowship. Thanks to all my friends who either read drafts or let me pester them with questions— especially Volker Bley, Thomas Kakalios, Sascha Mueller-Kraenner, Jorg and Eva Nadler, Miranda Robbins, Dan Badger, Jim McNeil, Stephen Holmes, James Fallows, Tony Judge, Linda Healey, and others I'm sure that I have shamefully left out. I'm grateful to Alexander Blankenagel for letting me teach at Humboldt in the spring of 2001—and sit in his office while he was gone. Thanks to Craig Kennedy at the German Marshall Fund for giving me an excuse to go to Germany in 1997. Thanks to Sam Boyd for heroic help with fact checks. Finally, I'd like to acknowledge my two he-roes, both recently deceased. Ah, I wish I could have shown them this book. The first of course is Leon Despres, my colleague and law partner who grew up in Paris and spoke all those languages and who even at age ninety (and over) kept our law practice going while I slipped off to Europe to eat dinner at night alone. The second is Sam Beer, friend, teacher, great man: who also just died, at age ninety-seven. Had Boswell found Sam Beer, he'd have ditched Sam Johnson. It was from Sam, first in his course, and then in his company, that I learned we can't just read history as a pile of facts—we have to keep going back to it to try out different ideas, try to place it in frameworks, even if none of these ideas or frameworks will ever fit. The important thing is to go on thinking and arguing and enjoying each other's company while we can, not so much from a love of learning as simply from a love of life.

Finally, thanks to André Schiffrin who kept after me to write this book—and did so even when for many years I'd be so lost in my real life as an American that I'd forgotten I'd ever been to Europe at all.

Index